'this rugby spellbound people'

RUGBY FOOTBALL IN NINETEENTH-CENTURY CARDIFF AND SOUTH WALES

'this rugby spellbound people'

RUGBY FOOTBALL IN NINETEENTH-CENTURY CARDIFF AND SOUTH WALES

Gwyn Prescott

Welsh Academic Press

Published in Wales by Welsh Academic Press, an imprint of

Ashley Drake Publishing Ltd
PO Box 733
Cardiff
CF14 2YX

www.welsh-academic-press.com

First Impression – 2011

ISBN
978-1-86057-117-6

British Library Cataloguing-in-Publication Data.
A CIP catalogue for this book is available from the British Library.

Typeset by White Lotus Infotech Pvt. Ltd., Puducherry, India.
Printed by MPG Book Group Ltd, Bodmin, Cornwall.

CONTENTS

Dedicated to the memory of my father Jim Prescott
(St. Peter's School, Cardiff Centrals and Grange Baptists)
and my mother Maud Prescott, who both loved rugby football.

FOREWORD

The title of this book derives from a report its author found in the *Irish Times* describing the crowd at the Wales v New Zealand game in December 1905 as 'this rugby spellbound people'. Throw 'spellbound' into a computer search engine and most likely it will cough up a film of that name. Gwyn Prescott, though, is more interested in Frank Hancock than Alfred Hitchcock. That's for the birds – though it seems that rugby already *was* in Cardiff when the first grandstand was erected at the Arms Park in 1881 'for the convenience of the spectators and the ladies in particular'. By 1898 there were complaints that they were monopolising it.

Some years ago I met Aeronwy Thomas, Dylan's daughter, at a concert at the London Welsh Centre in Gray's Inn Road given by the Pendyrus male choir (I was – am – a member and Aeronwy had married one). I told her I had once, with my friend Dai, written a book about Welsh rugby – a real conversation-stopper, this, when talking to the daughter of a famous poet, herself a writer – and we'd called it *Fields of Praise*. With just a flicker of a smile she replied, 'That's a good title', and moved on. How many times, I wondered, had Aeronwy read and recited her father' s immortal lines '… how it must have been after the birth of the simple light/In the first spinning place, the spellbound horses walking warm/Out of the whinnying green stable/On to the fields of praise'? Gwyn, whose daughter Sarah, he tells me, has been in love with 'Fern Hill' since childhood, was spellbound by the coincidence, though his Irish rugby correspondent can hardly have been aware of it, writing nine years before Dylan was born.

There weren't many green stables in late nineteenth-century Cardiff: that's what its explosive growth was all about, and Gwyn Prescott's study shows how rugby became a key component of the new urban culture that developed along with it. Fifty years ago a distinguished professor of Welsh history did indeed recognise that 'more organised sport was becoming popular' in Cardiff in the 1860s and '70s, providing as confirmation the death of two mountaineers on Mont Blanc. Fortunately sports history has developed apace since then. Prof William Rees can hardly be blamed for not knowing that by the 1890s there were over 200 rugby sides in Cardiff. I didn't either until Gwyn Prescott's research unearthed and listed them. Clearly the clubs in formal membership of the WRU were only the tip of a much bigger iceberg, and Gwyn has blazed a trail for other pioneers to push on into the probably equally active conurbations of Newport and Swansea to enable us to further fill out the national picture.

It is unlikely that anyone who turns to this book needs persuading of the social significance of the history of sport. Academic snobbery about sports history may still linger in some of the mustier recesses of the ivory tower, but Gwyn Prescott, a university teacher, has never shared it: he well knows that sport generally – Welsh and therefore Cardiff rugby in particular – is socially and historically determined. Sports history, perhaps more than most comparable kinds of scholarly endeavour, can easily be reduced to the unimportant and the trivial, the anecdotal and anodyne, the stunningly statistical and the microscopically close reading where 'the alleged try scored by the New Zealander Deans in the historic Welsh victory over the All Blacks in December 1905 is described with the scholastic antiquarianism of an analysis of medieval commotes' (the historian K.O., now Lord, Morgan reviewing *Fields of Praise* in the *Times Literary Supplement*).

Gwyn Prescott knows all this – though perhaps not that review (I never showed it to him). In this book he has brought off two major achievements. He recognises we need to know more facts, the raw data which only painstaking empirical research can uncover, because he is well aware that it is very often specific, even parochial, developments which determine the distinctive contours of sporting practice. He traces, from an exploration of a wide array of hitherto unused primary sources, the emergence and organisation of a robust infrastructure of socially inclusive teams and clubs in inner, dockside and suburban Cardiff; how many, where they played and how often. By the 1890s rugby football was contributing to an expressive local, civic, even national conscious-ness: Cardiffians, who have that endearing habit of equating Cardiff with Wales, were talking of rugby as 'the national game' as early as 1879. At the same time the author meticulously documents this unprec-edented growth without losing sight of the wider context and culture of the teeming townscape of late Victorian Cardiff (we can only speak of a *city*scape from 1905), thereby placing his book on a par with the two other major studies of 'coal metropolis' in its heyday by Martin Daunton (1977) and John Davies (1994).

Neither neckless nor shaven-headed, a living refutation of the claim that the thinking prop is some fabulous beast, Gwyn Prescott also confirms that while one does not *have* to be a player, a spectator or even an armchair aficionado to appreciate that rugby football has been hardwired into the popular culture and urban life of Cardiff for over 130 years, it cannot be a disadvantage actually to have picked up the ball and run with it. The author, a product of Cardiff High School and the HSOB, has serious form in a playing career that spanned the sixties, extending from captaining the Welsh Secondary Schools to a near-Blue at Cambridge and playing for Glamorgan Wanderers and for Penarth against the Barbarians. His brother Colin also captained the Welsh Youth and played at prop for Cardiff, Newport and Penarth. Gwyn's interest in the history of the game was kindled by his father, an avid working-class rugby follower who was a schoolboy and District player in Cardiff before the war. Prescott senior had been taken to watch the Blue and Blacks in the early 1920s by his part-Irish grandfather who had himself watched and played in Cardiff from the 1890s. With his family thus steeped in the sport Gwyn has always been conscious of the city's rugby heritage whose historical undergrowth he here reveals and probes. And time and again we are reminded how the importance of rugby football within Cardiff's urban culture was physically symbol-ised by the strategically central location of the Cardiff Arms Park and the commercial and public benefits reaped because of its sheer accessi-bility. As the *Western Mail* remarked in 1896, 'the value of this piece of ground to the Cardiff Football Club is really untold, and they will never rightly value it till they have to shift!'

How the late, great Bleddyn Williams of Cardiff and Wales, a rela-tive of the author's, would have savoured those prophetic words. The incomparable Bleddyn would have enjoyed reading Gwyn Prescott's book. So will you.

Gareth Williams
Pontypridd, November 2010

ACKNOWLEDGEMENTS

This book could never have been written without the help of numerous others. In particular, I have to thank Professor Gareth Williams of the University of Glamorgan who supervised the research on which the book is based. Like all good coaches, he always managed to keep me focused on getting the ball across the try line, not the easiest of achievements when dealing with a former prop-forward not used to handling the ball. Without his guidance, support and encouragement, this book would never have been completed. Whether it was providing sources, or drawing on his unrivalled expertise to comment on all aspects of the work, his help was invariably given freely and with his customary good humour. The happiest outcome of the research is that he is now a valued friend.

There are many others who, in a variety of ways, also helped me to conceive, develop and produce this book and to them all I offer my sincere thanks. They include: Professor Dai Smith, Dr. Andy Croll, Professor David Hillier and Professor Chris Williams, (University of Glamorgan); Professor Martin Johnes (Swansea University); Professor Mike Huggins (University of Cumbria); Dr. Julie Light (Cardiff University); Jed Smith and Sophie Walker (RFU Museum of Rugby); Martin Davies and Peter Owens (WRU); Bryn Jones, Katrina Coopey and colleagues (Cardiff Library); and Dr. Mike Bassett (Barry RFC), the late Peter Cronin (Cardiff), Richard Daglish (Liverpool), Angus Evans (Newport), Howard Evans (Cardiff), Amanda Gillard (London), Roger Goode (Cardiff), Bernard Green (Llandaff RFC), Dr. Andrew Hignell (Glamorgan County Cricket Club), Lindsay Jenkins (Barry), John Lyons (Narberth), Rupert May-Hill (Cardiff), Gareth Morgan (Australia), John Owen (Cardiff), James Prescott (Cardiff), Mike Price (Neath RFC), Gareth Thomas (Cardiff and District RU), Tudor Williams (Cardiff) and Martin Wills (Northampton). I am especially grateful to David Hughes, secretary of one of my old clubs, Penarth RFC, for allowing me to make use of the club archive.

Finally, of course, I have to thank my family. Sarah, Anna and Siân all provided their father – a product after all of the pre-computer age – with invaluable help in the drafting of this book. Sarah also gave immeasurable assistance in arranging for its publication. With her usual patience, and frequently having to draw on her degree in English, my wife Catherine has supported me wholeheartedly throughout. This book is as much theirs as it is mine.

Gwyn Prescott
Cardiff, May 2011

PREFACE

Given the popularity which rugby has always enjoyed in Wales, it is strange that there has been no detailed historical study of the sport at a local level. This book aims to remedy that with an investigation of nineteenth-century Welsh rugby which concentrates on the nature of the game in one urban area. It sets out to argue that from the earliest days Cardiff was at the centre of rugby in Wales and that rugby was also at the heart of the Victorian town's popular culture. This book is, therefore, the first in-depth study of its kind. The absence of any detailed research at this level has provided an opportunity to make a contribution to our knowledge not only of the history of sport in Wales but also of nineteenth-century rugby and sport in general. Drawing on previously unused sources, it provides some fresh insights into the origins and early years of the game in Wales. It also throws new light both on the significance of Cardiff to Welsh rugby in the nineteenth century and on the importance of rugby in Cardiff.

In seeking to achieve this, the early chapters set out the context for the game in Cardiff by exploring the origins of rugby in Wales and its subsequent development as a popular sport, up to and including the formation of the Welsh Football (Rugby) Union in 1881. The following three chapters then concentrate on Cardiff, examining the extent and nature of the club game, how it was organised, who played and administered it and the impact which rugby had on the town and its popular culture.

The final chapter concludes that rugby very rapidly became the main sporting interest in Cardiff and it experienced very little serious competition from other sports until the end of the century. For many newly arrived citizens, therefore, rugby was an easily accessible and speedy route into the social life of the community. Cardiff's distinctive economic and social structure influenced the particular way in which the game evolved in the town. At the grass roots, the game was dominated by neighbourhood clubs, largely involving working-class and lower middle-class players and administrators, rather than by institutional teams organised by social improvers. At the highest level of competition, an emphasis on civic pride meant that success on the field was more important than social exclusivity. The game was played and supported, therefore, by representatives of all classes within the town.

A range of sources was used to carry out this research. In the absence of any of relevant club records from the nineteenth century, the main primary source was the local press, in particular the *South Wales Daily News* and the *Western Mail*. These morning daily newspapers were published in Cardiff and circulated throughout south Wales. Therefore, as their coverage of rugby had both a Welsh and a Cardiff dimension, they were especially relevant to the study and so they were both thoroughly investigated from the late 1860s to 1900.[1] No previous study of rugby of this period has made use of this particular source in such depth. Other newspapers were also consulted where necessary.

As a research source, newspapers have their weaknesses and they have to be used with a degree of caution. They are written for a particular audience, time and locality. Sports coverage in the two Cardiff dailies was frequently variable and selective, leaving many topics unresolved, whilst reports may have suffered from uncorrected errors, bias and falsehoods. Nevertheless, they do provide, by far, the most comprehensive record we have of Welsh rugby during the period. Increasingly they came to articulate the local sporting culture and in doing so they helped to construct both a local and a national identity. However, they did not merely reflect the sporting context: they also contributed to it. Without this significant resource, the record of the personalities, clubs and institutions of Victorian Welsh Rugby would have been largely lost forever. Thanks to our ancestors who read, wrote and published their newspapers with such vigour, a great deal of that record is still accessible to us, if we are prepared to look for it and use it critically. There is much more valuable evidence about the game in Wales waiting to be discovered in the many newspapers of the time, particularly with regard to other parts of the country.

Contemporary football handbooks also proved to be very informative, as were copies of Alcock's *Football Annual*, another previously underused source for Welsh rugby. Other primary material included RFU and WFU minute books, as well as census returns, directories and biographical compilations which were used to identify individuals and their social background.[2]

A wide range of books and articles and several academic theses were consulted, though there has been surprisingly little detailed and academic research on nineteenth-century Welsh rugby. Of course, David Smith and Gareth Williams' brilliant tour de force, *Fields of Praise*, was not only the inspiration for this book but was also a constant and invaluable reference.

I am also most grateful to the following for their kind and generous permission to use their illustrations in this book: Cardiff Libraries, Howard Evans, Bernard Green, David Hughes, Lindsay Jenkins, Gaynor Jones and Gareth Thomas.

Contemporary sources invariably refer to "football" clubs rather than "rugby" clubs, so this style is consistently adopted throughout the book when discussing rugby clubs and unions in the nineteenth century, for example, Cardiff Football Club and Welsh Football Union. These, after all, are the names they called themselves and by which they were always referred to in the press at the time, whilst usages such as "Glamorgan RFC" and "South Wales Rugby Football Union" are simply anachronisms. It was because all local Victorian rugby clubs chose to call themselves just "football clubs" that, when the forerunners of Cardiff City FC were formed in 1899, they were forced to adopt the title "Riverside AFC". The name "Riverside Football Club" was already being used that season by an older established rugby club which played in the Cardiff and District league. In addition, following the practice in south Wales during the nineteenth century, all references in the book to the round ball version of football are qualified as "association" or "soccer". The word "football" is also sometimes used as a generic term describing all varieties of football. Finally, as Cardiff did not receive city status until 1905, it is described as a town in any reference before then.

Notes

1. The *Western Mail* was published from 1869 and the *South Wales Daily News* from 1872.
2. Unfortunately, WFU minutes before 1892 no longer survive.

ABBREVIATIONS

AFC	Association Football Club
C&DFU	Cardiff and District Football Union
CDFU	Cardiff District Football Union
FA	Football Association
FAW	Football Association of Wales
FC	Football Club
FU	Football Union
GAV	Glamorgan Artillery Volunteers
GRV	Glamorgan Rifle Volunteers
GWR	Great Western Railway
IFU	Irish Football Union (Irish Rugby Football Union)
IJHS	International Journal of the History of Sport
IRB	International Rugby Board
NU	Northern Union
RFC	Rugby Football Club
RFU	Rugby Football Union
RMA	Royal Military Academy
RU	Rugby Union
RWF	Royal Welch Fusiliers
SFU	Scottish Football Union (Scottish Rugby Union)
SWDN	South Wales Daily News
SWFC	South Wales Football Club
SWFU	South Wales Football Union
WFU	Welsh Football Union
WM	Western Mail
WMC	Working Men's Club
WRU	Welsh Rugby Union

1

INTRODUCTION

'The contagion will spread'

In December 1905, *The Irish Times* despatched a reporter to cover the All Blacks game in Cardiff. Only a little over thirty years earlier, apart from a few young middle-class blades who took exercise by occasionally playing with an oval ball, the game of rugby was barely known in the town. Yet following the historic Welsh victory over New Zealand, that Irish journalist memorably described the excited, good humoured and wildly enthusiastic crowds he witnessed that day in and around the Arms Park as "this rugby spellbound people". He went on to declare that the Welsh were "undoubtedly the best exponents of the game." [1]

How did this come about? How did a game which elsewhere was played predominantly by public schools and largely middle-class clubs become within a few years such a passion for people of all classes in Wales and in Cardiff in particular?

By the early 1880s, as will be shown, rugby was already putting down strong roots in south Wales. But a series of events in the middle part of that decade was to establish Cardiff as one of the aristocrats of the club game, and, in so doing, permanently embed rugby football into the popular culture and the very lifeblood of the town.

During miserable weather in February 1884, a decision was made by a selection committee in a hotel room in the centre of Cardiff which was to lead eventually to profound changes in the way rugby has been played ever since. The Cardiff club were due to play at Cheltenham College but, owing to the torrential conditions, only a few players bothered to turn up at the station. So a team was hurriedly cobbled together using some of the reserves who were also meeting at the station travelling to an away fixture at Chepstow. Despite this, Cardiff won the match at Cheltenham, partly due to the play of Frank Hancock, who was making his First XV debut at three-quarter. This new recruit was a highly talented player. Within two months, and after only five games for Cardiff, he won the first of his four international caps when he played for Wales against Ireland. [2]

When Frank Hancock came from Somerset to manage his father's new brewing interests in south Wales, he was already an accomplished club and county footballer, and he would shortly captain the town's rugby club in its most successful ever season. It was a fortunate set of circumstances which brought him to Cardiff at a time when his leadership and tactical skills could be used to lasting benefit for the game.[3]

Impressed with his performance at Cheltenham, the Cardiff selectors decided to keep him in the side for the following fixture with Gloucester. Perhaps not wishing to upset their fellow club-mates, they were reluctant to drop any of the regular three-quarters for a newcomer, so they came up with the inspired solution of selecting four, and thus a new system was born. The Cardiff selectors continued to experiment with four three-quarters during the rest of the 1883–4 season and the following year. They sometimes reverted to three players, but settled on the new formation by the end of 1884–5. By this time, other teams like Llanelli, Neath and Swansea were also occasionally selecting four three-quarters, demonstrating that Welsh clubs were already prepared to experiment with promising new ideas.[4] Even more junior clubs were willing to innovate at this very early stage. When Penarth played Canton in March 1885, both employed four three-quarters.[5] Hancock is often credited with "inventing" the system but Henry (Joe) Simpson, his captain in those two seasons, and another Englishman incidentally, was the first to adopt it.[6] It was Frank Hancock, however, who worked out the best method of applying the new four three-quarter formation and, in doing so, he produced a tactical advance which helped to transform the game.

In August 1885, he was unanimously elected captain to replace Simpson. Hancock had a reputation for being a disciplinarian and his impact on the club was immediate. Up to that season, Cardiff had enjoyed success, but lacked consistency. The chaotic circumstances surrounding his introduction to the club eighteen months earlier must have made him realise that a dramatic change in organisation was required if Cardiff were to achieve their potential.

After the four three-quarter system had eventually become universally accepted, other clubs began to claim that they had played four three-quarters before Cardiff and therefore had "invented" the system. Writing in 1948, W.J. Townsend Collins, the highly regarded rugby correspondent for the *South Wales Argus* and whose own playing career went back to 1876, identified two such clubs. He astutely added, however, "What is certain is that to Cardiff belongs the credit of having perfected the system."[7] Searching for some solace in England's defeat by Wales in 1899, *The Sunday Special* even claimed that it was an English invention. "The Welshmen ... have done splendid work in making Rugby football popular – even if they did obtain the system from the West of England clubs".[8] But, in any case, such claims entirely miss the point. It wasn't so much the mere placing of four men in the line-up which mattered: rather it was what was done with the new formation which was revolutionary. This was Hancock's – and Cardiff's – great legacy to the game.

Reducing the pack from nine to eight was potentially a great risk and initially it was strongly criticised and resisted by many pundits and clubs, even those in the generally more progressive north of England. For Cardiff, this reduction was particularly risky because they did not possess big forwards. Hancock's solution was to encourage them to concentrate on winning and transferring the ball to the half-backs as quickly as possible, rather than engaging in prolonged scrums and mauls, which was then the conventional role for the forwards. Though this may not appear particularly innovative today, it certainly was so in the 1880s. For some, it represented nothing less than the emasculation of rugby football. Even as late as 1899, Arthur Budd, a former inter-national and President of the RFU, was advising *Sporting Life* readers that English "decadence" began when they tried to imitate the Welsh three-quarter game and abandoned old style forward play.[9]

At this time, both half-backs "fed the scrum" and there was no spe-cialised outside-half. Instead of kicking or running with the ball, which was the usual practice, under Hancock the half-backs' responsibility was to move it quickly and accurately from the scrum to the three-quarters. Cardiff were lucky here since they possessed one of the finest passing half-backs of the era in William "Buller" Stadden, described as "brilliant" even by the largely Anglo-centric *Football Annual*.[10] The role of the centre three-quarters was to feed the wings as quickly as pos-sible with low, accurate passing. Facing only three opponents, the wings invariably had a clear overlap by the time they received the ball and the tries flowed easily. Hancock also stressed the importance of correct alignment and insisted the backs took their passes on the run. Simple ideas perhaps but somebody had to be the first to practise them.

The speed and accuracy of the passing of the ball confounded oppo-nents whose own attempts at passing in response were feeble in com-parison, often amounting to no more than lobbing the ball in the hope that someone would catch it. Only three teams managed to score against Cardiff all season. Used to a more sluggish style of play in which the ball was often tied up for minutes in mauls and in which combined passing was a relatively rare event, spectators are recorded as being bewildered by the speed of the play; some even had difficulty follow-ing the ball. On their way to their match at Stradey Park, the team were "saluted with a few stones and handfuls of mud".[11] However, after their comprehensive ten try victory, they were greeted with cheers as they drove back through the streets of Llanelli. Even local journalists were impressed. "Llanellyite" perceptively wrote:

> fifteen [Cardiff] players worked with a perfection of combination unexampled in the annals of Welsh football. Selfishness, that bane of good play, was never once perceptible ... the victorious team, not only should be the pride of Cardiff, but of the whole Principality, and strange it will be if their success does not stimulate to more scientific play the other teams of Wales, and operate to improve the exposition of the Rugby game generally.[12]

The "passing game" had arrived.

The results were astonishing. Of twenty-seven games played, only the last against Moseley was narrowly lost when it seems that nerves finally got the better of the players. An even more remarkable statistic is that while 131 tries were scored, only a mere four were conceded. Gareth Williams has described the new system as, "a concept as enterprising and innovative as the brash, self-confident society that invented it."[13] It is no surprise then that in such an enterprising society, other Welsh clubs quickly responded to the new system by adopting it themselves, some before the end of the season. Thus, as "Llanellyite" accurately predicted, before very long, the "Cardiff game" became the "Welsh game". English clubs like Gloucester, with regular fixtures against Welsh teams, also switched, but in the main it was initially resisted by many die-hards in the English, Scottish and Irish game. A not untypical response was that of *Pastime*'s rugby "expert" who wrote in 1885, "There is really not room for four three-quarter backs on an ordinary ground. In Jemmy [sic] Stokes's day the post used to be taken with some ease by *one*."[14] Players outside Wales seemed to struggle with the new system. Even as late as 1897, following Wales' 11-0 victory over England, "Old Stager" was able to boast about "swift, sharp, low passing, which seems easy to crack local players, as it is pleasing to the eye of the spectator, and which is so difficult for the premier backs in the three sister countries to acquire."[15]

One of the most common descriptions of the play of Hancock's team was its "machine-like" quality. To modern ears this may sound rather negative, conveying a sense of the mundane, the mechanical and the repetitive. However, at the high summer of Britain's industrialisation, which had so transformed the lives of Victorians, the analogy was both valid and complimentary. Combination, precision, speed and practice were the keys to the system's success. Unfortunately, the "scientific attack" theory proved difficult to transfer successfully to the international level, where teams were assembled at short notice with no opportunity for practice. In addition, in the early years, Wales simply did not have strong enough forwards to compete with the bigger nine men packs of the other nations. Only towards the end of the 1890s, with the emergence of the "Rhondda forward," were Wales finally able to prove conclusively the superiority of their system and silence its critics for ever. After Wales' decisive victory over England in 1899, the *Morning Leader* ran up the white flag at last and conceded defeat.

> Our methods, like our "rulers", are antiquated ... After Saturday's lesson the contagion will spread, and in a few years' time we will doubtless see the "Welsh game" played throughout England. We are a proud, if not pig-headed nation, but we will show wisdom even at this late hour by copying the superior method of our conquerors.[16]

The *Morning Leader* was right. That contagion was the basis of Wales' great success in the first "Golden Era" of the 1900s, which included the historically important victory over the first All Blacks, and it *did* eventually spread, not just to England but throughout the rugby world. This, therefore, is arguably Cardiff's greatest contribution to the game.

It is no exaggeration to claim that these events in Cardiff ultimately brought about a revolution in the way rugby was played. It led to the demise of the forward-dominated mauling game in which passes were made only infrequently. For the first time, it handed the attacking thrust to the backs, who had previously played a largely defensive tackling or kicking role. Some have suggested that one of the reasons why association football eventually began to eclipse rugby – at least in England – in the late nineteenth century was its greater fluidity compared to the more static handling code.[17] But this ignores how dramatically rugby changed after 1885. It was in Wales, and in Cardiff in particular, that these changes were first put into practice and exploited so well. There is no doubt that, in Cardiff *and* throughout south Wales, this new and exciting playing style contributed greatly to the enormous growth in the popularity of rugby, both as a game to play and to watch. Within four years of Hancock's groundbreaking season, the number of teams in the immediate Cardiff area alone rose from sixty to well over 200. Certainly for the next fifteen years, it far outstripped soccer in the locality.

Gwyn Nicholls, the captain of the Welsh team which defeated the All Blacks and regarded by many as the greatest player of the era, wrote about its impact in 1908:

> [Rugby's] process of evolution has been very marked during the last twenty years. ... all clubs nowadays *combine* more or less ... The new idea was originated and its virtues first demonstrated by the Cardiff team, which, under the captaincy of ... F.E. Hancock,

originated the four three-quarter game ... [it requires the] total merging of the player in the team. He is no longer even an [sic] unit, but rather an integral part of the whole.[18]

Forty years later, Townsend Collins – he was after all a Newport man – generously acknowledged:

> The "Cardiff tradition" has persisted till this day. No other club have played the four three-quarter game with such consistent success. Theory has been handed on from generation to generation ... players have been found to illustrate anew the value of judgement, unselfishness and accuracy in the combined game with eight men in the scrummage and four in the threequarter line.[19]

Both the success and the playing style of the club became matters of great pride for Cardiff's sports-loving citizens and so rugby became an important part of the popular culture of the town. It was, after all, the "Cardiff game". It is interesting too to note the extent to which Hancock's team mirrored the character of the fast growing town. Though all of the seventeen leading players lived and worked in Cardiff, only nine were born in the locality. One came from Pembrokeshire and another from north Wales. Two were Scots, while one Cardiff-born player was a member of the town's large Irish community. Four team members were English and it should not be forgotten that the four three-quarter system was both introduced and developed at the club by two of them. A third of the team was working class. The players were also substantially products of a local club system which flourished spectacularly during the late nineteenth century. The composition of Hancock's team was, then, a reflection of Victorian Cardiff society and as such it was a team with which the town's citizens could easily identify and proudly share in its success.

This book is concerned with many of the themes highlighted here: the extraordinary growth in the number of clubs in late nineteenth-century Cardiff; the take-up of the game by working-class players and its socially inclusive nature there; civic pride and the popularity of rugby; the wider impact of the game; and its contribution to local, civic and national consciousness. The story begins, however, with the arrival of "football" in south Wales in the 1860s.

Notes

1. *Irish Times*, 18 Dec. 1905.
2. See Andrew Hignell and Gwyn Prescott, *Cardiff Sporting Greats* (Stroud, 2007), pp. 163–4 for an account of Frank Hancock.

3. Remarkably, the Hancocks were not the only English brewing family to contribute to the sporting heritage of Cardiff. Joseph Brain helped to elevate Glamorgan County Cricket Club to first-class status, while other members of the Brain family have supported the Cardiff and District Rugby Union over the years and Brains still sponsor the District as well as the Welsh Rugby Union today. See Hignell and Prescott, *Cardiff Sporting Greats*, pp. 41–3 for an account of Joseph Brain.

4. *South Wales Daily News* (hereafter *SWDN*) and *Western Mail* (hereafter *WM*) Sept. 1884 to Apr. 1885 passim.

5. *SWDN* 17 Mar. 1885.

6. In 1884, Durham-born Simpson became the first man without an Oxbridge background to captain Wales.

7. W.J. Townsend Collins, *Rugby Recollections* (Newport, 1948), p. 13.

8. Quoted in *SWDN* 9 Jan. 1899.

9. Quoted in *SWDN* 21 Mar. 1899.

10. *Football Annual*, 1887 p. 168.

11. *SWDN* 16 Nov. 1885.

12. *WM* 16 Nov. 1885.

13. Gareth Williams, *1905 and All That: Essays on Rugby Football, Sport and Welsh Society* (Llandysul, 1991), p. 19.

14. Quoted in *SWDN* 30 Mar. 1885.

15. *SWDN* 11 Jan. 1897.

16. Quoted in *SWDN* 10 Jan. 1899.

17. Dave Russell, *Football and the English: A Social History of Association Football in England, 1863–1995* (Preston, 1997), p. 20.

18. E. Gwyn Nicholls, *The Modern Game and How to Play It* (London, 1908), pp. 9–11.

19. Townsend Collins, *Rugby Recollections*, p. 13.

2

FROM FOOTBALL TO RUGBY

'Neither dribbling fish nor handling fowl'

The remarkable popularity of rugby in Victorian Cardiff did not occur in isolation. It is necessary, therefore, to establish the context for this by exploring the introduction and consolidation of the game in Wales up to 1881, when the Welsh Football Union (WFU) was founded. In so doing, the hitherto unrecognised contribution which the town made to the earliest days of rugby football in Wales will be demonstrated.

Within a few years, the rapid expansion of the coal industry transformed nineteenth-century Welsh society. It also dramatically changed the country's sporting culture, for it was during this period of massive population growth, mainly the result of inward migration, that rugby football became the dominant sport in the south. In so doing, it helped to bind newcomers not only to their communities but also to their nation.

The arrival of rugby in Wales coincided with a period of extraordinary economic change. Between 1870 and 1914, south Wales became a centre of heavy industry of world significance. At no other time in its history was Wales more important to the British economy.[1] Though the expansion in steel and tin-plate production contributed to the spectacular growth experienced in this period, its main cause was the dramatic increase in the export-driven demand for Welsh coal. In 1840, Wales was producing four and a half million tons. By the 1870s, this had risen to sixteen million and by 1913 coal output reached fifty-seven million. The exploitation of steam coal in the Glamorgan and Monmouthshire valleys was well advanced by the 1880s but the continued expansion, largely due to the seemingly insatiable demand from the world's steam ships, was especially pronounced in the Rhondda. The anthracite areas of west Wales also saw an unprecedented expansion, mainly to meet domestic and commercial demands. By 1913, over half of all British coal exports passed through the ports of south Wales and there were over a quarter of a million men – almost one in three of the total labour force – employed in the industry.[2]

Initially, demand for labour was largely met from Wales itself, mainly by migration from the depressed countryside. Between 1851 and 1911, rural Wales experienced a net loss of population of 338,000: this was balanced by an inward migration into the south Wales coalfield of 366,000. From the 1890s, however, the migrants came increasingly from outside Wales, particularly from the west of England and the border counties.[3] By 1911, a fifth of Glamorgan's population and a quarter of Monmouthshire's had been born outside Wales, mainly in England.[4]

During every decade after 1850, there was a net gain through migration in the populations of Glamorgan and Monmouthshire. As David Smith and Gareth Williams argue, the massive migration into the area was highly significant as far as Welsh rugby is concerned. The industries of south Wales were labour intensive. Not only did coal have to be cut and steel and tin-plate manufactured, they also had to be carried to the ports and transferred onto ships, while their export had to be arranged through coal and shipping companies. Railway lines and port facilities had to be constructed. This all required a new workforce which had to be housed and serviced and, as a consequence, new urban communities sprang up in the valley areas, while port towns like Swansea, Newport and Cardiff expanded dramatically. This newly urbanised population also had to be entertained and it was here that rugby football had a special contribution to make.[5]

Rugby came late to Wales. By the 1860s, clubs playing according to rules based on those deriving from Rugby School had been established not only in England but also in Scotland, Ireland and even Australia. While there is no evidence to support Guy's Hospital's claim of an 1843 foundation date, England's oldest club, Liverpool was in existence by the 1857–8 season. The title of the oldest club in the world, though, is claimed by Trinity College Dublin and is supported by a newspaper report from as early as 1855.[6] However, it was only during the early 1870s that the Rugby School code began to have any noticeable impact in Wales, although there is evidence that sporadic games of hybrid "football" were being played across south Wales before then.

Jennifer Macrory reveals that because of the increasing numbers of pupils attending Rugby School by the 1840s, the customary practice of communicating the rules by word of mouth could no longer be relied upon.[7] Thus, in August 1845, and some eighteen years before the Football Association, the Rugby boys produced a printed booklet containing the "Laws of Football Played at Rugby School". These are the earliest written rules of football.[8] They were regularly updated and Adrian Harvey has revealed that they were made available to outsiders in 1859 when they were published in *Lillywhite's Guide to Cricketers*.[9]

The revised rule book of 1862 was the first actually written for the benefit of all players, whether at Rugby School or not. This had been produced because by the early 1860s, the handling game was expanding and demand for the rules was coming from emerging clubs like Liverpool, Blackheath, Richmond, and Manchester; from the universities; and from other public schools like Marlborough, Cheltenham, Clifton, Haileybury and Wellington.[10] In Ireland, laws were drawn up in Trinity College Dublin by an Old Rugeian, while in Scotland, public schools and clubs were also playing a form of rugby by the 1850s. In 1868 Edinburgh Academy produced the "Laws of Football As Played by the Principal Clubs in Scotland". The official historian of the Scottish Rugby Union claims that the first Scotland v England international match in 1871 may have been played under these laws.[11]

This illustrates that it would be a mistake to assume that all clubs and schools in the 1860s played to a common set of laws. Even teams favouring the handling game did not follow Rugby School's rules exactly. Blackheath, for instance, produced their own set of laws in 1862.[12] As Adrian Harvey points out, some clubs "were very catholic in their adoption of rules" and used elements of both rugby and association football in their games.[13] The *Football Annual* of 1868 lists the differences between the varieties of football being played at that time and it is clear that there were many variations, even between those playing a broadly similar type of football.[14] In his recent book on early football, Harvey usefully identifies five main categories which were played at this time. At the two extremes were those teams which only played a "pure" form of either association or rugby. Then there were those who played games which were based on one of these two codes but with some variations. Finally, some teams played a version of football which adopted rules from both codes.[15] Nevertheless, for those who preferred a handling game, it was the Rugby School rules which provided the substance and much of the terminology for the first set of laws drawn up by the RFU in 1871 and which became universally adopted soon after. The RFU minutes confirm this in their description of the laws as "Football Rules ... based upon the Rugby system of play".[16]

It has to be borne in mind in the following discussion, therefore, that before the mid 1870s clubs did not *necessarily* adhere to any single set of unified rules. It was common practice to adopt local variations, or compromise on rules, or even play under a variety of other codes. Harvey has discovered, for example, that during a remarkable five week period in 1863–4, Richmond first played Forest FC under Cambridge rules, the code most distinct from rugby, then Barnes under the new FA rules and finally Blackheath under rugby laws.[17] It should also be pointed out that up to the 1880s, it was by no means certain that association would eventually become the dominant version of football in Britain. In the north of England in the 1870s, for instance, rugby "towered" over soccer, according to Tony Collins.[18] It should not be a matter of any surprise, therefore, that rugby took root so strongly in Wales at that time.

Whilst football has ancient and popular roots, this book does not enter into any investigation or debate about the origins of the game of rugby football itself. David Smith and Gareth Williams argue in relation to the game in Wales:

> Bloodhounds roaming the centuries on the scent of the pedigree of Welsh rugby … have detected a number of exciting aromas, but they have managed to establish little more than that ball games have been a feature of the Welsh countryside for well over a millennium.[19]

As elsewhere in the British Isles, the existence of an earlier popular tradition of folk football may partly explain why rugby was eventually adopted readily and widely in Wales, particularly by the working class. Tony Collins refers to this as a "residual consciousness of older forms of football".[20] John Gouldstone argues that more sophisticated versions, some involving handling, were already being played by the working class in the first half of the century, while research by Adrian Harvey also demonstrates that, at that time, varieties of organised football with rules, referees and fixed teams were taking place outside the influence of the public schools.[21] There has recently been some debate in academic circles about the significance of such early, non-public school football.[22] It is possible that the eventual adoption of rugby in Wales was the result of a convergence of such working-class football with the public school game, though little evidence for it has so far emerged. David Smith and Gareth Williams refer to cnappan as the most plausible forebear of Welsh rugby, with which, they argue, it shared some "striking similarities … It engendered a vigorous community involvement and fierce inter-village rivalry; it was a game of throwing, tackling and kicking".[23]

Adaptations of cnappan or folk football may have been practised well into the nineteenth century. In the 1870s, there are reports of parish football games of an unknown nature still being played at Christmas near Cowbridge; whilst Shrove Tuesday football took place in the streets of Narberth in Pembrokeshire as late as 1884.[24] Richard Holt argues that when football was taken up in the industrial areas, it was often played in a way which might have been recognised by participants in an earlier version of folk football. Old rivalries too could be sustained through the new game.[25]

However, according to the official historians of rugby in Scotland and Ireland, though there may have also been a tradition of earlier folk football involving handling in those countries, it was predominantly pupils and masters – both returning locals and newcomers – from English rugby playing schools who introduced the codified version of the handling game there. In addition, it was through the public schools and universities, crucially located in the main urban centres, that rugby was eventually introduced to a wider Scottish and Irish public.[26]

The comparatively late arrival of rugby in Wales may, therefore, be partly explained by the absence of any large public schools and universities in the main centres of population at this time. The three public schools in south Wales were all located in rural areas – Llandovery, Brecon and Monmouth – and they were small compared to their English and Scottish counterparts. Between the founding of Llandovery in 1848 and 1875, for instance, there were never more than eighty boys at the school. By 1875 the numbers had declined to forty, whilst Christ College Brecon had fewer than a hundred boys in the years before 1881.[27] Cheltenham, on the other hand, had over 600 pupils as early as 1858.[28]

In addition, Monmouth and Brecon did not *formally* adopt rugby until the middle of the 1870s by which time the game was already starting to develop in Wales. Indeed, rather than initiating rugby in Wales, they may have taken it up because it was already beginning to be played locally. It is possible, then, that the contribution of these Welsh public schools to the *introduction* of rugby may not have been as crucial as is sometimes claimed, whilst private and grammar schools may have had a greater influence on the adoption of the game in Wales than is often acknowledged. On the other hand, as will be shown, all three south Wales public schools were playing *forms* of football before the 1870s and this perhaps matters more in terms of their influence than their formal adoption of a specific code. As an illustration of this, several prominent members of the very successful early Newport XV (1875–1879) had played a hybrid game, perhaps closer to association, at Monmouth before that school adopted rugby.

There were no universities in Wales until Aberystwyth was founded in 1872 – again a small institution located well away from the main urban centres – and Cardiff in 1883. The only higher education establishments which did contribute to the early game in south Wales were St. David's College Lampeter and Carmarthen Training College, both situated in rural west Wales. There were no large urban equivalents of Edinburgh and Glasgow Universities, founder members of the Scottish Football Union, or of Trinity College Dublin (1855) and Sydney University (1864), both of which were the first clubs in their respective countries.[29]

That Wales had a smaller middle and upper class was another contributory factor. There were relatively fewer former public school and university men returning home bearing rugby balls and copies of the laws. Nevertheless, it would appear that it *was* these men who were eventually instrumental in bringing the game to Wales. This happened not only across Britain but also throughout the rugby world.[30] It is no co-incidence that a swathe of rugby playing public schools is found in and around the west of England and many affluent south Wales families sent their sons to institutions such as Marlborough, Cheltenham, Hereford, Clifton, Sherborne and Blundell's. Old boys from these, as well as from Rugby School itself, of course, were involved in early Welsh rugby, an example of what Neil Tranter terms the "proximity to the culture hearth".[31] A similar process appears to have happened in north-east Wales, where, as Martin Johnes and Ian Garland demonstrate, it was old boys of Shrewsbury School who played a key role in introducing soccer there.[32] This is consistent with David Russell's work on the spatial differences in the preference for rugby or soccer in Yorkshire and Lancashire, where he found that this depended at least partly on the schools which the local elite attended.[33]

Jennifer Macrory shows that west country public schools were "sending out players in force by the 1870s" and she argues that the subsequent popularity of rugby in that region is attributable to this.[34] It is now widely accepted that the Welsh game was stimulated by an influx of rugby playing migrants from the west of England.[35] With regard to public school men, there is much truth in this and, indeed, Macrory agrees: "The west-country schools supplied much of the early support for the game in South Wales".[36] But as far as ordinary *club* players are concerned, this may need qualification. A study of the founding dates of west of England clubs reveals that very few were formed before the early 1870s.[37] Therefore, there is some doubt about the extent to which many experienced *club* players from that region were involved in the early *introduction* of rugby to Wales. On the other hand, there is absolutely no question that from the later 1870s onwards their contribution to the *evolution* of the Welsh game was significant.[38]

The official historians of the WRU place the first incursion of rugby into Wales in the rural west, following the arrival of Rowland Williams as vice-principal at St. David's College Lampeter in 1850. He was a contemporary at Cambridge of Albert Pell, the Rugbeian who is credited by some with introducing rugby to Cambridge in 1839. In 1858, Williams encouraged his students to take up "healthful exercise", including football. Initially, internal games were played but from the mid 1860s, "foreign" matches of an undefined football nature took place against school teams, in particular Llandovery. By the 1870s, when club rugby was beginning to take a firm hold, Lampeter College had one of the strongest teams in Wales, reaching the final of the South Wales Challenge Cup on one occasion. The College were also founder members of the WFU.[39]

An account of rugby at Llandovery College, published in the *Western Mail* in 1949, maintained that "football of a sort" was "probably" played there in the 1850s.[40] A recent history of the school refers to a claim that the first game between Llandovery and Lampeter was played as early as 1856, though there is no contemporary evidence for this. It also mentions an account by a Breconian, probably J.A. Parry-Price referred to below, who recalled playing against Llandovery at some time between 1864 and 1867.[41] David Smith and Gareth Williams' suggestion that these early matches were "a hybrid game" is confirmed by the following evidence in the school history relating to the introduction of formal rugby rules at Llandovery.[42]

After teaching at Merchiston Castle School in Edinburgh, Watkin Price Whittington took up a post at Llandovery in 1868. In a letter written thirty years later, he described how he introduced rugby there soon after arriving. He referred to the game it replaced as "a *sort* of Association without definite rule", though the *Llandovery School Journal* in 1926 claimed that rugby was "easily adopted" in the 1870s "because the old Rugby game had for years been played". Since Whittington arrived at Llandovery before the RFU's codification of the laws in 1871, it is possible that the version of rugby that he brought to the college was based on the 1868 *"Laws of Football As Played by the Principal Clubs in Scotland"*.[43]

Whittington's account illustrates the way in which the early game was spread, in this case by schoolmasters from England via Scotland and eventually to Wales. Rugby was adopted at Merchiston in 1858–9, at which time there were three masters at the school who had had contact with rugby in England, including one who had taught at Cheltenham.[44]

The evidence provided by Whittington, then, appears to confirm Llandovery College as one of the first rugby playing organisations in Wales. It is likely that Lampeter formally adopted rugby laws at around the same time. Kenneth Evans claims a college club was formed as early as 1866, but provides no source.[45] Like Lampeter, Llandovery College were founder members of the WFU and they competed in the early years of the South Wales Challenge Cup until 1881. However, though Llandoverians were frequently found in the ranks of many of the first Welsh clubs and international teams, their strongest influence on the early game may have been in providing good regular opposition for newly emerging teams. As was common practice in schools at the time, the college XV would regularly include masters, like Charles Prytherch Lewis (C.P. Lewis) and Thomas Judson, both of whom were capped by Wales as adult players of the college. In one game in 1882, the Llandovery College team included six current and future internationals.[46]

Jonathan Harris' study of Breconshire soccer notes a very early mention of football at Christ College Brecon in 1861, when six schoolboys challenged any six "gentlemen" from the town to a game. It would be some years, however, before the College would formally adopt rugby. J.A. Parry-Price, who had been at Brecon in the second half of the 1860s, recalled in 1931 that "Our football was somewhat feeble, the game played being a kind of soccer, but with no very stringent rules with regard to hands or offside."[47] Swansea Grammar School played football matches with Kilvey in March 1865 and twelve "gentlemen" of Swansea in 1871.[48] Another early game took place between a Bridgend School XIV and R. Randall's VIII in 1866. The school won by 3 goals to 1:

> due in great measure to the general good play and "charging" of Messrs Green, E.S. Thomas and W.W. Thomas. Messrs. E.F. Blosse, T.A. Rees and A.W. Stockwood also contributed … For the "eight", Messrs. R. Randall, R.C. Blosse, T.J. Morgan and P. Llewellin, worked hard and well; the first gentleman distinguishing himself in the "squashes". The disparity of numbers was counterbalanced by the prestige of the public school men playing with the "eight."[49]

The mention of "public school men" playing football in south Wales at this early time is instructive. Robert C. Blosse of the public school "eight" was at Marlborough at the time. His younger brother, Edward F. Blosse also attended this prominent rugby school soon afterwards, and he later became a member of the Cardiff club.[50] The references to "charging" and "squashes" may also imply that the game was a version of rugby, but it cannot be claimed that this provides conclusive proof. It *is* known, however, that Bridgend School had adopted rugby by the early 1870s. Welsh international, W.D. (Bill) Phillips, learned the game there and, when he retired in April 1885, he claimed to have played for fourteen years, suggesting he first played at the school in 1870–1.[51] There are also newspaper reports of the school playing rugby by 1872.[52] Bridgend was a boarding and day school which prepared boys for the public schools, professions and commerce. Sport was an important part of the curriculum. The boys received "every encouragement in Manly Exercises" and were provided with a "Gymnasium and a large Cricket Ground."[53] If most of the boys being prepared for public school went on to those in the west of England, then it would be reasonable to suppose that rugby became the preferred sport at Bridgend from an early date.

The contribution of the military – through garrisons, volunteers and military academies – in introducing the game to Wales has not previously been explored. Hignell reveals that the presence of military units helped to stimulate interest in cricket in south east Wales during the 1840s.[54] According to J.D. Campbell, the Royal Military Academy Woolwich was playing rugby by 1860 and the sport became popular in the Army during the 1870s.[55] The armed services were influential in spreading the game throughout the world, including Australia, Canada, New Zealand and South Africa and there is some, admittedly limited, evidence of their early involvement in Wales.[56] Between 1867 and 1869, the Royal Welch Fusiliers (RWF) were stationed at Newport, Brecon and Cardiff. As it happens, these were all centres of early Welsh football.[57]

In 1868, the RWF participated in perhaps the first ever football match at the Arms Park. Again, there is no certainty about the form of football which was played, but perhaps "scrimmages" suggests that it might have been a more robust version.

Yesterday the first match of football played upon the Cardiff Arms field, took place between a picked eleven of the Cardiff and Canton Cricket Clubs and fifteen of the 23rd Royal Welsh Fusiliers headed by Lieutenant Patterson and Ensign Gilbert … After about two hours of spirited play, the match resulted in a draw, neither party being able to effect a go [sic] kick, though the 23rd had decidedly the best of the match. Lieutenant Patterson was very conspicuous in the "scrimmages"… Messrs. Jones and Yorath on the Cardiff side, did their party good service, as did also Mr. Peter Robinson, of the Free Library.[58]

Cardiff cricket club had been re-formed the previous year and this is an example of the influence of cricket on early football in Wales, which others have noted.[59] The match clearly aroused local interest, for another was immediately arranged for the 28th March and this too was duly reported:

at the Cardiff Arms Park, the largest number of spectators we remember having seen present at any sports, watched the game throughout with unflagging interest … when time was called, the victory remained undecided, though, in the opinion of the major-ity of the spectators, the Cardiff Football Club might well have claimed Mr. Heath's first kick as a clear "goal" … For especially good play amongst the Fusiliers, we may mention Ensign Gilbert, Private Astbury, and Glass, each of whom gained a "touch down" … For the club, first praise is due to Mr. Bassett Jones,

while the play of Messrs. Hutchins, Rhys Jones, and Bell, were
deservedly admired. The "touch downs" for the club were gained
by the last two players.[60]

The references to touch downs may provide a further clue about the type
of football played. That the match attracted the largest ever sporting
crowd to the Arms Park clearly anticipated the hold which rugby was to
have in later decades on the public of both Cardiff and Wales. Whether
the cricketers actually formed a "Cardiff Football Club", however, must
remain an open question, in the absence of any further evidence.

No record of any further games played by the RWF has yet been
traced, though it is quite likely that they played other unrecorded
matches, particularly against the Newport club, which, as will be seen,
was in existence in 1867–8. What is certain is that RWF officers played
for this Newport team while stationed in the town. Though no direct
link between the RWF and Brecon has yet been established, it may be
no coincidence that a Brecon club existed by 1868. The club historians refer to a local press report that year of a game between a Brecon
thirteen and twelve "gentlemen" from Abergavenny, who won by a
drop-kick, suggesting they played a form of rugby. There were also further newspaper references to the club in 1868–9.[61] In November 1872,
Brecon arranged a match with the 94th Regiment, though bad weather
prevented it from being played.[62] That Brecon was a garrison town, as
well as being the location of Christ College, may account for the early
arrival of football there.

Local rifle and artillery volunteer corps were other military organisations which helped to spread rugby later during the 1870s and 1880s.
Tony Collins notes the contribution which Volunteers made to early
organised football in the north of England.[63] The Cardiff based 10th
Glamorgan Rifle Volunteers (GRV), for instance, were an early club
which participated in the South Wales Challenge Cup and they were the
first ever team to play against Newport at Rodney Parade.[64] Volunteers in
Aberdare, Neath, Newport and Swansea all had rugby teams from time
to time, while in rural Wales, both Breconshire and Builth Volunteers
played occasional games. It seems that many of the first players in
Wales were also Volunteers and there are a number of reports of matches
between Volunteers and "Civilians". When Cardiff drew the 10th GRV
in the 1878–9 South Wales Challenge Cup, they refused to allow any of
their Volunteer members to play for their opponents in the match.[65]

During 1913, W.J. Townsend Collins, under his pseudonym
"Dromio", wrote a series of articles in the *South Wales Argus* on the
history of Newport rugby club (founded 1874).[66] In these, he drew on
reports in the *Monmouthshire Merlin* relating to three football matches

which were played by an earlier Newport club against Abergavenny between November 1867 and March 1868. There was military involvement in the last of these, as three RWF officers played for Newport while Abergavenny drew on players from a local educational establishment preparing young men for the army and navy. "Dromio" was initially convinced that the game played in this series of matches was a close relative of rugby, citing fifteen a-side teams and references to "dodging" and "running". One of the match reports also mentions that Abergavenny forced "the Newport side to touch the ball behind their own goal".

Townsend Collins was able to speak to several players who had participated in these contests. Two assured him that the game they played *was* rugby. Conversely, however, another player informed him that it was "chiefly a dribbling game, and that the players were not allowed to pick up the ball on the run; but that they *could* run from a catch from an opponent's kick, or from a pass by the foot to the hands on the part of a fellow player ... a player could be tripped or hacked over." "Dromio" was later contacted by an old Newport player, who said that he had played a hybrid game himself at Monmouth, before the school adopted rugby. Although he did not participate in the Newport-Abergavenny matches, he suggested that the game may have been more closely related to association and that it was essentially football "without a qualifying title". "The object of the game was to score a goal by kicking the ball between the posts and there was no cross bar. No try could be scored. But players could handle the ball *and run* if they could catch direct from an opponent's or a comrade's kick (without the ball touching the ground)." Reluctantly, Townsend Collins came to the conclusion that it was a hybrid game, with elements of both rugby and association.[67] The Newport matches, therefore, probably fall into Harvey's fifth category of football which adopted rules from both codes.[68]

So whilst it is not possible to argue with any conviction that these early Newport games were "rugby", neither can they be used as evidence that association pre-dated rugby in south Wales, as claimed by one article on early Welsh soccer.[69] This contends that handling was not allowed in the 1867 Newport-Abergavenny game, but "Dromio" clearly established that running with the ball *was* allowed. The FA had abolished touch downs by this time, whilst running with the ball and hacking had been distinctly outlawed by the first FA laws of December 1863:

Law 9. No player shall carry the ball.
Law 10. Neither tripping nor hacking shall be allowed, and no player shall use his hands to hold or push an adversary.

Whatever rules the games were played under, they were not those of the Football Association.[70]

The Pontypool RFC history, drawing on reports from *The Free Press of Monmouthshire*, shows that at the end of their 1868 season, local cricketers discussed "taking up physical activities during the winter months to keep fit". Two of the main proponents were Arthur and Herbert James, the sons of the Rector of Panteg. Both were educated at Shrewsbury School (where association football was played) and Oxford. By October 1868, the cricketers had formed a football club and played their first match. The club drew up their own rules which were a mixture of rugby and association. The club history suggests that Pontypool's early matches were closer to association. This was confirmed during this research with the discovery of the club's entry in the 1871 *Football Annual* which describes Pontypool as playing a "modification of association". It is tempting to speculate whether this modification might have involved *some* handling, particularly as a report of a fixture against Panteg in *The Free Press* in January 1870 criticised the Pontypool players for frequently using their hands to stop the ball and push it along the ground before kicking it. In October 1871 a fixture with the Tredegarville club of Cardiff was announced in the press, but no report of the match appears to have survived. Since, as will be shown later, Tredegarville played both association and rugby at this time, it is not known which version was played in the fixture. Not until 12th October 1875 did Pontypool formally adopt rugby union laws, though that is not to say, of course, that they did not experiment with rugby before that date and the likelihood is that they did.[71]

The history of Trinity College Carmarthen reveals that the vice-principal and acting principal between 1868 and 1870 was Reverend Francis Marshall, the well known rugby author and administrator. Without providing any evidence, the college history suggests that Marshall was instrumental in bringing rugby to Carmarthen. Given Frank Marshall's influential place in early rugby football, this seems credible.[72] However, at a college alumni dinner in Leeds in 1892, one speaker referred to Marshall's taking "a very active part in cricket, forming a college club which has existed ever since", but unfortunately no reference was made to his setting up a rugby club.[73] Carmarthen Training College was indeed one of Wales' earliest rugby clubs but it was not regularly mentioned in the Cardiff press until 1876–7, several years after Marshall had left.

The sporadic, casual and hybrid nature of football in the 1860s in south Wales – "neither dribbling fish nor handling fowl" in David Smith and Gareth Williams' memorable phrase[74] – gradually began to give way during the following decade to a more organised version. Football was now played according to a recognised and unified set of rules, in particular those of the RFU, which became standard in Wales from the early 1870s. It was during this decade that Wales began to undergo the transformation in sporting culture which was experienced by the whole of Britain in the second half of the nineteenth century. This was partly the result of improved transport and communications, shorter working hours and higher wages.[75] In south Wales, the 1870s was a period of significant growth in organised rugby. By the end of the decade, not only were many members of the Welsh public playing and watching the game regularly, but the social background of the sport's participants was beginning to widen.

The 1871 *Football Annual* provides the first conclusive *contemporary* evidence of a club playing according to rugby laws anywhere in Wales. This lists "Tredegarville (Cardiff)" as having been founded in 1870 with a membership of fifty and playing at Sophia Gardens.[76] It may be significant that the club took the name of a small exclusive area of high status housing rather than that of Roath, the suburb in which it was situated.[77] The secretary was C. Prior of "Lansdowne", Tredegarville. He is also mentioned in C.S. Arthur's 1908 history of Cardiff RFC, where he is described as a teacher at Monkton House. This was a private school located in a large house in The Parade known as "Lansdowne". Arthur adds that the Tredegarville club was comprised mainly of old boys of that school. According to the *Football Annual*, the club played in an outfit of blue and white jerseys, white flannel trousers and blue velvet cap with white silk tassel. Together with the club's name and location, this indicates the likely social status of these early players. The *Football Annual* records Tredegarville as playing *both* rugby and association. Such an arrangement was not at all unusual at the time and several clubs were listed in early *Football Annuals* as playing under a variety of rules. An intriguing report in the *Cardiff and Merthyr Guardian* records Tredegarville's match with the "Cardiff Club" at Sophia Gardens on 21st December 1870, which they won by two goals and four rouges. "Rouges" refers to touch downs and since they had been abolished in association football for over three years, this brief report may perhaps record one of the very earliest club rugby matches played in Wales. The status of the "Cardiff Club" is unknown but entries in the *Football Annual* of 1871, 1872 and 1873 not only show that Tredegarville had some degree of permanence but they also provide the earliest *contemporary* evidence of an established club playing rugby in Wales. The discovery of the existence of this club at such an early time throws an entirely fresh light on the importance of Cardiff as a centre of the early game in Wales.[78]

The Cowbridge Grammar School history is vague about exactly when rugby was introduced there.[79] *Fields of Praise* says it happened in the early 1870s and this may be confirmed by a press report of a football match played on 26th October 1871 between the Grammar School and a team of Cowbridge "Gentlemen".[80] Shortly afterwards, on 8th November 1871, Shewbrooks' Club played the Science and Arts Club at the Arms Park and while the match reports provide no indication of the variety of football in this case, there is some circumstantial evidence to suggest that it may have been a form of rugby.[81] The headmaster of the Science and Arts School (later to evolve by many steps into Cardiff University) was James Bush, who also taught at Monkton House, and who was the father of the famous Welsh international Percy Bush.[82] Henry Shewbrooks was the headmaster of Monkton House school, which was often known by his name during the 1870s. Both played rugby and, indeed, James Bush had participated in the 1868 matches at Cardiff Arms Park against the Royal Welch Fusiliers.[83] Contemporary press match reports show that both men turned out regularly for the Monkton House school rugby team.[84] Shewbrooks, whose contribution to Welsh rugby has been largely over-looked, was born in Taunton and educated at London University and was probably already a rugby player when he came to Cardiff to open his school in 1870. Described on a number of occasions as "the father of South Wales football", he was reputed to have given lines to any pupils who were reluctant to play.[85] His obituary in 1905 claimed that he "was largely instrumental in introducing rugby into South Wales" and, whilst this may be an exaggeration, it does perhaps confirm that Monkton House was crucial in the establishment of rugby in Cardiff at the very least, if not in the whole of Wales.[86]

These events in Cardiff, Brecon, Cowbridge, Pontypool and elsewhere all predate, therefore, the fixture between Neath and Swansea teams on the 3rd February 1872, which is generally held to be the earliest press report of a Welsh rugby match. The centenary history of Neath RFC quotes the *Swansea and Glamorgan Herald* of 7th February:

> On Saturday a match was witnessed between Swansea and Neath clubs. The interest displayed was very great, although the result was undecided, both parties claiming to be victors. [87]

It is this 1872 match report on which Neath base their claim of being the oldest rugby club in Wales and "the birthplace of Welsh rugby" with a foundation date of 1871. Neath neatly side-step their opponents that day by arguing that Swansea did not formally adopt rugby until several years later. According to a later club historian:

As a result of that brief account, Neath are held to be the most senior of Welsh clubs ... because while the footballers of Swansea enjoyed a flirtation with the association game, the men of Neath stuck firmly with the rugger cause.[88]

This interpretation has never been seriously challenged and Neath's seniority and 1871 foundation date are both unquestioningly accepted throughout the game. However, the quoted match report tells us nothing about the version of football played that day and it makes no reference to any rugby features. The game *could*, therefore, have been contested under hybrid or even association rules and so the report provides no more convincing a case for the first ever rugby match in Wales than many of the earlier ones already discussed. Interestingly, Matthews' history of Swansea RFC claims that a later fixture against Neath in November 1872 *was* played under association rules, which suggests that Neath also continued to "flirt" with the round ball.[89] Perhaps of even greater concern is that there are no reports in the *Western Mail* or the *SWDN* of matches involving Neath until 1875–6 and the club does not figure in any of the comprehensive and well recorded early results lists of Llanelli until 1877–8 or Cardiff and Newport until 1878–9. Neither of the Neath club histories refers to any subsequent matches involving Neath until 1876–7.[90] So even if the 1872 match was played under rugby laws, there must be some doubt about whether the club enjoyed a continuous existence thereafter. Neath may well be the oldest rugby playing club in Wales, but stronger evidence than one brief match report from 1872 is required to provide conclusive proof.

Whenever the club *was* formed, it is generally accepted that Neath's founders were members of the professional middle class. David Smith and Gareth Williams say they comprised, "a consortium of ten: a doctor, a surveyor, a mining engineer and a veritable plague of solicitors, in the chamber of one of whose number ... the club's first meetings were held." These included Lewis Kempthorne, who had been at Llandovery and Thomas Whittington, who was educated at Merchiston Castle School and Edinburgh University. He became the first Welshman to play international rugby when he was capped by Scotland in 1873 when playing for Merchistonians.[91]

According to Matthews' history of Swansea RFC, the club was founded on 26th September 1872. It seems that initially association matches were played, including one against Neath on 23rd November 1872. Swansea *formally* adopted the rugby code on 17th October 1874 but this does not *necessarily* mean, of course, that the club had not previously played some games of rugby. Indeed, an early history, published only eighteen years after the event in 1892, claims that the

Swansea club's first game of rugby took place seven months earlier on 28th February 1874. Swansea's first known rugby match was against Llandovery College and the school featured regularly on their fixture lists for some years afterwards, suggesting that Llandoverians were closely involved in the early days of the rugby club.[92]

There are press reports of other games in 1872–3, involving Cowbridge Grammar School, Monkton House and Brecon. A match between Shewbrooks' and Bridgend School resulted in a win for Bridgend by "2 goals and 4 points to nothing", the reference to points suggesting tries or touchdowns.[93] By February 1873, a Llanelli club was in existence, playing internal matches at the New Park. The captain and founder was John Rogers, educated at Rugby School and a manager at his family tinplate works, while the secretary David Williams was a solicitor's clerk.[94] However, this early team disbanded for, as the club's latest historian has demonstrated, the present club was founded in November 1875, when Rogers was elected the first captain. The new secretary was another Rugbeian, William Nevill, a member of a local family prominent in shipping and industry.[95]

During the 1873–4 season, games of an uncertain nature were reported involving Christ College Brecon, Monmouth School, Brecon, Roath, Pontypridd, Swansea Collegiate School, Swansea Normal College and Arnold College Swansea. The Christ College matches were probably played under association type rules.[96] Monmouth had previously played a hybrid "dribbling game in a somewhat casual way," according to H.W. Peill, the master who introduced rugby there in November 1873 and who turned out for them against adult teams. This development was soon to have great significance for the game in Wales, as Old Monmouthians were very prominent members of the highly successful Newport sides of a few years later.[97]

Though there is no conclusive evidence, when "Roath (Cardiff)" met Pontypridd at Sophia Gardens in December 1873, they probably played rugby. It is quite likely that this was the Tredegarville club, or at least an offshoot of it. The game was drawn with no goals but there is reference in the match report to a touch down, not a feature of association football for over six years. Over half of the players who took part can be identified as active in rugby in later years. At least eight became members of the Glamorgan club. It is probable, therefore, that the game was played under a version of rugby laws. Census returns indicate that the participants in the 1873 match were predominantly members of the professional and commercial middle-class. Perhaps as a sign of the growing interest in the game, the match report also commented that "a goodly number of ladies honoured the players with their presence."[98] That a team existed in Pontypridd as early as 1873 seems to have previously gone unnoted. Pontypridd RFC celebrated their centenary in 1976, though a subsequent club history now firmly places the club's foundation as late as 1877–8.[99]

There is evidence that by 1873, if not earlier, the players who were to form the Cardiff Wanderers and Glamorgan clubs, the forerunners of Cardiff, were meeting at the Arms Park to play rugby. The precise origins of Cardiff's two predecessors have never been established. Surprisingly, historians of the club have shown no great interest in them, preferring to concentrate on 1876 as the club's foundation date. For this reason, a misconception has arisen that rugby came later to Cardiff than to other Welsh towns but, as has been shown, this was far from the truth. Unfortunately, the club's first historian is a little confusing in the matter of exact dates.

> It was in what I may call the *season of 1873–1874* that a number of young men ... banded themselves together and formed the first real club in the town and called themselves the Glamorgan Football Club. Mr. S. Campbell Cory was the prime mover and early in the *autumn of 1874* he sent out a circular letter stating that it was intended to form a club, and giving the names of about fifty players who had already consented to join. Those to whom circulars were sent were invited to apply for membership to Mr. Henry White ... Some of the players referred to in Mr. Cory's circular ... had in the preceding season formed themselves into a club for the purpose of playing football in the Cardiff Arms Park.[100]

It is significant that, in 1873–4 both Campbell Cory and Henry White played against Pontypridd for the Roath club, so there was probably a connection with this team and conceivably, therefore, with the earlier Tredegarville club. Glamorgan FC is the only Welsh rugby club listed in the 1875 *Football Annual* when its year of foundation is shown as 1873, though an account published some years later suggests 1872 for both Glamorgan and Cardiff Wanderers.[101] The *Football Annual* also records that Glamorgan played at the Arms Park, had a membership of 147 and wore dark blue jerseys with red collars and cuffs. C.S. Arthur relates that there were a number of Cheltenham College men amongst the first members. Solicitor's clerk Henry White, who was Glamorgan's secretary and treasurer, was born in Cheltenham and may have been a day boy at the college. Thomas Donaldson Selby was sufficiently prominent to be elected Cardiff's first captain in 1876. He played rugby for Cheltenham College and is described in the school's report in the 1874 *Football Annual* as "an honest player [who] makes good use of his strengths".[102] The Cheltenham College connection is also confirmed by subsequent regular fixtures between the school and Glamorgan and later Cardiff.

The first mention of Glamorgan FC in the local press does not appear until the beginning of the 1874–5 season. At around the same time, it seems that another separate group was also playing football, also at the Arms Park, and these players formed the Cardiff Wanderers club under the leadership of W.D. (Bill) Phillips.[103] There are many later references to his being only seventeen years old at the time, which would place the year of formation at around 1873. One of the pioneers of the Welsh game, Bill Phillips, the son of a public house licensee, was a railway company official. He founded the Wanderers shortly after leaving Bridgend School and was the club captain until the amalgamation of 1876. He later played five times for Wales, was an international referee and served on the WFU committee for many years. He also held many offices of the Cardiff club, including that of captain, and was widely referred to as the father of the club. [104]

It is possible that the Wanderers were based around ex-pupils of Bridgend School. Though there is no hard evidence, the Glamorgan club may have initially enjoyed a slightly higher status, perhaps based on a stronger public school contingent. Only a few of the Wanderers' matches were recorded in the press and contemporary reports suggest that they concentrated mainly, though not exclusively, on internal games, rather than playing what were then termed "foreign" matches.[105]

To summarise so far then, although there may have been an earlier version of folk or working-class football which subsequently converged with the public school game, it was predominantly the latter which was responsible for the eventual adoption of the handling code in south Wales. Though the Welsh public schools were small in size, there were several prominent rugby playing public schools in the west of England and it was old boys of these and their English and Welsh feeder schools who also helped to introduce the game to south Wales.

Football of an undefined nature was played from the 1850s at St. David's College Lampeter and from the 1860s at Llandovery College, Christ College Brecon and elsewhere. In the later 1860s, "clubs" at Newport, Abergavenny, Cardiff, Pontypool and Brecon emerged, though it seems they too played under a mixture of rules and were often short-lived.

Towards the end of the decade, as a result of the efforts of a master from a rugby playing Scottish public school, Llandovery College formally adopted the game, as Lampeter College probably did around the same time. By 1870, Tredegarville, the first recorded Welsh club playing under rugby rules, was in existence. Following the codification of the laws of the game by the RFU in 1871, schools and clubs throughout south Wales began to give up their earlier hybrid and compromise versions of football and play under a commonly accepted set of rules. Accounting for the take-off of rugby rather than soccer in the 1870s in south Wales, Martin Johnes argues that once a particular football code had gained an initial foothold in an area, then it was more likely that local sportsmen would take it up in preference to any rival.[106] It would appear that something like this did happen as, in the second half of the decade, the popularity of rugby increased dramatically, as we shall now see.

Notes

1. Kenneth O. Morgan, *Rebirth of a Nation: Wales 1880–1980* (Oxford, 1982 edn.), p. 59.
2. Morgan, *Rebirth*, pp. 60–7; D. Gareth Evans, *A History of Wales 1815–1906* (Cardiff, 1989), pp. 177–189; Chris Williams, *Capitalism, Community and Conflict: The South Wales Coalfield, 1898–1947* (Cardiff, 1998), p. 11.
3. Morgan, *Rebirth*, p. 7.
4. Williams, *Capitalism, Community and Conflict*, pp. 69, 86.
5. David Smith and Gareth Williams, *Fields of Praise: The Official History of the Welsh Rugby Union 1881–1981* (Cardiff, 1980), pp. 28–9.
6. JRA Daglish, *Red, Black & Blue: The First 125 Years of Liverpool Football Club (Rugby Union)*, Manchester, 1983, pp. 2–4; Adrian Harvey, "The Oldest Rugby Club in the World?", *Sport in History*, 26, 1 (2006), pp. 150–2.
7. Jennifer Macrory, *Running with the Ball: The Birth of Rugby Football* (London, 1991), pp. 92–3.
8. See Jed Smith, *The Original Rules of Rugby* (Oxford, 2007), pp. 9–37 for an account of the rules of rugby from 1845 to 1871, including the 1845 laws.
9. Adrian Harvey, *Football: The First Hundred Years: The Untold Story* (London, 2005), p. 49.
10. Macrory, *Running with the Ball*, pp. 86–101; Tony Collins, *A Social History of English Rugby Union* (London, 2009), p. 12; Graham Curry, Eric Dunning and Kenneth Sheard, "Sociological Versus Empiricist History: Some Comments on Tony Collins's 'History, Theory and the Civilizing Process'", *Sport in History*, 26, 1 (2006), p. 116.
11. Edmund Van Esbeck, *Irish Rugby 1874–1999: A History* (Dublin, 1999), pp. 10–12; A.M.C. Thorburn, *The Scottish Rugby Union: Official History* (Edinburgh, 1985), pp. 1–3; Sandy Thorburn, *The History of Scottish Rugby* (London, 1980), pp. 9–16.
12. Collins, *Social History*, p.13; see Nigel Starmer-Smith, *Rugby – A Way of Life: An Illustrated History of Rugby* (London, 1986), p. 15 for the 1862 Blackheath laws.
13. Harvey, *Football: The First Hundred Years*, p. 130.
14. *Football Annual*, 1868, pp. 55–75.
15. Harvey, *Football: The First Hundred Years*, p. 159.
16. RFU minutes 26 Jan. 1871; see Smith, *Original Rules of Rugby*, pp. 57–88 for the 1871 laws.

17. Adrian Harvey, "'An Epoch in the Annals of National Sport': Football in Sheffield and the Creation of Modern Soccer and Rugby", *International Journal of the History of Sport*, 18, 4 (2001), p. 69.

18. Tony Collins, *Rugby's Great Split: Class, Culture and the Origins of Rugby League Football* (London, 2006 edn.), p. 30; Tony Collins, "History, Theory and the 'Civilizing Process'", *Sport in History*, 25, 2 (2005), pp. 291–6.

19. Smith and Williams, *Fields of Praise*, p. 17.

20. Collins, *Rugby's Great Split*, p. 3.

21. John Gouldstone, "The Working-Class Origins of Modern Football", *IJHS*, 17, 1 (2000), pp. 135–147; Harvey, *Football: The First Hundred Years*, p. 91.

22. See Harvey, "An Epoch in the Annals of National Sport", *IJHS*, 18, 4 (2001), 53–87; Eric Dunning, "Something of a Curate's Egg: Comments on Adrian Harvey's 'An Epoch in the Annals of National Sport'", *IJHS*, 18, 4 (2001), 88–94; Adrian Harvey, "The Curate's Egg Put Back Together: Comments on Eric Dunning's Response to 'An Epoch in the Annals of National Sport'", *IJHS*, 19, 4 (2002), 192–9; Eric Dunning and Graham Curry , "The Curate's Egg Scrambled Again: Comments on 'The Curate's Egg Put Back Together'!", *IJHS*, 19, 4, (2002), 200–204; Adrian Harvey, "Curate's Egg Pursued by Red Herrings: A Reply to Eric Dunning and Graham Curry", *IJHS*, 21, 1 (2004), 127–131.

23. Smith and Williams, *Fields of Praise*, p. 18.

24. *Western Mail* 30 Dec. 1875, 30 Dec. 1879 (Cowbridge); Martin Johnes, *A History of Sport in Wales* (Cardiff, 2005), p. 9 (Narberth).

25. Richard Holt, "Working-Class Football and the City: The Problem of Continuity", *British Journal of Sports History*, 3, 1 (1986), p. 5.

26. Thorburn, *Official History*, pp. 1–4; Thorburn, *History of Scottish Rugby*, pp. 6–16, 323–6; Van Esbeck, *Irish Rugby*, pp. 1–24.

27. D.I. Gealy, "Sport at Llandovery: Rugby Football" in R. Brinley Jones (ed.), *Floreat Landubriense: Celebrating a Century and a Half of Education at Llandovery College* (Llandovery, 1998), p. 242; Danny James and P.O.J. Rowlands, *Brecon Rugby Football Club: One Hundred Years of Rugby Football 1879–1979* (Brecon, 1979), p. 15.

28. Timothy J.L. Chandler, "Games at Oxbridge and the Public Schools, 1830–1880: The Diffusion of an Innovation", *IJHS*, 8, 2 (1991), p. 181.

29. Thorburn, *Official History*, p. 4; Van Esbeck, *Irish Rugby*, pp. 15–16; Jack Pollard, *Australian Rugby: The Game and the Players* (Chippendale, Australia, 1994), pp. 21–5.

30. See Macrory, *Running with the Ball*, pp. 197–205.

31. Neil Tranter, *Sport, Economy and Society in Britain, 1750–1914* (Cambridge, 1998), p. 30.

32. Martin Johnes and Ian Garland, "'The New Craze': football and society in north-east Wales, c. 1870–90", *Welsh History Review*, 22, 2 (2004), pp. 279–280.

33. David Russell, "Sporadic and Curious: The Emergence of Rugby and Soccer Zones in Yorkshire and Lancashire, c 1860–1914", *IJHS*, 5, 2 (1988), p. 194.

34. Macrory, *Running with the Ball*, p. 183.

35. For example, Martin Johnes, *History of Sport in Wales*, p. 24.

36. Macrory, *Running with the Ball*, pp. 192–3.

37. Uel A. Titley and Ross McWhirter, *Centenary History of the Rugby Football Union* (London, 1970), pp. 202–4. This lists the foundation dates of all the clubs in membership of the RFU in 1970. In the west of England, only Bath (1865), Cirencester (1866) and Cirencester College (1868) claim to have been formed before 1870. References to clubs in early RFU minutes and editions of the *Football Annual* confirm the general point.

38. See Smith and Williams, *Fields of Praise*, p. 33.

39. Smith and Williams, *Fields of Praise*, pp. 22–3; D.T.W. Price, *A History of Saint David's University College Lampeter, Volume One: To 1898* (Cardiff, 1977), p. 152; Macrory, *Running with the Ball*, p. 142.

40. *WM* 1 July 1949.

41. Gealy, "Sport at Llandovery", pp. 241–3; see also H.A. Harris, *Sport in Britain: Its Origins and Development* (London, 1975), pp. 132–3.

42. Smith and Williams, *Fields of Praise*, p. 23.

43. Jones, *Floreat Landubriense*, p. 48 (letter); *WM* 28 July 1898 (Whittington introduces rugby); W. Gareth Evans, *A History of Llandovery College* (Llandovery, 1981), p. 70 (1926 Journal).

44. Thorburn, *History of Scottish Rugby*, pp. 10–12.

45. Kenneth Evans, "A Historical Study of the Formative Years of the Welsh Rugby Union 1870–1900" (M.Ed. thesis, University of Liverpool, 1981), p. 73.

46. *WM* 5 Dec. 1882. C.P. Lewis had already been capped and T.H. Judson won his first cap two weeks after this match. The other college players (all pupils) who later became Welsh internationals were E.P. Alexander, E.H. Bishop, A.A. Matthews and R.L. Thomas.

47. Jonathan Harris, "The Early History of Association Football in Breconshire", *Brycheiniog*, XXVII, (1996), p. 128. Harris quotes the *Brecon Journal* of 28 Mar. 1861, drawing on the earlier work of J.R. Boulton, 1969, *Brecon Football 1860–1880* (Brecon, 1969).

48. A.L. Evans, "Some Reflections on Local Sport", *Port Talbot History Society Transactions*, 13, 2 (1981), pp. 22–49 (Kilvey); David Farmer, *The Life and Times of Swansea R.F.C.: The All Whites* (Swansea, 1995), p. 1 (town gentlemen).

49. *Bridgend Chronicle* 26 Jan. 1866.

50. Anon, *Marlborough College Register From 1843 to 1904 Inclusive*, (Oxford, 1905), p. 169, 205; W.T. Pike (ed.), *Glamorgan Contemporary Biographies: Pike's New Century Series No. 20* (Brighton, 1907), p. 156 (R. Blosse); C.S. Arthur, *The Cardiff Rugby Football Club: History and Statistics, 1876–1906* (Cardiff, 1908), p. 21 (E. Blosse).

51. *South Wales Daily News* 13 Apr. 1885.

52. *SWDN* 29 Nov. 1872.

53. *Webster and Co.'s Postal and Commercial Directory of the City of Bristol and Counties of Glamorgan and Monmouth* (London, 1865), p. 40.

54. Andrew K. Hignell, *A "Favourit" Game: Cricket in south Wales before 1914* (Cardiff, 1992), pp. 38–42.

55. J.D. Campbell, "'Training for Sport is Training for War': Sport and the Transformation of the British Army, 1860–1914", *IJHS*, 17, 4 (2000), pp. 33–4.

56. Macrory, *Running with the Ball*, pp. 203–5; Titley and McWhirter, *Centenary History Rugby Football Union*, p. 94; Pollard, *Australian Rugby*, p. 21.

57. Rowland Broughton-Mainwaring, *Historical Record of the Royal Welch Fusiliers* (London, 1889), pp. 259–261; A.D.L. Cary and S. Stouppe McLance, *Regimental Records of the Royal Welch Fusiliers Volume II 1816–1914* (London, 1923), pp. 137–9.

58. *Bridgend Chronicle* 20 Mar. 1868.

59. W. Alan Thomas, *Cardiff Cricket Club: 1867–1967* (Cardiff, 1967), p. 13; Gareth Williams, *1905 and All That: Essays on Rugby Football, Sport and Welsh Society* (Llandysul, 1991), p. 129 (cricket and football).

60. *Bridgend Chronicle* 3 Apr. 1868.

61. See James and Rowlands, *Brecon Rugby*, pp. 11–14 for quotes from the *Brecon and County Times*.

62. *SWDN* 23 Nov. 1872. 94ᵗʰ may be a misprint of 24ᵗʰ Regiment.
63. Collins, *Rugby's Great Split*, p. 7.
64. W.J. Townsend Collins (ed.), *Newport Athletic Club: The record of half a Century 1875–1925* (Newport, 1925), p. 14; *SWDN* 17 Oct. 1877. The gate money from this match was donated to the Indian Famine Fund.
65. *WM* 2 Dec. 1878.
66. See Meic Stephens (ed.), *New Companion to the Literature of Wales* (Cardiff, 1998), p. 117 for a brief biography of Townsend Collins.
67. *South Wales Argus* 4, 11 Oct. 1913 (italics added); Townsend Collins, *Newport Athletic*, p. 10.
68. Harvey, *Football: The First Hundred Years*, p. 159.
69. Brian Lile and David Farmer, "The Early Development of Association Football in South Wales, 1890–1906", *Transactions of the Honourable Society of Cymmrodorion*, (1984), p. 195.
70. Geoffrey Green, *The History of the Football Association* (London, 1953), pp. 36–8 (FA laws 1863); Harvey, "An Epoch in the Annals of National Sport", p. 67; Macrory, *Running with the Ball*, pp. 171–180.
71. Edward Donovan, Arthur Crane, Allan Smith and John Harris, *Pontypool's Pride: The Official History of Pontypool Rugby Football Club 1868–1988* (Abertillery, 1988), pp. 28–31; *Football Annual*, 1871 p. 66, 1872 p. 65, 1873 p. 77.
72. Russell Grigg, *History of Trinity College Carmarthen 1848–1998* (Cardiff, 1998), pp. 197–8.
73. *WM* 5 Mar. 1892.
74. Smith and Williams, *Fields of Praise*, p. 30.
75. Tranter, *Sport, Economy and Society,* pp. 13, 32–6.
76. *Football Annual* 1871 p. 69, 1872 p. 66, 1873 p. 80.
77. Andrew K. Hignell, "Suburban Development in North Cardiff, 1850–1919: A Case Study of the Pattern and Processes of Growth in the Parishes of Llanishen, Lisvane and Whitchurch" (Ph.D. thesis, University of Wales, 1987), p. 168 (social status of Tredegarville).
78. Arthur, *Cardiff Rugby*, p. 9; *Cardiff and Merthyr Guardian* 24 Dec. 1870; Harvey, "An Epoch in the Annals of National Sport", p. 78 (rouges).
79. Iolo Davies, *"A Certaine Schoole": A History of the Grammar School at Cowbridge Glamorgan* (Cowbridge, 1967), p. 126.
80. Smith and Williams, *Fields of Praise*, p. 23; *WM* 28 Oct. 1871.
81. *WM* 9 Nov. 1871; *Cardiff and Merthyr Guardian* 11 Nov. 1871.
82. Venessa Cunningham and John Goodwin, *Cardiff University: A Celebration* (Cardiff, 2001), pp. 16, 156–174.
83. *Cardiff Times* 21 Mar. 1868.
84. See Andrew Hignell, *From Sophia to SWALEC: A history of Cricket in Cardiff* (Stroud, 2009), pp. 44–5.
85. *Welsh Athlete* 19 Oct. 1891.
86. *WM* 2 Jan. 1905.
87. Quoted in T. Dargavel, *Neath R.F.C. 1871–1971 Centenary Year* (Neath, 1971), p. [2]
88. Mike Price, *Images of Sport: Neath RFC 1871–1945* (Stroud, 2002), pp. [7] –11.
89. Brinley E. Matthews, *The Swansea Story: A History of the Swansea Rugby Football Club 1874–1968* (Swansea, 1968), p. 10.
90. Gareth Hughes, *The Scarlets: A History of Llanelli Rugby Football Club* (Llanelli, 1986), p. 13; Arthur, *Cardiff Rugby*, p. 24; Jack Davis, *One Hundred Years of Newport Rugby 1875–1975* (Risca, 1974), p. 180; Dargavel, *Neath RFC*, p. [4]; Price, *Neath RFC*, p. 11.

91. Smith and Williams, *Fields of Praise*, p. 24; Thorburn, *History of Scottish Rugby*, p. 27 (Merchistonians).

92. Matthews, *The Swansea Story*, p. 10; Farmer, *Swansea R.F.C.*, p. 1; *Cardiff Times* 1 Oct. 1892.

93. *SWDN* 23 Nov. 1872 (Brecon), 29 Nov. 1872 (Shewbrooks'), 6 Mar. 1873 (Cowbridge);

94. *WM* 12 Feb. 1873.

95. Gareth Hughes (ed.), *One Hundred Years of Scarlet* (Llanelli, 1983), p. 1; Gareth Hughes, *The Scarlets*, pp. v–vi, 7; Macrory, *Running with the Ball*, p. 192; A.T. Mitchell (ed.), *Rugby School Register Volume II From August 1842, To January, 1874*, (Rugby, 1902), p. 226 (Rogers), p. 277 (Nevill).

96. James and Rowlands, *Brecon Rugby*, p. 12; *SWDN* 13 Dec. 1873 (Brecon v Christ College); *WM* 20 Dec. 1873 (Roath v Pontypridd), 28 Feb 1874 (Swansea teams), 21 Mar. 1874 (Brecon v College).

97. H.C. Toulouse, *Monmouth School Rugby Football Club: One Hundred Years* (Newport, 1973), p. 9.

98. *WM* 20 Dec. 1873.

99. Desmond T. Jones (ed.), *Pontypridd Rugby Football Club 1876–1976* (Pontypridd, 1976), p. 1; Gareth Harris and Alan Evans, *The Butchers Arms Boys: The Early Years* (Neath, 1997), pp. 11–15.

100. Arthur, *Cardiff Rugby*, p. 7 (italics added).

101. *Football Annual 1875*, p. 149; *Cardiff Times* 3 Sept. 1892.

102. A.A. Hunter (ed.), *Cheltenham College Register 1841–1889* (London, 1890), pp. 122 (White), 283 (Selby); *Football Annual 1874*, p. 24.

103. *SWDN* 23 Oct. 1874 (Glamorgan), 30 Oct. 1874 (Wanderers and Arms Park), 18 Jan. 1875 (Glamorgan and Arms Park).

104. See Andrew Hignell and Gwyn Prescott, *Cardiff Sporting Greats* (Stroud, 2007), p. 129 for an account of Bill Phillips' career.

105. *Cardiff Times* 3 Sept. 1892.

106. Johnes, *Sport in Wales*, p. 18.

3

THE GAME IS ESTABLISHED

'The running business'

Whatever versions of football had previously been played in south Wales, there can be no doubt that by 1874–5, rugby had become the overwhelming choice of players. This was a pivotal year in the history of Welsh rugby: new clubs were springing up, the organisation of the game was improving and interest was spreading beyond the participants.

Matches were reported that season involving Brecon, Bridgend School, Cambria (Swansea), Cardiff Wanderers, Cowbridge Grammar School, Glamorgan, Lampeter College, Llandovery College, Newport, Pontypridd, Swansea, Swansea Grammar School and University College Aberystwyth. The Glamorgan club even had a large enough playing membership to field two teams on the same day in November 1874.[1] The number of participants still varied greatly, however. It is often asserted that rugby matches were contested by teams of twenty a-side until numbers were reduced to fifteen in 1876–7. However, the idea that because of a decision made that season by the RFU, Welsh clubs suddenly reduced their teams from twenty players to fifteen is simply to misunderstand the nature of the game at this time. It is quite evident that the usual practice was for clubs to compete with whatever number of players they had available. No single example of a Welsh twenty a-side match was traced in the local press in this research. In only two reported games – Glamorgan against Cardiff Wanderers in 1874 and Swansea against Llandovery College in 1876 – were the sides made up of eighteen players. Other matches normally involved teams of around twelve to sixteen players.[2]

During this season, newspaper reports began to comment on large attendances at matches. Several hundred, for instance, watched Cardiff Wanderers play Pontypridd in March 1875.[3] The novelty of the game to the public, however, was still apparent. When Glamorgan defeated Swansea at the Arms Park:

> The game was so attractive that on several occasions the spectators passed through the bounds, and in one instance, there was a

somewhat laughable spectacle presented by a scrimmage party becoming wholly surrounded by the general public, who, curious to see the mode in which the process was performed, closed round the opponents in scores.[4]

Within only a few years, as will be seen, Welsh spectators would be crowding onto the field of play with worse motives than mere curiosity.

A significant event took place in September 1874 with the foundation of the Newport club. This appears to have been at least partly an initiative of the Phillips family who had recently moved their brewing operations from Northampton. They brought with them, it is alleged, one of the first oval balls seen in the town which they had acquired in Rugby, where the family also had business interests. The club was founded at Thomas Phillips' Dock Road Brewery by his sons William (who attended Rugby School according to Macrory) and Clifford, together with a group of Old Monmouthians, including Charles Newman, later capped by Wales. As shown earlier, up to 1873, Monmouth School had played a hybrid football, closer perhaps to soccer, so it seems that association may have been initially adopted by the new club. However, there are no records of any soccer matches against other teams, so perhaps only a few "internal" games were played. In any case, the rugby playing Phillips brothers would not have been happy with this and Newport soon switched permanently to rugby, playing their first fixture against Glamorgan on 5th April 1875. H.W. Peill, who introduced rugby to Monmouth, is also believed to have been influential in the decision.[5]

It was also during the 1874–5 season that the first description of a rugby match and the response of the spectators to it appeared in the Cardiff press. The account is very illuminating in several respects and it is worth quoting in full.

[On] Saturday great interest was felt in a football match on Ynysangharad fields (kindly leant by Mr. Gordon Lennox) between the Cowbridge Grammar School and … Pontypridd … A commodious marquee had been erected on the ground for the convenience of the ladies. Soon after two o'clock the public began to arrive, and shortly afterwards the excellent brass band of Treforest, comprised exclusively of working men, entered the field … The game commenced about three o'clock … and was watched with eager interest by the hundreds that were present, who appeared highly amused. It appears the play was in accordance with the Rugby rules, and by these rules carrying the ball is a prominent feature of the game. This was much oftener done on

Saturday than kicking it ... But what afforded most amusement to
lookers-on was *the running business*. A red striped Cowbridgian
would succeed snatching the ball from the ground, and would then
endeavour by his fleetedness of foot to carry it towards his party's
goal [sic]. This was the signal for the "blues" to hurry from all
parts of the field and fall on the "coch" [red] like an avalanche:
Of course this would bring all the "reds" to the rescue of their
colleague with the ball, and all would fall, blue and red "in one
burial blent",[6] followed by roars of laughter from the spectators.
These incidents frequently happened to both parties, and created
much merriment. After an hour and a half the Pontypridd club
was declared the victor, having won three goals. The Cowbridge
boys struggled manfully, and the contest was of the hottest, but
they did not succeed in sending the ball over to the goal. It should
be stated, however, that [in] the preceding contests which took
place between the parties at Cowbridge, the school was victorious, so that this victory places the two clubs on equal footing.[7]

The game was evidently not the first between the teams, an earlier
one having been won by the school. The importance of local schools
in providing fixtures for the newly established clubs cannot be over-
emphasised. One week later, for instance, Cowbridge were entertaining
Glamorgan. During the following season, Swansea played Llandovery
College no less than five times out of their eleven fixtures.[8]

The match was actively supported by a prominent local industrial-
ist, Gordon Lennox, who provided the field on land near his home at
Ynysangharad House. A former player himself, he had been a member of the Pontypridd team which played Roath the previous season.[9]
Census returns indicate that many of the town team and officials were
drawn from the professional and commercial classes. There may be
further evidence of this in the reporter's comment that the Treforest
Band comprised only working men, while he makes no mention of any
working-class players actually participating in the game. This suggests,
therefore, that, even in the valleys, rugby was initially a middle-class
pastime.

Perhaps of greatest interest, however, are what may be the earliest
recorded references to the reactions of Welsh spectators to the game
in which "carrying the ball is a prominent feature". The hundreds who
attended were obviously enthralled and "highly amused" by this novel
"running business". It is hard for us to imagine now what it must have
been like to watch a new ball game for the very first time but this account
reveals something of the sheer thrill, excitement and enthusiasm it must
have aroused. Comments such as: "what afforded most amusement to

the lookers-on was the running business"; "roars of laughter from the spectators"; and "these incidents ... created much merriment" anticipate the sense of boisterous, humorous spectacle and theatre which has characterised Welsh rugby ever since.

That rugby continued to grow in popularity is revealed by the establishment of the South Wales Football Club (SWFC) in September 1875 at Brecon. The first secretary was H.W. Davies of Brecon, confirming the key position this club held in the early days of Welsh rugby.[10] Cardiff was very well represented on the committee by Campbell Cory, Thomas Selby, Fleming Thomas and Edward Fry, all members of the Glamorgan club. Though the SWFC could in no sense be described as a controlling body for the sport in Wales, it does mark an important step towards that goal. The club's initial objective was simply to provide members with an opportunity to play a better class of football against English teams.[11] This could be interpreted as an acceptance of the inferior status of Welsh rugby at this time: the only way Welsh players could compete well with English teams was to combine forces. However, another interpretation might be that, even at a very early stage in the development of Welsh rugby, and before working men were taking up the game in numbers, there existed a strong desire to *compete*. It must be noted that the organisation was a "club" and members were individuals rather than clubs, so early South Wales teams were not truly representative. A subscription fee of five shillings guaranteed that membership was restricted to the better off. Six fixtures against English teams were arranged for the inaugural season though not all were played.[12] Nevertheless, the first match involving a nominally "representative" Welsh team took place on 27th November 1875 in Hereford. Despite having to borrow three "substitute" players (one of whom was a future captain of Wales, James Bevan, then a pupil at Hereford Cathedral School), South Wales won.[13] However, defeat followed in the fixture with Clifton, played in front of hundreds of appreciative spectators at the Arms Park.[14] According to the Clifton club history, however, the return fixture was cancelled because South Wales were unable to raise a side.[15]

Another first was achieved this season with the earliest mention in the local press of an Anglo-Welsh fixture. This took place on 13th November 1875 at Cheltenham and it involved a Cardiff club. Though the 1876 *Football Annual* describes the team which played the College as "South Wales Ramblers", it is clear from the press report that their opponents were Glamorgan FC. The College won comfortably, not least because the Welsh club "had the disadvantage of not knowing the College rules", revealing that even at this late stage there might still be some variation in the rules adopted in matches. That the College had accepted this fixture, which was the forerunner of a long series of games with Cardiff, provides further evidence of the link between Cheltenham and the establishment of the Glamorgan club.[16]

New clubs such as Llandeilo, Llanelli, Neath, Panteg, Pontypool and Vale of Usk (Abergavenny) continued to emerge, or at least feature in the press for the first time. Llandaff can claim to be Cardiff's oldest club still in existence, since they were formed in early 1876, (several months before the merger which created Cardiff Football Club), though they appear to have played under the name of Ely until 1878. The founding of the Carmarthen town club this season has been attributed to the arrival of A.F. Laloe, formerly head of Cowbridge Grammar School, who took up the headship of Carmarthen Grammar School in June 1874.[17] Schools rugby continued to flourish. When Llandovery College defeated Lampeter College, in front of "an unusually large number of visitors", they demonstrated that training and skill could still overcome size and age.

> [Llandovery] counterbalanced their opponents' superiority in weight by their skill in "dodging" and passing on the ball, in which the Lampeterians were deficient, trusting as they did more to "big" kicks.[18]

During this season, Llandovery College lost only one of their five matches with Swansea, while Christ College Brecon decided to adopt rugby, playing their first fixture against the town in December 1875.[19] In Cardiff, Monkton House and the Cardiff Collegiate combined forces on several occasions as "United Cardiff Schools" to play local men's teams, anticipating the Cardiff Schools Union by nearly thirty years.[20]

Suggesting that players and spectators were beginning to take the game more seriously, particularly in matches between close rivals, the first indications of disagreement appear in press reports and correspondence. For instance, disputes occurred either during, or after, games between Glamorgan and Newport, Carmarthen and Llandeilo and Newport and a Cardiff scratch XV.[21] Nevertheless, the spectacle of the game continued to appeal to increasing numbers as evidenced by the 400 who attended this last match. When Newport secured a home victory over Swansea, the *Western Mail* commented:

> A good deal of excitement prevailed among the spectators as the various movements of the contestants were executed, and great enthusiasm prevailed when Newport was declared the winner ... *a large company was present, including many ladies. The game is becoming very popular.*[22]

Towards the end of the season, a dispute occurred in the *Western Mail* between the SWFC and the Football Association of Wales (FAW). This arose when the FAW announced that they had selected a team to play Scotland. SWFC officials protested that they knew nothing about this. The FAW reasonably replied that since Welshmen throughout England and Wales were aware of the arrangements, it was hardly their fault if the SWFC had failed to take notice of the announcements.[23] In their article on early Welsh soccer, Brian Lile and David Farmer refer to correspondence in *The Field* in 1876 about the establishment of a Welsh soccer team. They quote "Half-Back" who argued that association rules were those "chiefly adopted in the Principality". Lile and Farmer argue that this correspondence provides "confirmation of the early dominance" of soccer in Wales.[24] However, "Half-Back" evidently had little knowledge of what was happening in the south. As any close inspection of the Cardiff press will demonstrate, there were virtually no soccer clubs in south Wales at this time and certainly none at all of any standing. There can be no doubt about the dominance of rugby there by 1876.

The SWFC secretary's response to the *Western Mail* confirms the extent of the spread of rugby in south Wales by this time. He wrote that it was unlikely that players would travel to trials in the north from "Cardiff, Swansea, Neath, Merthyr, Pontypridd, Llanelly or even from Carmarthen or Brecon." The omission of Newport from his list is explained by the uncertainty over the status of Monmouthshire at the time.[25]

This was addressed by the SWFC in October 1876, when it was agreed that Monmouthshire should be considered part of south Wales and, therefore, anyone in the county was eligible to join. At the same meeting, it was also "unanimously resolved that the club should enter the Rugby Union challenge cup".[26] This resolution is highly significant, as it reveals that the club members – still overwhelmingly, if not wholly, drawn from the middle and upper classes – were keen to take part in competitive rugby and it is an early hint that Wales would travel a distinctly different path from that of the RFU. Unfortunately for the SWFC, events had already overtaken them. During 1875–6, the Royal Military Academy Woolwich had offered to present a cup for competition amongst RFU clubs. An RFU subcommittee drafted the rules but unfortunately the offer of the cup was then withdrawn by RMA Woolwich and the competition was kicked into touch for a century.[27]

The game continued to spread geographically in Wales and there were also signs that it was beginning to break out of its class boundaries. New clubs in Aberdare and Merthyr continued the expansion into the valleys. At first, these were probably mainly middle class in composition, however. The *Western Mail* reported that Aberdare included no fewer than six university men in a fixture with Roath in 1877, while Andy Croll's research on Merthyr reveals that players at this time were predominantly drawn from the commercial and professional classes.[28]

Even in north Wales the game took root though it was short-lived. In December 1876, Bangor was formed with a decidedly middle-class committee, who resolved "that the game be played according to the rules of Rugby Football". Unfortunately, the club switched to soccer the following year.[29] However, in the south, in the same month, developments were taking place which *were* to have a lasting effect on the Welsh game.

The occasion was the fixture between Swansea Reserves and Swansea Working Men's Club (WMC) in December 1876.[30] It is likely that some Welsh working men had already begun playing before this date, either by joining existing clubs, or by taking part in informal matches amongst themselves. There are allusions to such games in several club histories and whilst in all probability this did happen, the only proof for it is usually hearsay.[31] The match in Swansea, however, provides clear evidence of the early diffusion of the game to the working class and it therefore marks a very significant stage in the history of Welsh rugby. We can only speculate how this began to happen, but it is highly likely that an initial interest in watching the town team led to a desire to give the game a try. There appears to have been little resistance to this process and indeed, it is instructive that Swansea were prepared to offer the new club a fixture. Perhaps given the increasing keenness with which matches were being fought, they shrewdly recognised the potential advantage from doing so.

The press was beginning to reflect the "edge" which was creeping into the game. For instance, on the same day as the Swansea WMC match, Cardiff supporters were criticised for their "repeated plaudits of their own party exclusively [which] scarcely constituted a fitting welcome to the Swansea team".[32] Hardly bad behaviour by today's standards, but it was a sign perhaps that some of those watching the game in Wales were now coming from a different social and sporting background from those who adhered to any "gentlemanly" code.

It was the desire to produce a team which would best represent the town in an increasingly competitive environment which led Glamorgan and Cardiff Wanderers to merge and form the Cardiff Football Club in September 1876. Many accounts of this event incorrectly claim that the Tredegarville club was also a party to the merger. However, this club appears to have disbanded by 1876 and it is quite clear from contemporary reports that only Glamorgan and Cardiff Wanderers were involved.[33] Whilst these earlier clubs had originally been founded purely for the enjoyment of their members, the amalgamated club was now reconstituted to serve the interest of the town's honour. This was also happening in the north of England, where increasing inter-town rivalry meant that clubs were evolving into civic or community organisations rather than private institutions for young gentlemen.[34] A similar process was also at work in New Zealand, where – as in Wales – a significant expansion in the number of clubs, players and spectators was taking place. According to Geoffrey Vincent, there was a growing acceptance in New Zealand that rugby was a means for defending civic pride and protecting the "honour of the province" against external "enemies".[35]

Before long, both playing and non-playing members of Cardiff would be drawn from a much wider spectrum of society and the club would give supporters a focus for deep pride in their home town. Richard Holt argues that whereas the working class were anxious to identify emotionally with their town (soccer) club, this was less important to the middle and upper classes, who had alternative ties to schools and professions.[36] However, in the socially inclusive version of rugby which was emerging in south Wales, it was evident that enthusiastic support for the town was not restricted to the working class by any means. Regional, if not national pride, was also becoming more apparent. Playing in front of a crowd of 500, probably the largest to watch a game in the principality so far, South Wales were able to gain revenge over Clifton with a sound victory at Newport.[37] Another development this season which signified the changing nature of the Welsh game was Newport's decision to request entrance money. Wales' most go ahead club at this time charged the 200 spectators sixpence each to watch their first ever fixture with Cardiff in December 1876.[38] Within two years, supporters at Sophia Gardens were complaining to the press that Cardiff had followed suit.[39]

Ironically, it was an act by Welsh soccer authorities which helped to stimulate the process by which rugby became deeply rooted in the popular culture of south Wales. When the FAW placed a notice in the *Western Mail* in September 1877 announcing the inauguration of a Welsh Cup, they did so in the hope of encouraging soccer in an area which was already becoming a rugby stronghold.[40] Martin Johnes and Ian Garland argue that the introduction of the cup was to have a significant influence on the development of soccer.[41] However, its initial effect in south Wales was to indirectly help the growth of rugby. An immediate retaliation came in the form of a letter to the *Western Mail* from "Half Back" from the Vale of Towy (probably C.P. Lewis) suggesting the introduction of a rugby cup for south Wales because "all of its leading football clubs play the Rugby Union rules and not that of association." He accurately predicted that it would stimulate rugby in south Wales, "which yearly increases in popularity ... [whilst] it is so evident that association rules are far from popular here." Keen support for the initiative then came in a helpful letter from the Cardiff captain who "strongly advocate(d) the establishment of a football challenge cup for South Wales". The SWFC secretary replied that the proposal had already been discussed in committee and, as a result, a special meeting had been convened to consider it.

Perhaps appropriately, given the significance of the event, this meeting was held at the hostelry which gave its name to the Arms Park, the *Cardiff Arms Hotel*. On 22nd October 1877, the SWFC formally agreed to organise the competition. A fifty guinea cup was to be presented to the winners and clubs were invited to send in their entries before 3rd November. The speed with which the competition was set up suggests that the SWFC were anxious not to be beaten to the goal-line once again by the FAW.[42]

The inspired decision to promote the cup probably ranks only second in importance, if that, to the founding of the Welsh Union in 1881 in confirming rugby as the main sporting pastime of the south Wales public. Although the major clubs competed for only ten years, it was during that crucial period that Welsh rugby took off both in popularity and in playing standards.[43] The cup greatly stimulated these processes and it was in these early cup ties that the Welsh public's passion for the game, accompanied by a deep desire for success, first emerged in a significant way. Its popularity was a reflection of the competitive nature of working-class culture which fueled the partisan nature of the Welsh game. In 1897, the *Western Mail* was certain about the significance of the cup to Welsh rugby: it had generated "intense partisanship" and "attracted a following for the various clubs that [has] never since left them."[44] The South Wales Challenge Cup was also the forerunner of numerous county and local cup competitions which sprang up over the following twenty years. For example, knock-out cups were subsequently organised for clubs in Monmouthshire, Pembrokeshire, Cardiff, Llanelli, Neath, Newport, Swansea, Aberavon, Blaenavon, Ebbw Vale, Morriston, Treherbert and elsewhere.

The introduction of a club competition is noteworthy, however, for another reason. The Welsh game was barely out of its infancy in 1877, but it was already sufficiently ambitious and self-confident to innovate, when administrators in older and more established rugby playing areas were reluctant to do so. As we have seen, two seasons earlier, the RFU missed the opportunity to introduce a national competition. Then again in 1878, the Calcutta Cup was initially offered for annual club competition. However, displaying a keen lack of enthusiasm, the Union rejected this proposal, according to RFU minutes, because of "difficulties of all clubs playing together", whatever that meant. The RFU did, however, inform the Calcutta club that the Union "would accept the cup as a gift to be played for annually by the representative teams of England and Scotland".[45] The RFU minutes also reveal that the issue of a challenge cup was unsuccessfully raised again in 1881.[46] The failure to introduce a competition was probably a big mistake by English officials. In Tony Collins' view, the lack of a national focus at club level was a major reason why soccer eventually overtook rugby in popularity in England.[47]

The Scottish Union's original objectives included provision for a cup, but at their first AGM in 1873, they quickly dropped the proposal.[48] Similarly the Irish Union rejected a national cup competition in 1882.[49] There was a different attitude to competition in the north of England, however. Tony Collins reveals that the Yorkshire Challenge Cup, involving sixteen invited clubs, was "hurriedly organised for December 1877".[50] As in Wales, improving the standard of play was an important motive. It is remarkable to note, though, that Wales introduced their cup before Yorkshire, where the game was much more advanced at the time. The first round in Wales was completed *before* 1st December, so it was only by a matter of weeks, but the South Wales Challenge Cup can claim seniority.[51] That it was in Wales that the first major rugby competition for open clubs in the British Isles took place is surely evidence that something different was stirring there.

The first competition did not proceed without difficulties, however. There were eighteen entrants but some teams withdrew without playing. Though some matches were held on neutral grounds, this did not necessarily obviate a long journey and this prospect still caused some teams to scratch. Match dates were left for clubs to arrange and Cardiff's defeat at Carmarthen was blamed on the home club for responding so late that the visitors only had one day's notice of the fixture, forcing them to take a weakened team. This tie also resulted in a dispute over a vital score, which Cardiff threatened to take to the RFU for resolution. These matters were fully played out in correspondence in the press.[52] Cardiff's experience of the competition over the years was an unhappy one, involving frequent disputes, crowd misconduct and foul play. As a result, they eventually pulled out permanently in 1883, from which time the competition began to lose some momentum.

A major area of contention which arose before the cup had barely got off the ground was the question of eligibility of players. There were accusations that some clubs were strengthening their teams by bringing in outsiders. It was a matter of particular importance to C.P. Lewis, the rugby master at Llandovery College, who was clearly concerned about the effect this might have on the school's prospects in the competition.[53] H.W. Davies confirmed the eligibility rules of the cup in its first season. As in cricket, he wrote, a man could play for any club as long as he was a bona fide member. "In town matches too, it has always been understood that the same man may play for more than one club ... [but] no player will be allowed to compete in the cup ties for more than one club".[54] In subsequent seasons, however, cup rules limited selection to those who lived within a radius of a club's ground. So, reflecting the increasingly competitive environment, from its very inception the cup became embroiled in argument and dispute.

Despite these difficulties, from the outset it was a success in its primary objective of stimulating interest in the game. This matches similar events in Yorkshire where, following the introduction of their cup, new clubs sprang up everywhere and rugby quickly became embedded in the local culture. Tony Collins argues that attendance at Yorkshire cup matches also gave the working class one of the few opportunities to express their local pride.[55] In its account of the first Welsh final, the *Western Mail* reported that the cup had "aroused the greatest interest throughout [south Wales] and the ties ... have been most eagerly awaited". The final was played in front of a crowd of perhaps 2,000, easily the largest to attend a match so far. The occasion even merited comment in a *Western Mail* editorial, which described the game as "perhaps the most exiting football match which has ever taken place in the district." The victorious Newport team received a wildly enthusiastic welcome by a huge crowd on their return home with the all the attendant rituals which were to became the customary response to cup success over the following decade.[56] The celebrations later included a special banquet at which the local M.P. presided and during which the cup was filled with champagne and handed round to the tune of *Rule Britannia*.[57] The joy in Newport was matched by the disappointment in Swansea, where at least one player was verbally abused for his poor performance. Rugby was fast becoming ingrained in Welsh urban culture.

The cup channelled competitiveness between towns into a relatively structured format with a clear winner. However, the increased levels of foul play and dispute, which it also encouraged, were regularly used as arguments against repeated calls for the introduction of an official Welsh league from the late 1880s onwards and they delayed its introduction for a hundred years. Nevertheless, at a lower level, the demand for competition was met by a proliferation of cups and leagues by the 1890s. The WFU, however, took no direct responsibility for these, so they were not co-ordinated in any structured way and were left to local unions to organise. Nevertheless, this still contrasted with the attitude of the RFU which regularly refused consent for county unions to run competitions.[58]

The appeal of the game continued to breach social barriers. New clubs at Aberavon, Blaenavon, Cwmavon and Maesteg probably relied substantially on working men for their teams. Boilermakers at the Uskside Works in Newport formed a club.[59] Youngsters outside schools were also being attracted to the game as evidenced by the games organised between Cardiff, Newport and Roath boys' teams in 1877.[60] Crowd trouble was increasing. In matches between Neath and Cwmavon and in the cup semi-final between Newport and Llandovery College supporters spilled onto the field and disrupted play.[61] When Swansea WMC played Neath, "A great deal of noisy feeling was shown by the spectators and, as usual, the play was hampered by their crowding in over the touch-line and round the goal ... the scrimmages at times [were] dangerously rough".[62]

As the decade drew to a close, these trends continued. Attendances at matches rose substantially, with Newport, in particular, regularly attracting large crowds of several thousands. In 1879, for example, 2,000, 3,000 and anything between 5,000 and 8,000 spectators were reported to have watched them play Manchester Rangers, Neath and Blackheath respectively. For this last game, supporters lined the walls, fences and tops of houses.[63] Even local clubs sometimes found themselves playing in front of a hundred or so spectators. For example, during their inaugural season, when Pontymister played Newport Crusaders, over a hundred visiting supporters turned up.[64] Though press reports of crowd sizes must always be viewed with scepticism, such figures nevertheless indicate a trend of increasing fascination amongst the wider south Wales public. The prospect of watching an exciting football match, however, was not the only attraction. Neil Tranter argues that gambling was one of several reasons for the increasing interest in attending sporting events. Certainly, frequent references to betting were beginning to appear in reports of major Welsh matches, though there seems to have been no concerted efforts to stop the practice. For instance, at the 1879 South Wales Challenge Cup final at Sophia Gardens, "a number of sporting gentlemen were present on the field ... Betting ... was freely indulged in". Rugby, then, also provided new opportunities for gambling and this must have stimulated the fervour, aggression and occasional violence of some of the spectators.[65]

Though hard evidence of the process is difficult to locate, the growing enthusiasm for watching the game contributed to the increased level of participation. The most successful Welsh side of the 1870s were Newport, who remained undefeated in their first five seasons, during which time they were twice winners of the Challenge Cup. Townsend Collins explains that:

> the success of the team led to an outburst of enthusiasm for the Rugby game at Newport. It was taken up by schoolboys, it extended beyond the then somewhat exclusive circle of the Newport club, and new clubs were formed in the town ... *The little band of players had done more than found a club, they had established a game.*[66]

By 1880, many new clubs had appeared in the town and its neighbourhood, for example, Alexandra Rangers, Caerleon, Caerau Park Rovers,

Clytha, Excelsiors, Gas Yard Rangers, Gold Top Rangers, Lliswerry, Maindee, Maindee Star, Newport Albion, Newport Crusaders, Newport Rovers, Newport Wanderers, and Royal Oak.[67] A good example of the diffusion from spectatorship to participation is that of the Pontymister club which was formed in November 1879 by local cricketers. Forty took part in the first practice and the majority "had never played before, but they have taken great interest in watching the movements of the Newport team and ... [they] did their best to emulate their powerful neighbours."[68]

Of particular significance for the future of the game in the town, local youngsters were enthusiastically taking up rugby, either with junior teams, like Newport Rovers for whom Arthur Gould first played, or for a variety of educational institutions, such as Caerleon Industrial Schools, Newport Grammar School and Stow Hill Board School.[69] Following Newport's cup final victory in March 1879, it was claimed that every school in the town had its team.[70] Of course, such events were not restricted to Newport and similar developments were to be found throughout south Wales, in particular in the major towns, though it was probably in Newport that they first emerged.

This investigation into the origins of Welsh rugby supports David Smith and Gareth Williams' view that it was mainly public school old boys who were the founder players of the earliest clubs, with their "ranks ... stiffened by the ever-increasing self-confident class of solicitors, doctors, clerks, and engineers".[71] But now the game was reaching out beyond these groups to the lower middle class and to the fringes of the working class. Both Cardiff (as will be shown later) and Newport were still predominantly socially exclusive clubs at the end of the decade. A correspondent to the SWDN replied to an earlier press "accusation" that Newport had included "artisans" in their team which had defeated Cardiff in the 1879 cup final. The writer identified the occupations of all fifteen players and there were no artisans. The Newport team comprised four partners in local businesses, four clerks, two draughtsmen, two civil engineers, a mining engineer, an accountant and a student.[72] However, even in the Newport and Cardiff clubs, such exclusivity, in playing personnel at least, if not in administration, would soon change. Their close rivals, Swansea, were already including working men in their team. After their victory in the 1880 cup final, they returned to the Swansea Workingmen's Institute, where ten of the team were members.[73] Townsend Collins locates the arrival of working men in the Newport team shortly afterwards.

> There was no more striking feature in ... 1880–1 ... than the broadening of the bounds of selection. With the rise of new clubs

it was recognised that the town club were duty bound to make the team as far as possible representative of the playing talent of the town.

He also claimed that Newport's subsequent success was accounted for by its lack of class distinction and by the acceptance that the club was a town institution and a symbol of civic unity.[74]

Elsewhere, working men were playing the game in greater numbers. Clubs were not only springing up in Newport but also in Cardiff and Swansea and these were not located exclusively in middle-class districts. Given their proliferation, neither could they have been exclusively middle class in membership. It is known that a club existed in Felinfoel by 1877. According to the Scarlets' club history, it had been set up by Llanelli's first secretary, William Nevill who "prevailed upon men who worked in his father's foundry ... and colliers living in Felinfoel to turn out". Unfortunately no date for this is mentioned and this account is based on recollections published in 1934.[75] Llanelli may have begun to include working men earlier than many. Though it relates to the mid 1880s, the response of "Old Stager" to a suggestion that the club was composed entirely of colliers is revealing. "I fail to see that it matters two-pence-half-penny whether a team is made up of gentlemen or sweeps, provided they play an honest and fair game". He listed the occupations of the 1886 Llanelli cup winning team. There were no colliers, but ten were clearly working class. As well as two ironworkers and two tinplaters, the other occupations were painter, plasterer, plumber, blacksmith, saddler and stonecutter. Two schoolmasters, a chemical factor, a clerk and a (presumably idle) Cambridge graduate made up the rest of the side.[76]

Teams were also beginning to appear in the overwhelmingly working-class coalfield valleys. In March 1879, there are press reports of the Mountain Ash club playing Mountain Ash Temperance. The latter were described as mainly "underground workmen" who had begun playing only three weeks earlier.[77] Whilst examples of exclusively working-class clubs at this time are difficult to identify with certainty, the existence of teams such as Neath Institute and Llandovery Working Men's Club, and pub sides like the Crown, Mountain Ash and the Star, Aberdare is evidence that rugby was beginning to infiltrate working-class culture across south Wales.[78]

The SWFC became less exclusive in composition in April 1879 when it changed its constitution so that clubs, rather than individuals, were to comprise its members. This was reflected in a change of name to the South Wales Football Union (SWFU). However, as Gareth Williams argues, it is important to recognise that the *control* of the game, particularly at the level of the SWFU/WFU and the senior clubs, remained very firmly in the hands of the middle class throughout the century and beyond.[79] For instance, Maurice Ivor Morris of Briton Ferry, the first secretary of the reconstituted SWFU, had been educated at Cheltenham College. Morris appears to have been a better cricketer than rugby player and it may have been through his influential rugby contacts, like J.T.D. Llewellyn, C.C. Chambers, C.P. Lewis and Lewis Kempthorne with whom he played in the South Wales Cricket Club, that he secured the appointment.[80] Eric Dunning and Kenneth Sheard have recently acknowledged that their earlier contention that the Welsh game was administered by the lower middle and working classes was mistaken. However, as will be shown later in relation to Cardiff, it was these classes who would soon begin to dominate in terms of playing numbers and even control of neighbourhood clubs.[81]

The widening of interest in rugby raised the level of competitiveness with which matches were fought and this led to increased disruption both on and off the field. Similar trends were noted by Stuart Barlow in his research into early rugby in Rochdale.[82] Evidence that Welsh rugby was diverging from any public school code (if it had ever adhered to it in the first place), is contained in a letter to the *Western Mail* in 1880 from "An Old Cheltonian" who criticised the conduct of the Welsh game. He first complained about the frequency with which letters appeared in the press disputing match results. Then he attacked the players who continually argued with umpires and referees. "You never see this in matches in England", he claimed, because the transgressors would be dismissed from the field. The game in Wales, on the other hand, was "a series of disreputable squabbles". Though English rugby was not quite so free of disputes as Cheltonian alleged, his comments probably do record the Welsh rugby public's increasing divergence from the ethos of the game's gentlemen founders. There were no responses to his letter.[83]

Cheltonian was right about the growing level of disputes, however. There were, for instance, several major disagreements involving senior clubs, particularly in the cup, where increasing partisanship often led to disorderly crowd behaviour. When Newport suffered their first ever cup defeat in a contentious match against Swansea in 1879, they threatened to appeal to the RFU, after the SWFU upheld the referee's decision over a disputed score. So disgruntled were they by this, they even held onto the cup at the end of the season until forced to hand it over. This event no doubt helped to convince the Newport secretary, Richard Mullock, that a Welsh Union was needed. Much of the trouble in this game was caused by the crowd spilling onto the field and obstructing players and officials.[84] This also happened in a later match with Cardiff, when the Newport team walked off the field after a disputed try. Here the crowd frequently surrounded the players and "the scene became one of uproar and confusion".[85]

Even the theology students and their supporters at Lampeter had a fearsome reputation. In one cup tie, they were accused of biting and hitting a Cardiff player during a maul. This match ended in the inevitable dispute.[86] In the subsequent replay, up to fifteen minutes were wasted in arguments. Even though the "clerical element was well represented", there was much "avowed partisanship", particularly as some of the Lampeter supporters chose to claim that the game was a contest between the Welsh and the English, wrongly accusing Cardiff of having only two Welsh-born players.[87] When Swansea later defeated Lampeter in the final, they too received the "same objectionable treatment ... as Cardiff [had]" from the Lampeter supporters.[88] During a match between Newport and Cardiff reserves, a supporter ran on the field and struck the Cardiff umpire. The perpetrator justified his actions by claiming his victim had kicked a Newport player in a previous match.[89] Bridgend supporters were accused of "disgraceful", but unfortunately unspecified, behaviour after losing to Cowbridge Grammar School, while against the 10th GRV, Bridgend frequently interrupted play with "unruly conduct."[90] Cheating also went on. In a game against Bridgend, Neath Abbey players kept pushing the posts out of perpendicular every time their opponents attempted a goal kick, "anything but a gentlemanly act" according to a correspondent to the *SWDN*.[91]

The more enterprising administrators sought new ways of appealing to an ever wider audience. One was Newport's secretary, Richard Mullock, who was particularly adept at this. To attract more spectators, Newport became the first Welsh club to arrange fixtures with strong English clubs. In 1879, they promoted a "Football Week" involving several important matches. These included a victory over the South of Ireland and Newport's first ever defeat since 1874, at the hands of Blackheath. In December 1878, Newport arranged the first recorded floodlit game in Wales played against Cardiff under electric lights.[92] This was only eight weeks after the earliest ever floodlit rugby match at Broughton on 22nd October.[93] Here again is evidence of the willingness of Welsh rugby to experiment to widen the appeal of the game. Had Newport gone ahead with their initial proposal to play a practice match under lights on the 5th October, they might have been able to claim to be the innovators of this form of rugby.[94]

For the 1878–9 cup, the SWFU introduced new regulations restricting teams to selecting players from within a ten mile radius. They also decided, in the absence of any specification in the RFU laws, to adopt a standard pitch size of 120 x 75 yards.[95] These were relatively small matters, but they do indicate that Welsh rugby was beginning to develop a degree of independence from the RFU. The SWFU continued with an ambitious programme of fixtures but turning out the strongest teams was still a problem, with away games being particularly difficult. There was an enormous variation in the composition of SWFU teams from match to match, with no apparent consistency in selection. A fixture with Cheltenham College could not be fulfilled because of a cup clash. However, a good win was achieved over the visiting South of Ireland team in November 1879, which might be considered the first real "representative" match played in Wales. The status of this touring side is in some doubt. The official Irish historian says that it was Munster and that they received a severe reprimand from the IFU for travelling to Wales without permission. Strangely, he places the tour in 1881 but in describing the three fixtures played, it is clear that it was the 1879 tour to which he referred.[96] Similar unofficial Irish teams returned to play against South Wales and leading Welsh clubs, including Cardiff, for several more seasons and this undoubtedly fuelled the appetite for greater international competition.

Welsh rugby changed out of all recognition during the 1870s. A minority leisure pastime was becoming the passion of a wider public. This was well summed up by the *SWDN* at the very end of the decade following Newport's defeat by Swansea in the 1879 cup.

To the uninitiated it is quite a remarkable feature to notice the interest taken by the inhabitants generally in the result of these periodical contests, but the fact is that they have grown to look upon the matter as one where the credit of the town is at stake ... in South Wales ... the rivalry between the leading clubs has added much to the interest taken in [rugby] by the general public. [97]

Wales in Union

The 1880–1 season marked a major turning point in the development of Welsh rugby, for in that year the WFU was formed and Wales played her first international. Technically, the first Welsh XV was an unofficial one, since the Union was not brought into being until several weeks later but the match has traditionally been accepted as a full international. Besides, Scotland played three officially recognised internationals against England before the Scottish Union was founded in 1873, so there is precedence for this. These events are well covered in *Fields of Praise*.[98] However, this study has provided an opportunity to return to 1881 and examine that year in rather more depth than David Smith and Gareth Williams were able to do. Whilst their general argument is confirmed, on some points of detail, there is new evidence to consider, especially with regard to the role of Richard Mullock. The creation of the Welsh Football Union cannot be considered in isolation from the circumstances surrounding the 1881 international at Blackheath, so these will first be examined in some detail.

The season opened with a remarkable letter to the press which criticised the SWFU secretary, M.I. Morris, for not arranging a general meeting in accordance with the constitution.[99] This was remarkable because the letter writer was Richard Mullock and it was just the kind of complaint that he would receive when he later became secretary of the WFU. The SWFU meeting was eventually held when Sam Clarke of Neath was appointed the new secretary. Mullock's growing irritation with the existing administration cannot have been improved when the SWFU organised an East v West trial in which, apart from one Newport Crusader and three Bridgend players, the fourteen-man East team included ten from Neath![100] Players from the Cardiff and Newport clubs either appear to have been ignored or they deliberately made themselves unavailable for some reason. Either way, it suggests all was not well within the South Wales Union and perhaps their absence is an indication that Mullock was beginning to make his own plans for a match with England.

It is generally accepted that an informal meeting had been held in March 1880 at the *Tenby Hotel* in Swansea when discussions were held about arranging an international with England. David Smith and Gareth Williams disprove the previously widely held view that it was here that the WFU was founded. They also establish beyond any reasonable doubt that the clubs which were believed to have attended were identified retrospectively, and therefore incorrectly, simply by listing the clubs (or in some cases the place of residence) of the players who represented Wales in the first international.[101] Though no written confirmation of the *Tenby Hotel* meeting has survived, there is new evidence which suggests that it may have happened. In the 1881 *Football Annual*, Mullock wrote as the new WFU secretary:

> Some time previous to the formation of this Union, *and after consultation with the leading clubs*, International matches were arranged with England and Ireland.

Of course, "consultation" does not necessarily mean that a meeting of clubs was actually held. Perhaps Mullock was simply trying to deflect criticism by claiming that his actions were based on a consensus of clubs. However, this is the nearest that we have at present to a corroboration of the *Tenby Hotel* meeting. Though writing only a few months after the event, when describing the actual foundation of the Welsh Union, Mullock places it in Swansea and not Neath where it was held in March 1881.

> At a meeting at *Swansea* in March last it was decided that such a Union should be formed. At the same time the South Wales FU was dissolved and its Challenge Cup handed over for competition by any club belonging to the Welsh Football Union.[102]

Was Mullock confusing his meetings?

Whether as a result of the *Tenby Hotel* meeting or of his "consultations", Mullock presumably felt he had a sufficient mandate to proceed. It is significant that Newport appeared for the first time amongst the forty-one clubs represented at the RFU AGM on 25th October 1880 and they were the only Welsh club to do so.[103] There can be little doubt that Mullock attended the meeting to sound out English officials and he must have made a favourable impression. Only four days later, the press reported, "The Rugby Union committee want to arrange an international match between England and Wales to be played at Newport in February next." Since this appeared in a newspaper report about Newport, it almost certainly came from the hands of Mullock, no doubt with an element of "spin", particularly regarding the venue for the fixture.[104] Nevertheless, only a few weeks afterwards on the 30th November, the RFU minutes record:

> A letter from Mr. R. Mullick [sic] of Newport Monmouthshire was read proposing a match with Wales – after considerable discussion it was proposed by L. Stokes [and] seconded by J. McLaren That the challenge be accepted – the match to be played in London on 8th Jan.[105]

Because the Welsh team performed so badly in the first match against England, a great deal of criticism has been levelled against Mullock, some of it justified, some of it not.[106] He arranged a trial at Swansea for 29th December 1880. Virtually all accounts of the events leading up to the international say that the match did not take place and this is often presented as an example of Mullock's incompetence. Yet, as the *SWDN* reveals, the match *was* held. It was admittedly not a great success, though Welsh trials throughout the nineteenth century rarely were. In this case, there was too much individual, selfish play with little passing of the ball. Nevertheless, at least five, perhaps six, of the eventual Welsh XV took part and a good spread of clubs was represented.[107]

However, the RFU decided on the 30th December that the international match would have to be postponed until the 22nd January and a subsequent meeting reported that "the Wales committee" had accepted this. A severe frost resulted in further delays and at one point the RFU, brazenly revealing their priorities, warned Mullock that the game might have to be cancelled because they were looking for new dates to accommodate Scotland and Ireland.[108] However, it was eventually fixed for the 19th February. These delays caused problems for Mullock's selections, but it also meant that during the seven weeks between the trial and the match, there were plenty of opportunities to publicise the team. The frequently asserted view that some players were unaware that they had been selected is therefore hard to believe. On at least three occasions, the team appeared in the local press. There *were* admittedly some variations in these teams and, given two postponements, injuries and unavailability this was perhaps inevitable. What is surprising is how *few* changes there were. The team published on 13th January contained thirteen of the eventual side plus one reserve who played; that of the 12th February (a squad of seventeen) also had thirteen; and that published on the 19th February had twelve of the team plus the three reserves who subsequently played.[109] Thus, the selection was not as haphazard as usually claimed. What is invariably ignored, by those who criticise the apparent disarray in the Welsh match organisation, is that only twelve of the originally selected England XV played on the day.[110]

C.P. Lewis (Llandovery College), a gifted player who later captained Wales, is alleged to have refused to take part in the match.[111] This may be true, particularly as he may have been closely associated with the officials of the SWFU, which was effectively being by-passed by Mullock. His name does not appear in any of the published team lists, so he may have made Mullock aware of his opposition to the game from the outset.[112]

It is widely believed that some players had not even been notified of their selection and that, as a result, Wales were forced to include men from amongst the spectators on the touchline. Precisely *who* these men were, however, no-one has ever established. This version is based on the recollections of Richard Summers. Speaking on the BBC some fifty years later, he recalled:

> When we got to the changing room, we discovered that we were two men short, their invitations apparently having gone astray. However, we picked up two 'Varsity men with Welsh qualifications, and they agreed to fill vacancies on condition that they were allowed to play three-quarter.[113]

This account does not fit entirely well with the contemporary evidence. The (two) three-quarters who played at Blackheath were the captain James Bevan of Cambridge, who had always been in the team, and Edward Peake of Oxford.[114] Peake was originally selected but was then dropped to reserve to accommodate a more experienced player, Robert Knight. On the morning of the international, the *SWDN* published the Welsh team, of whom three did not play. Those who came into the side as replacements were Edward Peake and the forwards Edward Treharne and Godfrey Darbishire. Since all three were *named reserves*, the idea that Wales had to rely on players from the touchline can surely be dismissed.[115] Indeed, that Wales arrived *with* reserves is to Mullock's credit. Despite having far more in terms of playing resources and administrative experience, England twice travelled to away matches without reserves around this time and on both occasions were forced to pick up players locally. This happened in Ireland in 1880 when one player suffered badly from the effects of sea-sickness and in Scotland in 1881 when Henry Taylor missed the train.[116]

Two of the men who dropped out the Welsh team were Oxford Blues. Robert Knight was a half-back from Bridgend and an old boy of Cowbridge Grammar School, whilst three-quarter Arthur Evanson came from Llansoy in rural Monmouthshire.[117] His older brother, Wyndham Evanson, became the third Welsh-born rugby international when he was capped by England in 1875. A Blue in 1879, Robert Knight missed the December 1880 Varsity Match because of injury, which might possibly explain his absence at Blackheath. His selection, however, was a logical one: he had just been appointed term captain of the University and he would also have renewed his Oxford half-back partnership in the Welsh team with his fellow Blue, Leonard Watkins. Marshall and Jordan's history of the Varsity Match claims that Knight turned down a Welsh cap in the hope of being selected for England, though he never was. Evanson, on the other hand, *was* later capped by England and was regarded as an outstanding international three-quarter. It would appear then that Mullock was justifiably keen to select two Welsh-born Oxford Blues who were of, or very near, international standard for England. It is doubtful if there were any more experienced players available than these two Welshmen and it made good sense to invite them to play. Unfortunately, it seems the promise of a possible English cap meant more than a guaranteed Welsh one.[118] It is difficult to see these particular selections as evidence of Mullock's maverick policy when it is remembered that, when the first ever *officially* selected Welsh team was picked to play the North of England a year later, both Knight and Evanson were again included, though they again withdrew.[119]

John Brooks of Pontypridd is often regarded as one of the unluckiest Welshmen of all time because, as he later claimed, despite being picked for Wales, he was never informed of his selection.[120] This, however, cannot be sustained by the evidence. He did not take part in the trial, he had never previously represented South Wales and, importantly, his name is not included in any of the Welsh team lists published before the match. Indeed, his name does not appear in any published *Pontypridd* team in the *SWDN* or *Western Mail* until several years after the 1881 match. It is difficult, therefore, to see how he could have been considered for selection at this time.

Where Mullock might justifiably be criticised is in his choice of some players who were little known in Wales and who did not appear to have a particularly strong rugby pedigree. It is quite evident that his primary concern was to select players who had experience of playing in England or against English teams. This perhaps was not such a foolish policy, for there cannot have been any realistic hope that Wales would defeat England, whatever side was picked. What was wrong with the policy was that some of these "English" players were simply not good enough. Another criticism is that Mullock ignored the justifiable claims of players from other clubs, Swansea, Neath and Llanelli in particular, while Newport, with six players, and Cardiff, with four, were well represented. Despite the fierce rivalry that already existed between Cardiff and Newport, it does seem that there may have been some collusion between the east Wales clubs and it is quite likely that Cardiff officials were also involved in the team selection. Even before the match took place, complaints were made about Mullock's team.[121] That there was a cup semi-final on the day of the international does not exonerate him for failing to pick anyone from Llanelli and Swansea, as players from these two clubs were also omitted from the earlier team selections for the two postponed dates.[122] There is little doubt that Mullock included too many men with little proven ability and he could have found some players of a better standard from within the personnel playing regularly in Wales.

An examination of the social background of the first Welsh XV reveals few surprises. It would be three years yet before the first genuinely working man, Cardiff's William Stadden, would win a Welsh cap. The team was made up predominantly of students. Three (Bevan, Lewis and Newman) were at Cambridge and two (Peake and Watkins) at Oxford. Treharne was a medical student and Summers was studying prior to joining the Army. Garnons Williams, whose family were Breconshire landowning gentry, was a serving Army officer; Darbishire was a north Wales civil engineer and Rees was a farmer and solicitor. Mann was articled to a land agent while the remainder, Girling, Harding, Phillips and Purdon were all clerks. The team, then, was representative only of the middle class and the gentry. There were no artisans. In addition, of the fifteen, seven had been born outside Wales: Bevan in Australia; Purdon and Mann in Ireland; and Darbishire, Girling, Harding and Peake in England.[123] An investigation by Martin Johnes and Ian Garland into the social composition of the first Welsh international soccer team in 1876 provides an interesting comparison. They found that it was mainly middle class in character but, unlike the first rugby team, there was *some* working-class representation in the Welsh XI including a miner, a stonemason and a chimney-top maker. Nevertheless, they conclude that the "social networks of the middle-class FAW" would have determined the broadly middle-class make-up of the team. Similar networks in the administration of Welsh rugby guaranteed the social character of the 1881 XV, especially given the selection policy with regard to experience in England.[124]

Even though the match against England was an embarrassing disaster, it nevertheless had a long-term beneficial outcome. One immediate response was an understandably irate letter to the press asking if it was "a private team, got up by Mr. Mullock".[125] Sam Clarke replied that the SWFU had had nothing to do with it and that "Mr. Mullock was one of the committee who selected the Welsh team".[126] However, even *before* these letters were published, as *Fields of Praise* reveals, the *Athletic World* of 24th February was reporting that "The Welsh are, I understand, about to form a Union". Coming so soon after the 19th of February, this resolution can only have been made by interested parties at the *Princess of Wales* public house in Blackheath, where the Welsh and English teams assembled. The next time they would all get together again would be on the 12th March for the Cardiff v Llanelli cup final held at Neath, so it was decided to convene the meeting then and there.[127]

At that meeting, "after considerable discussion", it was unanimously resolved to form the Union and Mullock was elected secretary also by a unanimous vote. In addition, the meeting also charged Mullock with arranging the selection of a team to play Ireland before the end of the season. The clubs reported as being represented at the Neath meeting included Bangor, Brecon, Cardiff, Llandeilo, Llanelli, Merthyr, Newport, Pontypool and Swansea. Two others were "Lampeter" and "Llandovery". A careful scrutiny of the reported club matches around 1881 and of Mullock's list of "principal" clubs, referred to below, strongly suggest that these must have been the college teams rather than the town clubs. Indeed, Lampeter College had been runners-up in the South Wales Challenge Cup final only a year earlier, while Llandovery College had been semi-finalists in 1878. Nevertheless, though neither of the town clubs had played in the cup, both were accorded "founder member" status by the WRU and, as such, took part in the centenary celebrations. So too did Bangor, though the club history acknowledges that there was no rugby club in the city at the time. Bangor's inclusion was probably an attempt to demonstrate that the new Union embraced the whole of Wales. It is possible that Godfrey Darbishire attended the meeting as a representative from north Wales, as he was appointed one of three vice presidents of the Union for 1881–2. One of the other first vice-presidents was Edward Fry, a former captain of Cardiff, perhaps confirming that his club was closely involved in the various negotiations which took place during the previous year.[128]

A few months later, writing on behalf of the WFU in the 1881 edition of the *Football Annual*, Mullock recorded the "Principal Rugby Clubs" in Wales. The town clubs of Lampeter and Llandovery were not included though the college teams were, confirming their standing at the time. The clubs listed by Mullock were Abergavenny, Aberdare, Bangor, Bridgend, Cardiff, Carmarthen, Carmarthen College, Chepstow, Denbigh, Lampeter College, Llandeilo, Llandovery College, Llanelli, Neath, Newport, Pontypridd, Pontypool and Swansea. A club was formed in Denbigh in 1880. It is possible that his list includes some clubs which joined the Union after 12th March 1881.[129]

In this article, Mullock argues that, during the previous two years, the game had made rapid progress in south Wales and had become very popular, "but unfortunately the style of play has not improved". Whilst this was perhaps an attempt to divert attention from his team selection, it was evidently Mullock's expectation that the new Union would lead to improvements in playing standards. The WFU had also been formed, he wrote, "to promote a greater amount of sociability and good fellowship between the clubs." He may have been less confident about this aspiration. Mullock went on to explain that a match with Ireland had been arranged for the 9th April 1881 and a team was selected, but the IFU then cancelled the fixture because "no ground could be obtained".[130] This seems a feeble excuse by the Irish and it was the first in a series of problems which Wales were to experience in international match arrangements with Ireland in the early years.

To sum up, then, Mullock was a key figure in the development of the game in Wales. He was secretary of Newport when they became for several seasons the most dominant club in Wales. He generated increasing interest in the game there with a number of initiatives, particularly by promoting a series of attractive matches with teams from outside Wales. During his stewardship at Newport, rugby spread like wildfire there, both in terms of spectators and new clubs and it can be justifiably argued that Newport became the first community in Wales to develop a deep obsession with the game. It was his ambition and persistence which led to Wales becoming accepted as international opponents. This was no easy task, especially given the somewhat condescending manner with which Wales was treated at the time, not merely in sporting circles. Mullock's ability to arrange the international match almost single-handedly raises the question as to why the SWFU had not previously done so. Did they lack the ambition, confidence or even ability to do this themselves? Mullock also recognised that, if Wales were to achieve anything beyond mere county standard, it was necessary to establish a national ruling body responsible for all aspects of the game. Huw Richards neatly sums up the man. "Mullock's entrepreneurial skills were not matched by his administrative efficiency."[131] He certainly had his faults, which included a tendency to go his own way, slack financial management and, at times, poor administration and record keeping. It is probably no coincidence that the earliest WFU minutes begin in 1892, the year in which he resigned as secretary. However, his failings were surely outweighed by the crucial contribution he made to the establishment of Welsh rugby on firm foundations. This was acknowledged by his contemporaries, who after all were in a better position to judge him than we are, when they unanimously elected him as the Union's first secretary. He deserves a more balanced assessment than the excessively critical judgements which are sometimes made.

The 1880–1 domestic season was characterised by continuing growth in the numbers playing and watching rugby and, as a consequence of this, by increasing press coverage of the game at all levels. Competition was getting keener and, especially for cup matches, players were taking the game more seriously by practising and training. However, disputes on the field were becoming more common and there were more crowd disturbances involving pitch invasions and even violence against visiting teams.

Welsh rugby had travelled a long way in a decade. Evidence of the game's expansion can be found in the columns of the *Western Mail* and *SWDN*. During the 1880–1 season, these two newspapers alone referred to over a hundred teams in their columns. As they were based in Cardiff, they probably under-reported teams elsewhere in Wales particularly in the west, so the actual total may have been much higher.[132] Four thousand spectators attended the cup tie between Newport and Cardiff and large crowds watched that between Swansea and Llanelli. At the cup final in Neath, "thousands ... surrounded the ropes ... [while] as many were stationed outside", seated on railway trucks or in the upper windows of surrounding houses. In a preview of this match, an editorial in the *SWDN* spoke of "the growing popularity of this favourite game".[133]

Neil Tranter believes that, given the number of football matches played in Britain, incidents of crowd misconduct were atypical.[134] Most rugby games in Wales, too, probably passed off without any serious trouble. Nevertheless, there does appear to have been an increase in the number of unpleasant incidents. In the Neath-Bridgend cup tie in

December 1880, the visitors were pelted with turf, though whether this was because Bridgend played like "semi-savages", as the *Neath Gazette* claimed, is not clear.[135] One of the worst incidents of the season occurred in the cup semi-final at Newport, when Cardiff recorded their first ever win over their arch rivals. The pre-match anticipation for the meeting between "the two best clubs in Wales" was intense. "The two towns had been well placarded" and the teams widely publicised. Fighting broke out between players but it was Cardiff's disputed winning try which caused the crowd to erupt. After the match, the "mob surrounded the pavilion", where they verbally abused the Cardiff team. As the players left the ground, some were kicked and beaten and one was pulled off a cab. The angry supporters even attempted to throw the try scorer into the river. The Cardiff press was outraged, of course. For the *Western Mail*, "the disturbance was a disgrace to the town and to the noble game of football." The *Star of Gwent*, on the other hand, ignored these incidents but thought, "It was most unbecoming ... of the visitors to claim a try". Evidently, partisanship was no longer merely confined to club supporters: after all, the reputation of the whole town was now dependent on success in these encounters.[136]

For example, when the *Llanelly Guardian* previewed the cup match against Bridgend in February 1881, it announced, "We notice that several of the players are in offices and shops, and we appeal to their employers to permit special facilities for this important match, *as the honour of the town is at stake*."[137] Although Llanelli's later victory over Swansea was only a semi-final match, the team was, nevertheless, given a huge welcome on returning home, including a torchlight procession headed by the local band.[138]

Pitch invasions were another way in which supporters were beginning to display their displeasure and even to influence the outcome of matches. The Llanelli-Bridgend tie was frequently disrupted by disputes during which spectators rushed onto the field to participate in the arguments. The game came to an abrupt end with the field full of spectators.[139] The cup final at Neath ended when Cardiff scored a try against Llanelli well into extra time. Hundreds ran on to the field: Cardiff supporters to celebrate and Llanelli supporters to protest. A number of fights broke out and the Cardiff umpire, schoolmaster Henry Shewbrooks, had to be escorted off the field by the police. The match ended in chaos with Cardiff unable to take the conversion and Llanelli unable to use the final couple of minutes to attempt to equalise.[140] The *Western Mail* commented:

> owing to the animosity which is excited by the contests for the challenge cup several of the leading clubs in the South Wales

Football Union contemplate withdrawing from the competition; and it is probable that the "rowdyism" displayed at Neath on Saturday last will precipitate their decision.[141]

It was hoped that the new Union would prevent such incidents in the future, but following more violent matches, Cardiff permanently withdrew from the competition in 1883 and this began the process of the South Wales Challenge Cup's decline. The Welsh game was in desperate need of greater control, both to develop its enormous potential and to deal with the wilder excesses of its growing number of adherents on and off the field. From 1881 onwards, though it was not always successful in doing so, Wales now had a Union which could, at least, attempt to achieve these objectives.

In summary, rugby became the clear choice of footballers in south Wales by the mid 1870s. The number of clubs, players and spectators was increasing substantially and the game's organisation was evolving. Formed in 1875, the SWFC changed from a members club to a more democratic union of clubs in 1879. This body was responsible for introducing both representative and cup rugby to Wales. Though it was largely, if not entirely, dominated by the middle and upper classes, its membership nevertheless displayed a keen interest in competitive rugby. The South Wales Challenge Cup had an immediate and dramatic impact on the development of Welsh rugby as a cross-class sport. In particular, it appealed to the competitive nature of working-class culture and it stimulated strong and lasting club loyalties and partisanship. Associated with this, clubs evolved from private institutions run for the enjoyment of a few young gentlemen into standard bearers of the town's honour. In an increasingly competitive environment, civic pride now mattered, but there was also a downside. By the end of the decade, match disputes, foul play and crowd disturbances were becoming more commonplace.

By the later 1870s, rugby had expanded from the coastal and market towns into the industrial hinterland; the first working-class clubs began to emerge; and working-class players began to appear in previously socially exclusive teams. Youths and schoolboys were also taking up the game, particularly in Newport where the success of the town team resulted in an explosion of interest and participation in the game. Major club matches were now attracting crowds of several thousand, one consequence of which was the gradual monetisation of the game in Wales, as admission charges became standard practice.

Though his role has often been criticised, there is no doubt that Richard Mullock was primarily responsible both for introducing international rugby to Wales and for establishing the Welsh Football Union in 1881. These were very powerful symbols of the immense changes experienced in the Welsh game during the previous decade. By 1882, it was possible for the press to proclaim, "it is now a recognised fact that football is the national outdoor game of the Welsh".[142] It was within this wider context, then, that rugby came to dominate the sporting culture of late Victorian Cardiff. This is the subject of the following chapters.

Notes

1. *Western Mail* 24 Nov. 1874.
2. *South Wales Daily News* 23 Nov. 1874 (Glamorgan), 7 Feb. 1876 (Swansea).
3. *SWDN* 12 Mar. 1875.
4. *SWDN* 18 Jan. 1875.
5. W.J. Townsend Collins (ed.), *Newport Athletic Club: The record of half a Century 1875–1925* (Newport, 1925), p. 11; Jack Davis, *One Hundred Years of Newport Rugby 1875–1975* (Risca, 1974), pp. 60–1; Brian Glover, *Prince of Ales: The History of Brewery in Wales* (Stroud, 1993), pp. 124–5; Mike Brown, *Brewed in Northants* (Longfield, Kent, 1998), pp. 48–9; Jennifer Macrory, *Running with the Ball: The Birth of Rugby Football* (London, 1991), pp. 192–3; David Smith and Gareth Williams, *Fields of Praise: The Official History of the Welsh Rugby Union 1881–1981* (Cardiff, 1980), p. 25.
6. This is an allusion to a line in Byron's *Childe Harold's Pilgrimage*, where he refers to the Field of Waterloo: "Rider and horse, – friend, foe, – in one red burial blent!"
7. *WM* 16 Nov. 1874 (italics added).
8. Brinley E. Matthews, *The Swansea Story: A History of the Swansea Rugby Football Club 1874–1968* (Swansea, 1968), p. 11.
9. *WM* 20 Dec. 1873.
10. Smith and Williams, *Fields of Praise*, p. 44.
11. *Brecon County Times* 2 Oct. 1875 quoted in Danny James and P.O.J. Rowlands, *Brecon Rugby Football Club: One Hundred Years of Rugby Football 1879–1979* (Brecon, 1979), p. 13; Bob Harragan and Andrew Hignell, *C.P. Lewis: The Champion Cricketer of South Wales* (Cardiff, 2009), p. 74.
12. *WM* 15 Oct. 1875.
13. *WM* 30 Nov. 1875.
14. *SWDN* 24 Jan. 1876.
15. Frank C. Hawkins and E. Seymour-Bell, *Fifty Years with the Clifton Rugby Football Club 1872–1922* (Bristol, 1922), p. 8.
16. *Football Annual* 1876, p. 50; *WM* 15 Nov. 1876.
17. T.L. Evans, *Carmarthen Rugby Football Club Centenary Year 1874–1974* (Llandeilo, 1974), p. 1.
18. *WM* 2 Dec. 1875.
19. Matthews, *The Swansea Story*, p. 11; James and Rowlands, *Brecon Rugby*, p. 13.
20. *SWDN* 17 Dec. 1875; *WM* 29 Jan. 1876.
21. *WM* 20 Dec. 1875 (Glamorgan), 11, 13 Jan. 1876 (Carmarthen), 7, 8 Mar. 1876 (Cardiff XV), Townsend Collins, *Newport Athletic*, p. 12 (Cardiff XV).
22. *WM* 20 Mar. 1876 (italics added).
23. Smith and Williams, *Fields of Praise*, pp. 31–2; *WM* 2, 3, 10 Mar. 1876.

24. Brian Lile and David Farmer, "The Early Development of Association Football in South Wales, 1890–1906", *Transactions of the Honourable Society of Cymmrodorion* (1984), pp. 195–7.
25. *WM* 15 Mar. 1876.
26. *WM* 13 Oct. 1876.
27. F. Marshall (ed.), *Football: The Rugby Union Game* (London, 1894 edn.), p. 86; O.L. Owen, *The History of the Rugby Football Union* (London, 1955), p. 251. Unfortunately, the RFU minutes relating to the RMA Woolwich cup proposal have not survived, as there is a gap from 1872 to 1877.
28. *WM* 21 Dec. 1877 (Aberdare); Andrew J. Croll, *Civilizing the Urban: Popular Culture, Public Space and Urban Meaning, Merthyr c. 1870–1914* (PhD thesis, University of Wales, Cardiff, 1997), pp. 222–3.
29. R. Wendell Edwards, *100 Years of Rugby Football in Bangor* (Bangor, 1980), pp. 1–3.
30. *WM* 13 Dec. 1876.
31. See, for example, Anthony J. Moses and Brenda C. Moses, *A History of Dinas Powys Rugby Football Club and its Associations with the Village, 1882–1982* (Risca, 1982), p. 1 which refers to young farm-workers and quarry workers playing in the village by 1882, though no records of this exist. The first reported game took place there in 1889.
32. *WM* 19 Dec. 1876.
33. *WM* 23 Sept. 1876; C.S. Arthur, *The Cardiff Rugby Football Club: History and Statistics, 1876–1906* (Cardiff, 1908), pp. 9–10.
34. Tony Collins, *Rugby's Great Split: Class, Culture and the Origins of Rugby League Football* (London, 2006 edn.), p. 15.
35. Geoffrey T. Vincent, " 'To Uphold the Honour of the Province': Football in Canterbury c. 1854–c. 1890", in Greg Ryan (ed.), *Tackling Rugby Myths: Rugby and New Zealand Society 1854–2004* (Dunedin, 2005), pp. 14–30. See also Greg Ryan, *The Contest for Rugby Supremacy: Accounting for the 1905 All Blacks* (Christchurch, 2005), pp. 13–51 for early rugby in New Zealand.
36. Richard Holt, "Working-Class Football and the City: The Problem of Continuity", *British Journal of Sports History*, 3, 1 (1986), p. 10.
37. *WM* 22 Jan. 1877.
38. *WM* 5 Dec. 1876; Townsend Collins, *Newport Athletic*, p. 13.
39. *SWDN* 12 Nov. 1878.
40. *WM* 12 Sept. 1877.
41. Martin Johnes and Ian Garland, " 'The New Craze': football and society in north-east Wales, c. 1870–90", *Welsh History Review*, 22, 2 (2004), p. 284. See also Peter Corrigan, *100 Years of Welsh Soccer: The Official History of the Football Association of Wales* (Cardiff, [1976]), pp. 4–5.
42. *WM* 21 Sept., 11, 15, 24 Oct. 1877. The *Cardiff Arms Hotel* was demolished in 1878.
43. See Appendix 4 for the cup winners and runners-up from 1878–9 to 1897–8.
44. *WM* 25 Oct. 1897. See also Smith and Williams, *Fields of Praise*, pp. 1–5 for an account of the cup's impact.
45. RFU minutes 22 Jan. 1878. See Uel A. Titley and Ross McWhirter, *Centenary History of the Rugby Football Union* (London, 1970), pp. 99–102 for a detailed account of the origin of the Calcutta Cup. The Hospitals Cup was introduced in 1874–5 but, of course, was not a competition for open clubs. See Owen, *History of the Rugby Football Union*, p. 251.
46. RFU minutes 10 Jan. 1881.

47. Collins, *Social History*, pp. 43–4.
48. A.M.C. Thorburn, *The Scottish Rugby Union: Official History* (Edinburgh, 1985), pp. 4–6.
49. Edmund Van Esbeck, *Irish Rugby 1874–1999: A History* (Dublin, 1999), pp. 32–3.
50. Collins, *Rugby's Great Split*, p. 20.
51. *WM* 7 Nov. 1877. The draw for the first round is accompanied by the statement that the "ties must be played off on or before the 1st of December".
52. *WM* 29 Nov., 1, 3, 12 Dec. 1877.
53. *WM* 24 Nov. 1877.
54. *SWDN* 16 Nov. 1877.
55. Collins, *Rugby's Great Split*, pp. 21–2. See also Collins, *Social History*, pp. 25–6; David Russell, "'Sporadic and Curious': The Emergence of Rugby and Soccer Zones in Yorkshire and Lancashire, c. 1860–1914", *IJHS*, 5, 2 (1988), p. 195.
56. *WM* 4 Mar. 1878. See also Smith and Williams, *Fields of Praise*, pp. 1–2 for an account of such rituals.
57. *WM* 25 Apr. 1878.
58. Collins, *Social History*, pp. 44–5.
59. *WM* 17, 25 Jan. 1878.
60. *WM* 24 Dec. 1877, 3 Jan. 1878.
61. *SWDN* 18 Mar. 1878 (Neath), 18 Feb. 1878 (Newport). Eifion Morgan, *Llandovery RFC Centenary 1881–1981* (Llandovery, 1981), pp. 5–8 contends that it was the town and not the College which played Newport in the cup. The press report does refer just to "Llandovery" though they are referred to as boys. There can be no doubt from earlier references to the College in the cup draw and in SWFC meetings that it was not the town which played this fixture. There is other evidence to support this. Llandovery College competed every year in the cup until 1881.
62. *SWDN* 25 Mar. 1878.
63. *WM* 27 Oct. 1879 (Manchester); *SWDN* 17 Mar. 1879 (Neath); *WM* 21 Nov. 1879, *SWDN* 21 Nov. 1879 (Blackheath).
64. *Star of Gwent* 6 Feb. 1880.
65. Neil Tranter, *Sport, Economy and Society in Britain, 1750–1914* (Cambridge, 1998), pp. 52–4; *SWDN* 10 Mar. 1879).
66. Townsend Collins, *Newport Athletic*, p 19 (italics added).
67. *WM, SWDN* and *Star of Gwent* 1879–1881 passim.
68. *Star of Gwent* 28 Nov. 5 Dec. 1879.
69. *SWDN* 5 Nov. 1878 (Caerleon); *Star of Gwent* 5 Dec. 1879 (Grammar); *SWDN* 19 Mar. 1880 (Stow Hill).
70. *SWDN* 10 Mar. 1879. This is quoted in full in a later chapter.
71. Smith and Williams, *Fields of Praise*, p. 24.
72. *SWDN* 14 Mar. 1879.
73. *WM* 8 Mar. 1880.
74. Townsend Collins, *Newport Athletic*, pp. 20, 38.
75. Gareth Hughes, *The Scarlets: A History of Llanelli Rugby Football Club* (Llanelli, 1986), p. 9.
76. *SWDN* 12 July 1886.
77. *WM* 8 Mar. 1879; *SWDN* 10 Mar. 1879.
78. *WM* 16 Apr. 1879 (Neath), *SWDN* 5 Jan. 1880 (Llandovery), 25 Nov. 1879 (Crown and Star).
79. Gareth Williams, *1905 and All That: Essays on Rugby Football, Sport and Welsh Society* (Llandysul, 1991), pp. 16–17.

80. *WM* 21 Apr. 1879 (Morris); A.A. Hunter (ed.), *Cheltenham College Register 1841–1889*, (London, 1890), p. 257; http://cricketarchive.com/Archive/Scorecards/108/108412. htmlhttp://cricketarchive.com/Archive/Scorecards/108/108412.html (SWCC)

81. Eric Dunning and Kenneth Sheard, *Barbarians, Gentlemen and Players: A Sociological Study of the Development of Rugby Football* (Oxford, 2005 edn.), pp. 189, 249–250.

82. Stuart Barlow, "The Diffusion of 'Rugby' Football in the Industrialized Context of Rochdale, 1868–1890: A Conflict of Ethical Values", *IJHS*, 10, 1 (1993), p. 57.

83. *WM* 28 Feb. 1880. See Tony Collins, *Social History*, pp. 32–3 for disputes in English rugby.

84. *SWDN* 15 Dec. 1879; *WM* 15, 26 Dec. 1879; *SWDN* 27 Mar. 1880; *Star of Gwent* 30 Apr. 1880.

85. *WM* 10 Nov. 1879.

86. *SWDN* 25 Feb. 1880.

87. *SWDN* 1 Mar. 1880.

88. *WM* 3 Mar. 1880.

89. *Star of Gwent* 5 Dec. 1879.

90. *WM* 22 Oct., 7 Dec. 1878.

91. *SWDN* 20 Feb. 1880.

92. *SWDN* 17 Dec. 1878.

93. John Griffiths, *Rugby's Strangest Matches: Extraordinary but true stories from over a century of rugby* (London, 2000), pp. 9–10.

94. *WM* 16 Sept. 1878.

95. *SWDN* 3 Oct. 1878.

96. Van Esbeck, *Irish Rugby*, pp. 33–4.

97. *SWDN* 15 Dec. 1879.

98. Smith and Williams, *Fields of Praise,* pp. 34–45.

99. *WM* 5 Aug. 1880.

100. *SWDN* 5 Nov. 1880.

101. Smith and Williams, *Fields of Praise*, pp. 37–8. Despite this evidence, many sources still incorrectly give 1880 as the founding date of the WRU.

102. *Football Annual* 1881, p. 169 (italics added).

103. RFU minutes 25 Oct. 1880.

104. *WM* 29 Oct. 1880; *Star of Gwent* 29 Oct. 1880.

105. RFU minutes 30 Nov. 1880.

106. See, for example, Martin Johnson, *Rugby and All That* (London, 2001), pp. 41–4.

107. *SWDN* 30 Dec. 1880.

108. RFU minutes 30 Dec. 1880, 10 and 25 Jan. 1881.

109. *WM* 13 Jan., 12 Feb. 1881; *Star of Gwent* 14 Jan. 1881; *SWDN* 10, 19 Feb. 1881.

110. *WM* 12 Jan. 1881 (original English team); John Griffiths, *The Book of English International Rugby 1871–1982* (London, 1982), p. 30 (England XV v Wales).

111. *WM* 1 July 1949.

112. As was common practice at the time, Lewis, who was a master at Llandovery, played regularly for the college team. See Harragan and Hignell, *C.P. Lewis* for an account of his life and sporting career.

113. Quoted in John Reason and Carwyn James, *The World of Rugby: A History of Rugby Union Football* (London, 1979), pp. 39–40.

114. Bevan was presumably selected as captain as, having played for Cambridge University since 1877, he had the most experience of playing against strong English teams.

115. See Huw Richards, *The Red and the White: The Story of England v Wales*, (London, 2009), pp. 12–20 for a recent account which adopts a revised view of the events of 1881. He reveals that the Welsh team was also published in *The Sportsman*.

116. *SWDN* 19 Feb. 1881 (selected Welsh team); Smith and Williams, *Fields of Praise*, p. 40 (Welsh XV); Griffiths, *English International Rugby*, p. 26 (Ireland v England), p. 31 (Scotland v England).

117. *WM* 16 Apr. 1878 (Cowbridge GS); 1881 Census (Evanson's birthplace).

118. Howard Marshall and J.P. Jordan, *Oxford v Cambridge: The Story of the University Rugby Match* (London, 1951), p. 34 (Knight); Ross McWhirter and Andrew Noble, *Centenary History of Oxford University Rugby Football Club* (Oxford, 1969), Blues Biographical Section, pp. [20] (Evanson), [35] (Knight); Titley and McWhirter, *Centenary History Rugby Football Union* (London, 1970), Biographical Section, p. [33] (Evanson).

119. *WM* 7 Jan. 1882.

120. Gareth Harris and Alan Evans, *The Butchers Arms Boys: The Early Years* (Neath, 1997), pp. 23–4; Gareth Harris, *Taff Vale Park: Memories Lost in Time* (Pontypridd, 2000), pp. 177–180.

121. *WM* 14, 18 Jan. 1881; *SWDN* 12 Feb. 1881.

122. *WM* 13 Jan. 1881. One of the reserves selected for 22nd January, however, was G.L. Morris of Swansea.

123. 1881 Census; Smith and Williams, *Fields of Praise*, pp. 39–41; John M. Jenkins, Duncan Pierce and Timothy Auty, *Who's Who of Welsh International Rugby Players* (Wrexham, 1991).

124. Johnes and Garland, "The New Craze", pp. 287–8.

125. *WM* 28 Feb. 1881.

126. *WM* 3 Mar. 1881.

127. Smith and Williams, *Fields of Praise*, pp. 41–6.

128. *WM* 15 Mar. 1881.

129. *Football Annual* 1881, p. 171–2; *North Wales Chronicle* 8 Oct. 1881.

130. *Football Annual* 1881, pp. 169–172. Mullock's account of the unplayed fixture with Ireland is confirmed by Van Esbeck, *Irish Rugby*, pp. 33–4.

131. Huw Richards, *The Red and the White*, p. 16.

132. See Appendix 1 for a list of rugby teams in Wales in 1880–1.

133. *SWDN* 12, 14 Mar. 1881.

134. Tranter, *Sport, Economy and Society*, p. 47.

135. W.A.D. Lawrie, *Bridgend Rugby Football Club: The First Hundred Years* (Bridgend, 1979), pp. 18–20.

136. *WM* 20 Dec. 1880; *SWDN* 20 Dec. 1880; *WM* 25 Oct. 1897; *Star of Gwent* 24 Dec. 1880.

137. *Llanelly and County Guardian* 6 Jan., 24 Feb. 1881 quoted in: Gareth Hughes (ed.), *One Hundred Years of Scarlet* (Llanelli, 1983), pp. 25–7 (italics added).

138. *WM* 21 Feb. 1881.

139. *SWDN* 14 Feb. 1881.

140. *SWDN* 14 Mar. 1881.

141. *WM* 14 Mar. 1881.

142. *SWDN* 6 Mar. 1882.

4

THE CLUBS

'In Cardiff and district surely their name is legion'

Rugby in nineteenth-century Wales is often portrayed as a cohesive and socially inclusive sport, which enjoyed mass support across the classes and which therefore became a cornerstone of Welsh popular culture. The following chapters will consider the validity of this view by examining in detail the impact which rugby football had in the largest town in Wales.

At the beginning of the century, Cardiff was a small, insignificant market town with a purely local trade and a population of just 1,870. Within a hundred years, however, it had become not only the regional capital of south Wales but also one of Britain's largest ports and a trading centre of worldwide importance.[1] This astonishing change was acknowledged by a Board of Trade report in 1908.

> There is no more interesting study in town growth and development than Cardiff. At the Census of 1851 it was a place of some 20,000 inhabitants with no influence in commerce and no reputation. Now, it is one of the most thriving cities in the country, a centre of trade and commerce and a great port. In every respect the development has been remarkable.[2]

Though Cardiff began exporting iron from Merthyr following the opening of the Glamorganshire canal in 1798, its rise as a major port and regional centre was based on the expansion of the coal trade. From around 1850, coal began to overtake iron as the main staple of the south Wales economy and Cardiff became its main place of export. It also began to replace Bristol as the commercial centre for south Wales. By 1871, Cardiff had overtaken Merthyr to become the largest town in Wales.[3]

By the 1880s, south Wales dominated British coal exports and Cardiff dominated the south Wales trade. In 1870, three million tons were exported from Cardiff; by 1900 the figure had risen to nearly eight million.[4] However, though Cardiff developed a range of commercial and recreational services as it evolved into the regional capital, it never became a centre of manufacturing. Nevertheless, at the end of the century, it was being described as both the "metropolis of Wales" and the "coal metropolis of the world".[5] Indeed, the town's rugby players were often referred to as the "Welsh Metropolitans" at this time.

Between 1851 and 1911, Cardiff's population grew from 20,000 to 182,000, an astonishing rate of increase, which was not matched by any other major town in Britain, apart from Middlesbrough.[6] Following the construction of new docks, the populations of neighbouring Penarth and Barry also expanded, as shown in Table 2. Barry, in particular, grew phenomenally and, by 1913, it had even overtaken Cardiff in tonnage of coal exports.[7]

These events led to immense changes in the way of life of the town and its surrounding area, including an unprecedented enthusiasm for organised sport and overwhelmingly for rugby football. Commenting on the "lovers of the popular winter pastime" in 1890 the *SWDN* said of them "in Cardiff and district surely their name is legion."[8] Strangely, then, histories of Victorian Cardiff largely or, in some cases, completely ignore the impact that rugby had on the social, cultural, economic and civic life of the town.[9]

This chapter therefore aims to assess the importance of the game in Cardiff by examining the extent and nature of the participation. This will be done by establishing, for the first time, the number of teams in the Cardiff area up to 1900 and by attempting to trace their origins and background. The organisation of the game and the social class of its participants; and the social and economic impact of rugby on the life of the town will be explored in later chapters. Finally, an attempt will be made to assess the importance of rugby in the popular culture of Cardiff in the late nineteenth century.

In order to provide a measure of the growth of the game in the nineteenth century, every local team mentioned in the *South Wales Daily News* and *Western Mail* was recorded for each season between 1870 and 1900. The results of this exercise are shown in Table 1 and Figure 1.[10] In addition, the list of those traced for 1895–6, the season with the highest number of teams, can be found in Appendix 2. These figures include clubs from Penarth and Barry, as well as those from within the administrative boundaries of the modern city and its surrounding villages. This was done because clubs and players from these neighbouring port towns have always been an integral part of "Cardiff and District" rugby, where they have regularly contested both friendly and competitive matches. Penarth, for instance, were winners of the Cardiff District Challenge Cup for three seasons, while Barry were founder members of the Cardiff and District Football Union. From the earliest days, players from Penarth and Barry have represented Cardiff teams, while Cardiff men have often played for Penarth and Barry sides.[11]

Attempting to record the number of clubs in this way over such a long period is not without difficulties. Apart from simple human error, negative micro-films and missing and defaced editions, the reliability of the collected data has to be questioned. Some clubs may have changed their name during the season while others may have had their names reported incorrectly, both of which would inflate totals. Unfortunately, there is often no way of reliably dealing with this, though where such incidents were clear, the results were adjusted. However, a surprisingly large number of clubs ran second XVs and though these were noted (see Appendix 2), they have not been included in the overall totals in Table 1, partly because some club reserve teams played under a separate name. Therefore, any such inflation of the figures might be roughly offset by the exclusion of these second teams. There is no doubt that many of the teams recorded were transitory and did not play regular fixtures throughout the season. However, distinguishing regular from transient teams is not easy since some regular clubs rarely featured in the press. In addition, such teams were still an important part of the local rugby culture, even though they were transitory. It should also be pointed out, of course, that the activities of some, possibly many, teams never reached the columns of the local newspapers at all.

Both Alan Metcalfe and Mike Huggins, in their respective studies of early association football, noted a very high annual turnover rate of clubs.[12] This was also true for the rugby clubs of Cardiff. As a result, except for a very limited number of major clubs, it proved impossible to trace the progress of individual teams over the period. Newspapers were surprisingly uninformative about the bewildering frequency with which clubs changed their names, merged, split, disbanded and re-formed. Michael Bassett's very useful and well researched account of early rugby in Barry reveals just how complex the process of club turnover could be.[13] Nevertheless, no other similar detailed study of Welsh club rugby has previously been undertaken and it is believed that, despite the limitations of the data, they are sufficiently reliable to confidently draw conclusions not only about the extent but also, as will also be shown, about the nature of club rugby in Cardiff and Wales in the late Victorian period.

An examination of the results shown in Table 1 and Figure 1 suggest there were five phases of the development of the game in the Cardiff area during the last three decades of the nineteenth century.

1870–1 to 1876–7. In this phase, the game was initially established in the town. The number of clubs never reached double figures and rugby was played only by an elite minority.

1877–8 to 1883–4. This was a period of slow but gradual growth, as the game began to gain some popularity and reach out to the lower middle and working classes.

1884–5 to 1889–0. During these five years, the game took off. This was a period of rapid growth with the number of teams increasing five times in as many years to well over 200. Both the success and the style of play of Hancock's team in 1885–6 had an impact, particularly on the numbers of school and street teams in following seasons. Working men were now playing in large numbers.

1890–1 to 1896–7. This was the high summer for Cardiff (and Welsh) rugby teams in terms of their complete domination of the sporting scene. Wales secured their first victory over England in 1890 and in 1893 they won their first Triple Crown. Cardiff were playing attractive rugby against the best sides in the country. The number of teams in the Cardiff area consolidated at an average of over 200 each season. Working-class players dominated in terms of playing numbers.

1897–8 to 1899–1900. In the previous phase, participation in the game had probably reached a level of saturation which could not be sustained, so the final years of the century saw a process of rationalisation and contraction, though the number of clubs was still substantial. For the first time, rugby faced serious competition from association football, which was at last beginning to attract adherents in substantial numbers.

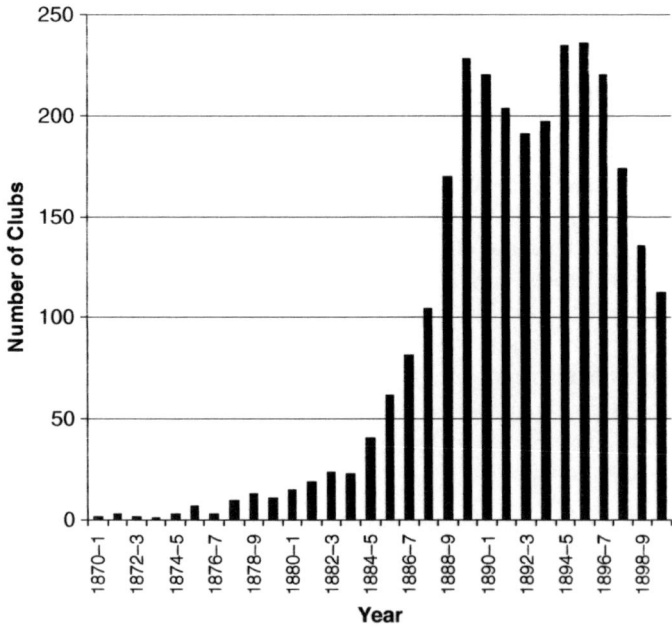

Figure 1: Annual Numbers of Cardiff and District Rugby Teams[14]

Table 1: Cardiff and District Rugby Teams Recorded in Local Press[15]

Year	School	Church	Work	Public House	Street	Neighbourhood	Misc.	Total
1870–1						2		**2**
1871–2	2					1		**3**
1872–3	1					1		**2**
1873–4						1		**1**
1874–5	1					2		**3**
1875–6	3					4		**7**
1876–7						3		**3**
1877–8	2					7	1	**10**
1878–9	3	1	1			7	1	**13**
1879–0	2					7	2	**11**
1880–1	2					13		**15**
1881–2	3					16		**19**
1882–3	2	1	1		1	18	1	**24**
1883–4	2		2	2	2	14	1	**23**
1884–5	3		5	4	4	21	4	**41**
1885–6	4	2	9	2	8	34	3	**62**
1886–7	12	4	3	1	8	52	2	**82**
1887–8	13	6	7	2	11	60	6	**105**
1888–9	10	16	19	4	19	97	5	**170**
1889–0	19	10	25	7	40	115	12	**228**
1890–1	16	15	26	8	41	105	9	**220**
1891–2	6	11	25	7	33	115	7	**204**
1892–3	7	11	28	1	38	100	6	**191**
1893–4	3	22	29	5	31	100	7	**197**
1894–5	6	17	35	6	25	136	10	**235**
1895–6	2	25	43	7	23	125	11	**236**
1896–7	7	22	24	4	27	129	7	**220**
1897–8	4	19	21	2	18	104	6	**174**
1898–9	3	14	13	1	8	86	11	**136**
1899–0	4	12	4		7	79	8	**114**

Perhaps the most important causal factor accounting for this astonishing growth in participation in the game was the dramatic demographic change which occurred in the area over the period, in particular during the 1880s and 1890s when Cardiff's population doubled.

By themselves, the figures in Table 2 do not adequately explain the growth in the number of clubs – why would Cardiff's many new citizens necessarily take up rugby? Indeed, the eventual establishment

Table 2: Population of Cardiff and District 1871–1901[16]

Census Year	Cardiff	Penarth and Barry	Total
1871	57,400	3,600	61,000
1881	82,800	6,700	89,500
1891	128,900	25,700	154,600
1901	164,300	41,200	205,500

of association football in Cardiff was at least partly the result of the efforts of migrants from soccer playing areas in England and Scotland. Nevertheless, with rugby firmly entrenched as the preferred sport of both the working and the middle classes in the town by the 1880s, it offered an immediate opportunity for immigrants to identify with their new community and to integrate into its social life. As David Smith and Gareth Williams have shown, rugby helped immigrants to develop a sense of their Welsh identity. [17]At the same time and at the urban level, it also provided newcomers – through their allegiance to their town team – with a sense of *local* pride and of belonging to their adopted place. Richard Holt argues that the supreme appeal of (association) football lay in its expression of civic pride and identity. The massive expansion of Britain's towns created new problems of identity for their inhabitants. He suggests that, as far as *playing* football was concerned, the neighbourhood was all important. But the inhabitants of streets were also the citizens of new cities and they also needed a cultural expression of their urbanism which went beyond the immediate ties of family and locality.[18] What was true of the English centres of professional soccer was just as true of the rugby playing towns of south Wales, in particular Cardiff, which now had one of the best teams in the country.

Before examining the findings of the research, it might be useful here to consider the position of association football in the town. In contrast to many other parts of Britain, there was very little organised soccer in south Wales before the mid 1890s.[19] With only a tiny handful of association teams in Cardiff during the 1880s, rugby was able to take-off with very little competition.

It is a widely held view, even in some rugby reference books, that Cardiff began life as a soccer club but press reports of 1876 make it quite clear that the new club was formed to play rugby.[20] It is also indisputable that both Cardiff's forerunners, Glamorgan FC and Cardiff Wanderers were rugby clubs and there is no hint of their ever having been founded to play association football. It is difficult to establish where this myth originated as there is absolutely no contemporary evidence for it.[21] Articles published in 1892 on the origins of the leading

Welsh clubs referred to the possibility that Swansea and Newport may have briefly had soccer roots but no such suggestion was made about Cardiff. Nor does either of the club's two official histories, the first of which was published in 1908, make any reference at all to this clearly erroneous claim. [22]

Founded in 1881–2 and initially based around the clergy at Roath church, St. Margaret's was the first association club in Cardiff. For a number of years, St. Margaret's was Cardiff's *only* soccer club and so they often had difficulty in finding opponents, even having to rely on one occasion on the members of the Cardiff club to give them a game, which the rugby players won 4-2. "There was not a large attendance."[23] Such was the lack of interest locally in soccer that in 1883 a supporter informed the press that it was "useless to form a club in Cardiff" unless other clubs were set up in the neighbourhood.[24] A newcomer from Birmingham complained shortly afterwards that "since coming to Cardiff I have not found one club playing the Association game."[25] The limited impact of soccer in the region meant that when North Wales played the South in 1884, the most southerly players came from as far away as Welshpool and Oswestry.[26] Following the one-all draw in the 1885 international with England, "Old Stager" remarked that in south Wales, "Association football is almost, if not entirely, at a discount."[27] In 1887, he was able to report *some* growth, but while he noted "no fewer than four clubs" in Cardiff, there were then over eighty rugby teams in the town.[28] The four clubs were Cardiff Scottish, Cardiff Villa, White Star and St. Margaret's. Some months later, the first three of these amalgamated to form the first Cardiff AFC but this club had little success and it soon folded.[29]

Two years later in 1889, the town still had only four soccer clubs.[30] However, on one Monday during the same season, the local press recorded forty-two rugby matches involving seventy-seven Cardiff district teams.[31] A local football handbook for 1890–1 published fixture lists for some seventy Welsh rugby teams, thirty-seven of which were based in Cardiff, but the only soccer teams whose fixture lists were included were those of St. Margaret's First and Second XIs.[32] It seems that, at a time when association football was booming elsewhere, it was just being kept alive in Cardiff by a small handful of enthusiasts.[33] Looking back ten years later, by which time the game was beginning to grow in popularity in Cardiff, one soccer official recalled the difficulty he had in 1891 in finding shopkeepers who could even supply balls for his new club. "To carry one of those funny round balls through the streets … [was to run] the gauntlet of curious onlookers".[34]

Even by the early 1890s, the local organisation of soccer was still poor. The *SWDN* reported in October 1890 that the "isolated effort [in Cardiff] … to awaken interest in the association game, has not so far been attended with any large measure of success." "Socker Player" from London complained to the same paper in January 1891 that he could never find any information on league matches in south Wales whilst "Association Enthusiast" responded, "The game has not yet attained to [sic] great popularity in Wales ... It is only recently that any interest has been taken".[35] The South Wales League was established in 1890–1, but it was not well organised at first. Of the thirteen teams which entered, only seven remained by the end of the season. The sole Cardiff representatives, St. Margaret's, played only one league match, prompting one correspondent to comment, perhaps with some justification, "they might as well not be in it". He added that neither Newport nor Swansea possessed a club of any significance.[36] Cardiff AFC then re-formed in August 1891. However, they received virtually no gate money and in 1895 they dropped out of both the Welsh Cup and the South Wales and Monmouthshire Cup. The club then collapsed after being expelled from the Western League for failing to complete their fixtures.[37]

Therefore, against this background of initial public indifference to soccer and its poor organisation, rugby in Cardiff, and in south Wales generally, had virtually a free run for over twenty years. But interest did at last begin to stir during the later 1890s. Even though there was not a great deal of local soccer to report initially, the *SWDN* began to give greater coverage to the game in England, particularly after the formation of the Football League in 1888. As a result of the influence of teachers who had been educated at soccer playing training colleges, Cardiff's elementary and higher grade schools started taking up the game from around 1895.[38] In addition, the continual flow of migrants to Cardiff during the 1890s included many newcomers who had already acquired a love of association football before they arrived. Almost all of the St. Margaret's team in 1890, for instance, had learned the game outside Wales.[39] In 1893, the *SWDN* observed, "Geordies and Caledonians, "Sockers" to a man, who hold aloof from the [Arms] Park nowadays will suffice to keep the other game going."[40] The number of association teams in Cardiff began to grow steadily from around 1893–4 but, nevertheless, the game still lagged behind in popularity. By 1900, there were probably as many soccer as rugby teams in Cardiff, although many of these were junior clubs and at this time there were no "first class" soccer outfits equivalent to Cardiff rugby club. Attendances at club rugby matches in Cardiff at the end of the century still far outstripped those at soccer. As Martin Johnes puts it, association football was not "able to claim such a pivotal role in working-class culture" as rugby. However, as he also shows, it was during the following decade that soccer quickly began to rival rugby's pre-eminence.[41]

Though soccer was a potential competitor for the hearts and minds of local sportsmen, rugby enjoyed a different relationship with cricket. Many of the first football clubs were founded by cricketers wanting to keep active during the winter months. In south Wales, Pontypool and Pontymister are two examples mentioned earlier, while, as we have also seen, cricketers were responsible for bringing an early version of football to Cardiff in the late 1860s.[42] It is also evident from a comparison of club team and membership lists that many local sportsmen during the 1870s and 1880s played for Cardiff at both cricket and rugby.[43] Whether cricket had any major influence in the formation of rugby teams in Cardiff in the boom years of the 1880s and 1890s, however, is open to question. In his book on cricket in south Wales, Andrew Hignell provides a chronological list of the founding dates of cricket clubs from 1785 to 1890.[44] This reveals that over thirty Cardiff cricket clubs were in existence before similarly named rugby clubs. However, merely sharing a name does not necessarily prove any relationship. Moreover, a mere thirty out of the many hundreds of rugby teams which were formed at this time represents only a very small proportion. This suggests that cricket's influence on club formation may not have been particularly strong, in Cardiff at least. On the other hand, of course, some rugby clubs could have been formed by cricketers who chose to adopt a different name, but finding much evidence for this may now be virtually impossible. It is conceivable that from the 1880s, given rugby's popularity by then, the process was occasionally reversed. For instance, the Blue Anchor, Hayes, Radyr, Rookwood Rangers, and Star cricket clubs all appeared the season *after* similarly named rugby clubs. Of course, there were always strong informal individual links between the two sports and a review of cricket match press reports will identify many names of prominent and less prominent rugby footballers from the area.

Analysis of Cardiff's Clubs

If it is difficult to estimate the number of teams accurately, then any attempt to categorise them reliably is even more problematic. Research into nineteenth-century English soccer, cricket and rugby has identified the existence of teams with a variety of origins, including schools, churches and chapels, workplaces, public houses, streets and local communities.[45] But, as Dave Russell reminds us, such categories are inevitably loose and overlapping, while Martin Johnes advises caution when assuming that a link with an institution is necessarily suggested by a club name.[46] Even with a good knowledge of the social history and geography of the town, categorising Cardiff's rugby clubs based on their names alone is not straightforward. "St. Peter's", for instance, could be a school, street or parish team, whilst "Cambrian" might be a workplace, pub or neighbourhood club. There might be some uncertainty, therefore, about the precise numbers shown in each category but, despite the inherent difficulties in this approach, it is believed that the findings are sufficiently robust to make comparisons with earlier studies and to draw generalised conclusions.

Drawing partly on D.D. Molyneux's unpublished research on late nineteenth-century cricket and soccer in Birmingham, Tony Mason refers to three particular pre-existing institutions which played an important part in the origin of soccer clubs. These were churches and chapels; workplaces; and public houses.[47] However, none of these categories seems to have been quite so important in the formation of rugby teams in Cardiff, where the evidence appears to support Holt who emphasises the importance of locally organised "neighbourhood" clubs.[48] The research still has to be carried out for other rugby areas of Wales but it is likely that Cardiff was not noticeably different from the rest of the country in this respect.

However, before investigating these categories in Cardiff in detail, it is first necessary to comment on the issue of "junior" teams. The term was used throughout the period in a loose and sometimes confusing way. As a consequence, no attempt has been made to categorise them separately. Many clubs described themselves as such, for instance, Canton Juniors and Roath Juniors. Whilst these were probably examples of boys or youths teams, they were not all necessarily so. Sometimes the term was used merely to distinguish the club from a more senior one in the locality. Adult sides are often described as "junior" clubs in the contemporary press. For example when the Cardiff and District Football Union introduced leagues in the 1890s, the first and second divisions were described as "senior" and "junior" respectively.[49] Until recently, the Welsh Junior RU (later retitled the Welsh Districts RU) was the name of the body which represented adult clubs which were not in membership of the WRU.[50] Sometimes "junior" was used to describe a club's second XV, but the existence of a junior club in a locality did not necessarily mean that such a team was attached to a senior one. Usually they were separately run organisations (e.g. Cardiff Juniors were unconnected with Cardiff FC). The issue is further complicated by those many juvenile teams which did *not* incorporate junior into their title, such as Melingriffith Stars.

During the 1889–90 and 1891–2 seasons, rugby reports in the *South Wales Daily News* and the *Western Mail* provided the age profiles of fourteen local clubs (only three of which, incidentally, described themselves as "junior"). These were: Bute Engineers Second XV (15–16); Cardiff Juniors (16); Canton Rovers (11–13); Clyde Rovers (15); Criterion (14–16); Grangetown Red Stars (15–17); Llandaff Yard Stars (14); Longcross Juniors (13–14); Melingriffith Stars (12–16); Railway Street Crusaders (12); Rennie Stars (10–12); Saltmede Rangers (14); Star Juniors (13–14); and Tongwynlais White Stars (14–15).[51] The ages range from ten to seventeen years, so there appears to have been no attempt to standardise formal age groups at that time. Presumably clubs arranged fixtures as best as they could with those of a similar profile. However, matches between boys or youths teams and adult clubs were not uncommon. In 1892, for instance, the boys of Penarth United surprisingly defeated the Cardiff Police team.[52]

It might be assumed that, by their very nature, such teams were ephemeral but some, at least, were as well organised as their adult counterparts. Despite having an average playing age of only fifteen, Clyde Rovers still published their twenty-six fixture programme for 1890–1 in a local football handbook. Only some of these matches appear to have been against other junior teams.[53] Canton Rovers (11–13) were reported to have won all of their twenty-two fixtures in 1889–90, and they were also undefeated during the following season. Their secretary was then only fourteen years old.[54] In 1889–90, Railway Street Crusaders (12) not only appointed a captain and vice-captain but also had a secretary and treasurer.[55] The apparent independence of these sometimes very young Victorian rugby footballers contrasts with the modern practice of close supervision of junior players.

As early as 1877–8, there are references to under-fifteen matches being played by Cardiff against Newport and Roath.[56] Evidence of the organisation of junior matches is very hard to locate but an early example from Newport in March 1879, when the captain of the winning team was only twelve years old, reveals a surprising degree of sophistication.

To such a height has the rage for football grown that in most of the schools of the town clubs have been formed, and these juveniles draft regulations, send out challenges ... to play a match on a given date with all the formalities attendant upon clubs whose members embrace those of riper years. Only on Saturday two school clubs ... styled Green versus Chandler [played each other]. A field had been engaged ... the ground properly marked out, goal posts erected, a systematic plan of battle arranged with captains, backs, quarter backs, half backs, three quarter backs and forwards regularly drawn out ... some of the combatants underwent an enforced training in anticipation of the event.[57]

There is no reason to suppose that such arrangements were at all unusual elsewhere in south Wales. Richard Holt reminds us that Victorian Britain was a very young society with about a third of the population aged under fourteen, so it is no surprise, therefore, that many of the teams catered for young players.[58] From 1896–7, the Cardiff club successfully instituted an age restricted junior cup competition, which regularly attracted entries from around sixteen teams, with the final being played at Cardiff Arms Park.[59] In addition, an under-nineteen league was organised by the Cardiff and District Football Union in 1899 and another for under seventeens followed soon afterwards. Such age restricted competitions, however, were frequently plagued by disputes about the use of over-age players.

Undoubtedly, the personnel of junior clubs must have overlapped with those of *school teams*. Schools made up only a small percentage of the total number of teams in the period, though their impact on the game in Cardiff, through the development of players, was far greater, of course, than is suggested by the figures in Table 1. As demonstrated earlier, the role of schools in the early development of rugby in Wales was crucial. Private schools in the locality were heavily involved throughout the period and they made a significant contribution to the game. Monkton House, in particular, under the guidance of Henry Shewbrooks, was a highly regarded rugby nursery for Cardiff.[60] Several Welsh internationals began playing at such institutions, for example, Frank Hill, George Young and William Cope (Monkton House); Albert Hybart and Norman Biggs (Cardiff Collegiate); and Percy Bush (St. Mary's Hall and Penarth Collegiate). The Wesleyan School also produced several prominent Cardiff players, including at least two internationals, Percy Bennett (Cardiff Quins) and Syd Nicholls, whilst his more famous brother, Gwyn Nicholls, probably began his illustrious rugby career there.[61]

However, it was not until 1885–6 that the elementary schools, which educated children up to the age of fourteen, began to have any noticeable influence on Cardiff rugby. That they had any at all during the nineteenth century appears to have been largely unrecognised. Carl French's study of the Welsh Schools RU, which was formed in 1903, suggests that there was little rugby organised by the elementary schools at this time because of the lack of school playing fields and because of the emphasis placed on physical drill rather than organised games.[62] However, discussing the forthcoming 1888–9 rugby season, the *Cardiff Argus* reported that "Every school in the neighbourhood has now its football club among its students and those belonging to different schools often have matches arranged between them".[63]

Whilst this might be an exaggeration, at least twenty-three elementary school rugby teams in the Cardiff area were identified in the press from the mid 1880s onwards.[64] It may be no co-incidence that the number of school teams playing the game increased markedly in 1886–7, the season which followed "Hancock's year," Cardiff's most successful season.[65] It is evident, therefore, that rugby *was* played by elementary school teams in Cardiff in the nineteenth century. In the light of French's observations, the likelihood is that, as in the earlier example from Newport, these teams were largely run by the boys themselves outside school hours. Certainly, their opponents were not always restricted to other school sides and this may suggest that the teams were generally not supervised by schoolmasters, until around the time the Cardiff Schools Rugby Union was established a few years later.

Cardiff's first secondary school, which catered for pupils aged twelve to seventeen, also played rugby. A recent biography of Gwyn Nicholls suggests that, while he *may* have attended Cardiff Higher Grade School at Howard Gardens, he could not have learned his rugby there, since it was a soccer school.[66] This conclusion is understandable since the voluminous school history claims that football was first played there only in 1896 and that the code adopted then was association.[67] However, newspaper reports confirm that, within weeks of the school opening in 1885, the Higher Grade was turning out rugby teams, though no doubt these were organised by the boys themselves. This continued throughout the nineteenth century and there is no evidence in the press that soccer was being played at the school before 1896. Whether or not Gwyn Nicholls was an old boy, the Higher Grade produced a Welsh international before him in Frank Mills (Swansea and Cardiff), a distinction which is unrecorded in the school history.[68] From 1896–7, Penarth County School was another local secondary school which began to appear in press rugby reports.

The Cardiff Teachers AFC was one of a small number of soccer clubs to emerge in Cardiff in the early 1890s. Their existence should have acted as a warning to the rugby authorities that soccer might eventually be taken up in local schools. In 1895–6, for the first time in over ten years, there were no elementary school rugby matches mentioned in the press and it cannot be a co-incidence that the first reported schoolboy soccer matches took place that season. Shortly afterwards, members of the Cardiff Teachers club initiated the establishment of a Cardiff Schools Association League. By 1899–1900, eleven schools were taking part and there was also a seven team schools league for Barry and Penarth. Rugby had clearly failed to take advantage of the lead it had built up in Cardiff's schools and it allowed the initiative to pass to the rival code, at least for the time being. This represented a major capture by soccer in Cardiff and it contributed greatly to the subsequent growth of the game there. In 1900, it was being claimed that the league had done much to promote soccer in Cardiff.[69] It may be significant that when Barry Grammar School and Cardiff High School opened in 1896 and 1898 respectively, they were both *initially* soccer schools.[70] In response to the growing interest in soccer amongst local youngsters, the Cardiff club donated a cup for competition for boys under seventeen in 1896, "a step in the right direction and one that should be followed in other districts in South Wales" in the opinion of the *SWDN*.[71] However, not until December 1902 was the Cardiff Schools Rugby Union formed and, whilst it was a very healthy offspring with twenty-three schools playing in three divisions, rugby's initial overwhelming advantage had undoubtedly been surrendered.[72] Local rugby administrators had clearly failed to take heed of the *Western Mail*'s warning as early as 1894 that "Association legislators are a bit energetic and only need half a chance to find their way to the front".[73]

Tony Mason suggests that almost a quarter of soccer clubs in England may have owed their origin to religious organisations.[74] A rather different picture emerges in Cardiff rugby, however, where throughout the 1890s *church teams* comprised only around 10% of the total. It should also be remembered that, as Richard Holt suggests, "parish" teams may often have been in reality neighbourhood clubs run without any particular church involvement.[75] Throughout south Wales, the number of clubs with religious affiliation or foundation was relatively small. Unlike English soccer and rugby league, there are no examples in Wales of major rugby clubs with church or chapel origins. St. John's Canton is the first church name to appear in the Cardiff press in 1878–9. Such early references were rare, though by the 1890s church based teams were more frequently mentioned. From the mid 1890s, the numbers were boosted by Boys Brigade, Church Lads Brigade and YMCA teams.

Of course, there may have been some clubs whose connection with a church was not evident in their name and who are not, therefore, included in the totals, but this would also apply to the data collected in other comparable research. The figures suggest, therefore, that "muscular Christians" did not have a particularly prominent role in organising rugby in Cardiff. Some historians like Dunning and Sheard, and also Adair, have argued that church groups may have regarded soccer as more "civilised" and so this might explain their reluctance to reach out to the working class by establishing rugby clubs.[76] Gareth Williams suggests that far from curbing disorderly behaviour and violence, rugby could incite it. It could also encourage drinking.[77] For these reasons then, Gareth Morgan contends, some nonconformists in particular were sceptical about the "moralizing influence" of the game.[78] In his study of rugby in Rochdale, Stuart Barlow points to the game's intrinsic violence as a deterrent to missionary zeal. He also reveals a remarkable

similarity to Cardiff when he concludes that churches provided "a significant, though *relatively minor* input into the diffusion of the sport"
in Rochdale.[79] However, Daryl Adair's argument that "the class based
nature" of rugby alienated working-class parishioners, causing "muscular Christians" to abandon rugby, cannot explain the church's relatively low level of involvement in the socially democratic game played
in Cardiff and south Wales.

The majority of the religious institution teams in Cardiff were
connected with the Church of England, for example, St. Agnes,
St. Andrew's, St. German's and St. Mary's but increasingly the period
saw the emergence of Roman Catholic parish teams, which were to have,
and indeed still do have, a strong and distinctive influence on the strength
and character of Cardiff rugby. Cardiff's large Irish community was overwhelmingly working class and its origin lay in the flood of immigrants
who arrived during and immediately after the Famine in the 1840s and
1850s. Their lives were largely ones of squalor and poverty but by the
late 1880s, living conditions had improved sufficiently for their descend-
ants to be able to take up sport in their spare time.[80] The first Catholic club,
St. David's, appeared in 1887–8 and, within a couple of years, it had become
one of the strongest in Cardiff and had joined the WFU. Amongst its playing membership were many with Irish surnames, though these would have
been mostly Welsh born, since large scale Irish immigration had ceased
by this time.[81] Dai Fitzgerald was the most prominent product of this club
and he was twice capped by Wales from Cardiff in 1894. Although born
in Cardiff, he was often referred to in the press as an Irishman and it was
rumoured – perhaps unreliably given his working-class background – that the
Irish selectors were interested in him. He was not the only St. David's man to
join Cardiff, as by 1891–2 there were five former players in the senior club
and it appears that these and other defections led to the club disbanding.[82]
But St. David's were replaced by other strong Catholic parish teams like
St. Paul's and St. Peter's, who would attract hundreds of supporters to
their matches. Both became leading clubs in Cardiff during the 1890s.[83]
St. Paul's were based in Newtown, one of Cardiff's early Irish communities,
and were sometimes referred to as "the Irishmen" in match reports, while
their teams and officers were dominated by men with Irish surnames.[84]
Located in Roath, a place of later Catholic Irish settlement, St. Peter's were
first mentioned in the press in 1888.[85]

There does not appear to have been any obvious religious segre-
gation in fixtures and, in any case, the establishment of Cardiff and
District leagues in 1894–5 ensured this could not happen. For example,
in 1896–7, St. Peter's completed their twenty-four match season without
defeat and almost all of their fixtures were against clubs with no obvious
Catholic or Irish affiliation.[86] From the 1890s, "Cardiff Irishmen" were

not only representing their town, but also Wales, and consequently they were becoming heroes of the wider community. After Dai Fitzgerald, the son of Irish parents, scored all Wales' points in the 7–0 victory over Scotland in 1894, he was chaired by supporters through the streets of Cardiff.[87] Rugby allowed Cardiff's Irish, perhaps for the first time, to visibly display their commitment to their home town and to Wales.[88] An in-depth study has not been undertaken here, but it appears that, although there may have still been antipathy and even occasional hostility to this community in general, rugby playing Catholics of Irish descent experienced nothing like the level of prejudice encountered by their soccer counterparts in Scotland.[89] The experience in Cardiff, however, was mirrored in Liverpool, where recent research on Irish soccer clubs there has shown that they suffered from no discernable hostility and, indeed, the sport acted as a bridgehead with the local community.[90] Though ignored by J.V. Hickey in his study of the Irish in Cardiff, Paul O'Leary briefly comments on rugby's role as a means of assisting the social integration and assimilation of the Irish into the wider community of both Cardiff and Wales.[91] The contribution of rugby to this process in Cardiff warrants further study.

It perhaps comes as a surprise to discover that there were also several teams with a nonconformist background in Victorian Cardiff. The conventional view is that Welsh chapels were vehemently hostile to football and there is plenty of evidence to support this.[92] However, the existence of several apparently chapel based teams indicates that, in Cardiff at least, opposition from nonconformists may not always have been total. Perhaps disapproval of rugby was less strong in the larger urban centres, where a more tolerant attitude to sport may have prevailed, as Tony Mason noted was the case in England.[93] This appears to be supported by Gareth Morgan's study of the Welsh religious "Revival" of 1904–5 which reveals that it had little impact on rugby in Cardiff.[94] The existence during the 1880s and 1890s of teams such as Bethany, Loudoun Wesleyans, Merthyr Street Mission, Presbyterians, Wesleyan Rovers, Wesleyans and Zion Harlequins may therefore suggest a greater level of tolerance than is often supposed.[95] However, these were almost certainly junior sides.

The extent of direct involvement of church officials in local rugby is difficult to assess. The St. Peter's club history records that its first secretary in 1888–9 was also secretary of the Catholic Young Men's Society, while the earliest team photograph of 1896–7 includes the St. Peter's rector who was the club president. This may indicate that the rugby club had at least the approval of the parish church, though the extent of its support and involvement can only be guessed at.[96] However, though Hickey makes no specific reference to sport in his study of Cardiff's

Irish community, he shows that local Catholic clergy took the lead in developing a range of parochial social activities and institutions in Cardiff.[97] So their participation in rugby may have involved more than merely giving their approval. He also argues that such activities and institutions helped to unite the Irish community as they spread out into the districts and suburbs of the town. If parish rugby matches contributed to this, then presumably the clergy supported them. The pronounced attachment to rugby of Cardiff's Catholic schools and parishes, therefore, may originate in the clergy's conviction that the sport could contribute significantly to the wider acceptance of the Irish Catholic community.

Hard evidence of the influence of Anglican clergy in Cardiff is also difficult to establish. In 1896, the local vicar was a vice-president of St. Andrew's, but then so was the landlord of the *Flora* public house.[98] Pentyrch, not a "church based" team as such and, in the nineteenth century at least, very much a rural village club, was founded in 1883 by the local schoolmaster and vicar, Morgan Thomas. A "muscular Christian", Reverend Thomas took his pupils to watch games at Pontypridd and was also keen on cricket.[99] Llandaff began using the Bishop's Field, which adjoins the Cathedral, in 1876 and, since this land is owned by the Church, the club presumably played there with its blessing.[100] However, apart from Boys Brigade and Church Lads Brigade teams, it is quite likely that many church clubs were largely organised by their members for their own recreation, rather than by the clergy as an instrument of social control. As Tony Collins appositely puts it, many such teams operated "under little more than a flag of convenience".[101]

The number of *workplace teams* in Cardiff was never very substantial and they did not enjoy a high position in the rugby hierarchy. From the mid 1880s, in most years, works teams comprised around 10 to 15% of the total, peaking at 18% in 1895–6. However, many of these were not regular sides, playing perhaps a few fixtures or even only one. It was common for groups of employees to play together for charity and examples include bakers, butchers, cabmen, clothiers, coal-trimmers, hairdressers, printers, publicans, sail-makers, shoemakers and theatre staff. Since Cardiff is not situated on the coalfield, it is no surprise that there were no teams of colliers. Coal-trimmers, of course, were dock workers. Though such teams were essentially ephemeral, their sheer range and number does give support to the argument that rugby was integral to the day-to-day life of the Victorian town. These games were not restricted to working men, and occasionally employees in banks and in the offices of merchants and shipowners would take part in them. Andrew Croll demonstrates that a similar wide range of social classes were involved in such matches in Merthyr.[102]

The extent and character of Victorian workplace teams depended, of course, on the structure of the town's economy. Cardiff's prosperity then was almost entirely based on its strategic position in the coal trade, on which many in the workforce, including those in the commercial sector, were highly dependent. Remarkably, there was little manufacturing in the town and most industrial activities were relatively small scale. There was no equivalent, for example, of the Lancashire cotton mill. Most of the waterside labour force was casual and the dock company did not employ men directly.[103] This was not a good environment, therefore, for the creation of work-related clubs.

Cardiff's few industrial activities, however, were reflected in some of the teams of the time. These included the Dowlais Iron Company (Dowlais Magpies, Dowlais Iron Works); railway rolling stock manufacturers (Western Wagon Works, Gloucester Wagon Works); timber importers and suppliers (Bland's Deal Carriers, Roath Saw Mills, Cardiff Steam Joinery); grain millers and brewers (Spillers, Anglo-Bavarian Brewery Rovers); paper manufacturers (Ely Paper Mill); engineering companies (Hill's Dry Dock, Tubal Cain Foundry); and tinplate manufacturers (Melingriffith).[104] Not one of these, however, had any significant impact on local rugby.

Of those workplace teams which enjoyed some longevity, the main occupational groups were shop assistants and uniformed employees like railway and post office staff and, to a lesser extent, the police. Railwaymen often used their place of work around which to organise their soccer in England and they seem to have been active in Cardiff rugby too.[105] Both the Taff Vale Railway and the Great Western Railway had regular teams and there were also many instances of occasional matches involving various branches of these and other companies, including Barry Railway. Unlike most dock workers, who were hired by a large number of employers for short periods, railwaymen tended to be employed permanently by one company.[106] This may explain why railway teams were better organised, played to a higher standard and survived longer than most other works teams.

In the mid nineteenth century, Cardiff replaced Bristol as the commercial centre for south Wales.[107] This too was reflected in the town's rugby provision. As Cardiff's service economy expanded to meet the demands of its growing hinterland, so too did the number of teams coming from this sector. The impact of the Saturday half-day on the growth of football has been well documented, but nevertheless many of those who were employed in service industries, of course, still had to work on Saturday afternoons. However, they were not denied the opportunity of playing rugby in Cardiff as there was a thriving Wednesday rugby scene. Some teams drew on groups of employees, for instance, one

Crowd congestion in 1895 forced some journalists to report the match from a tree at the Arms Park.

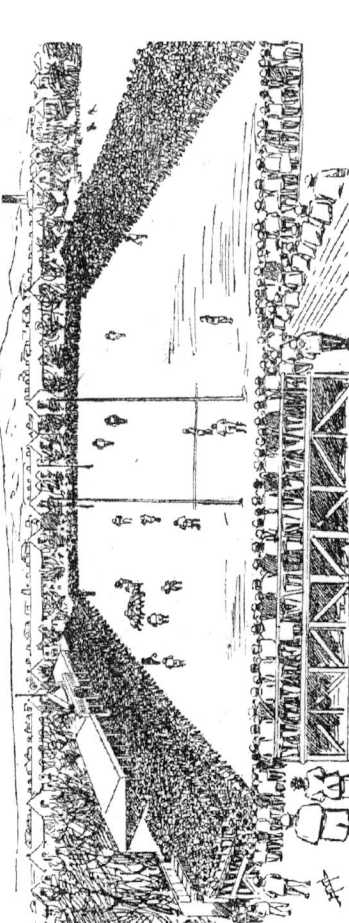

Rugby at the heart of Victorian Cardiff – the Arms Park in 1895 from the Westgate Street end. This would have been approximately the view from the *Grand Hotel* balconies.

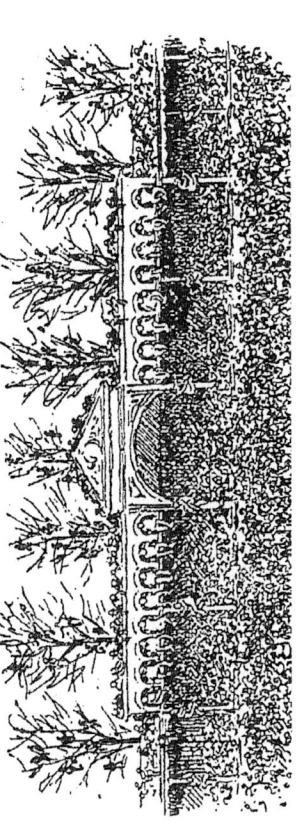

A packed Arms Park grandstand in 1895, with supporters watching from the roof and surrounding trees, presumably unable to stroll out for a pint whenever they felt like it.

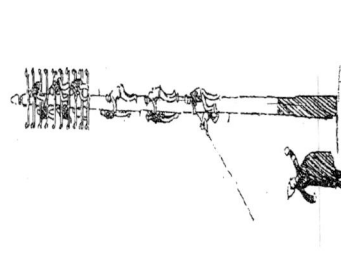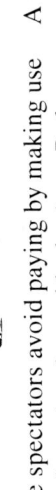

Agile spectators avoid paying by making use of a telegraph pole outside the Arms Park.

A line-out is called in an early match.

A well-dressed Victorian match official oversees a scrummage.

Cardiff in 1880–1 with the South Wales Challenge Cup. "The father of South Wales football", Henry Shewbrooks (Umpire) is standing third from left, while "the father of the Cardiff club", William D. Phillips (Captain) is seated with the ball.

The ground-breaking Cardiff team of 1885–6.
Back: A. Duncan; A. Bland; A. J. Hybart; J. Sant; A. Emery; G. Young; A. F. Hill; H. J. Simpson; W. Treatt. Middle: W. Jones; H. Hughes; C.S. Arthur; F. Hancock (Captain); W. Douglas; Q.D. Kedzlie; A.J. Stuart. Front: D. Lewis; J. Mahoney; W. Jarman; W. Stadden.

S. Campbell Cory (Glamorgan FC Captain 1874–5).

Thomas Donaldson Selby (Glamorgan FC Captain 1875–6, Cardiff Captain 1876–7).

William D. Phillips (Cardiff Wanderers Captain 1874–6, Cardiff Captain 1879–81, 1882–3, Wales).

Frank Hancock (Wiveliscombe, Cardiff Captain 1885–6, Somerset, Wales).

Edward Fry (Glamorgan FC, Cardiff Captain 1877–8).

Alexander Duncan (Glamorgan FC, Cardiff; Proprietor of the *South Wales Daily News*).

Raoul Foa (Cardiff Captain 1878–9).

William Stadden (Bute Dock Rangers, Canton, Cardiff, Dewsbury, Yorkshire, Wales).

The first Welsh XV in 1881. Back: W. D. Phillips (Cardiff); G. Harding (Newport); R. Mullock (Newport); F. Purdon (Newport); G. Darbishire (ex-Manchester); E. Treharne (Pontypridd); R.D.G. Williams (Newport). Middle: T. A. Rees (ex-Llandovery College); E. Peake (Chepstow and Newport); J. Bevan (Cambridge Univ. and Newport); B. Girling (Cardiff); B. Mann (Cardiff).
Front: L. Watkins (Oxford Univ. and Cardiff); C. Newman (Newport); E. J. Lewis (ex-Llandovery College); R. Summers (ex-Cheltenham College).

There was a strong Cardiff contingent in the first ever Welsh XV to defeat Scotland in 1888. Back: J. Meredith (Swansea); A. Gould (Newport); R. Powell (Newport); A. F. Hill (Cardiff); T. P. Jenkins (London Welsh); A. Duncan (Cardiff); W.H. Howell (Swansea and Cardiff).
Middle: G. Bowen (Swansea); A. Bland (Cardiff); T. Clapp (Newport); O. Evans (Cardiff); W.H. Thomas (Cambridge Univ.); T. Williams (Swansea); W. Stadden (Dewsbury, ex-Cardiff).
Front: E. Roberts (Llanelli); Q.D. Kedzlie (Cardiff).

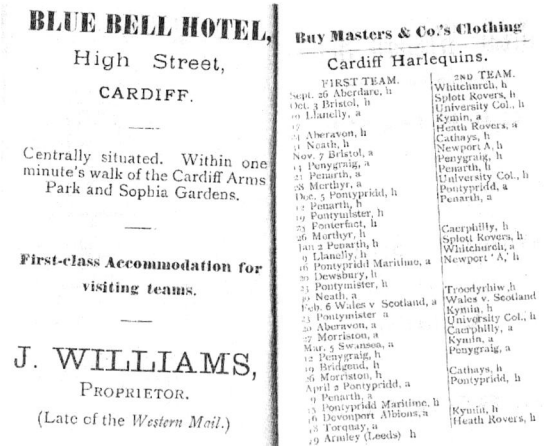

An 1891–2 handbook advertisement for the "centrally situated" *Blue Bell* (renamed the *Goat Major*). The adjoining page shows that Cardiff Harlequins had a strong fixture list by this season, though the Cardiff club was a notable absentee.

Amongst the many facilities offered in this 1891–2 handbook advertisement for the *Grand Hotel* were season tickets to view matches from the balconies. Alongside is Llanelli's varied fixture list, which included eight matches against north of England teams.

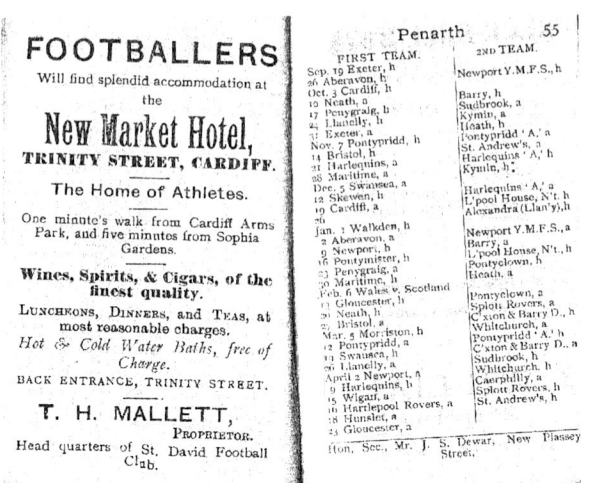

An 1891–2 handbook advertisement for the rugby-friendly *New Market Hotel* (renamed *O'Neill's*) reveals that Thomas Mallett was then the proprietor. The Cardiff and District F.U. was founded here in 1892. The accompanying fixture list was Penarth's most ambitious so far, and this season, two of their players, Richard Garrett and George Rowles, won Welsh caps.

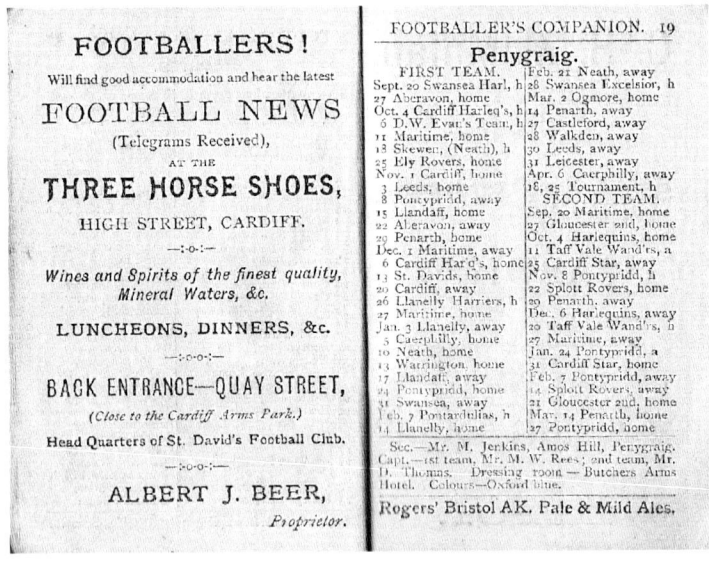

This 1890–1 handbook advertisement for the *Three Horse Shoes* made a strong appeal to rugby followers. Penygraig, whose fixture list is shown alongside, became the first valleys club to achieve senior status for a period.

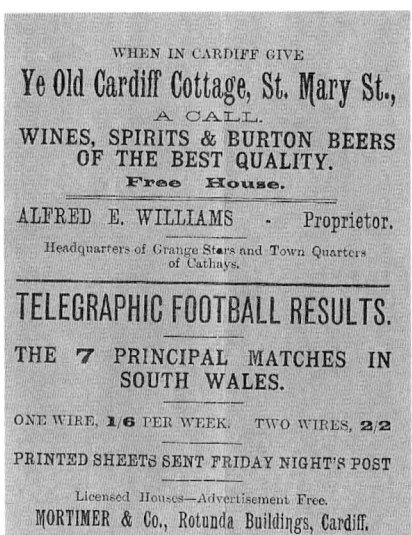

Advertisements in an 1894–5 handbook for the *Cardiff Cottage*, headquarters of two teams; and for a telegraphic service which kept pub users informed of the results of the principal Welsh matches.

The Harlequins Ground, Roath in 1899 being used by Cardiff High School cricketers. It was developed in 1892 by Cardiff Harlequins, who defeated Neath, Llanelli, Swansea, Bath and Bristol here during the 1890s.

Though this, and the following, photograph was taken in the early 1900s, it gives a good impression of what the character of a late Victorian Arms Park crowd would have been like.

The Arms Park was not a totally male world. Two female supporters can be seen in the front left of the picture. One is wearing a large white hat, while there appears to be another standing behind her.

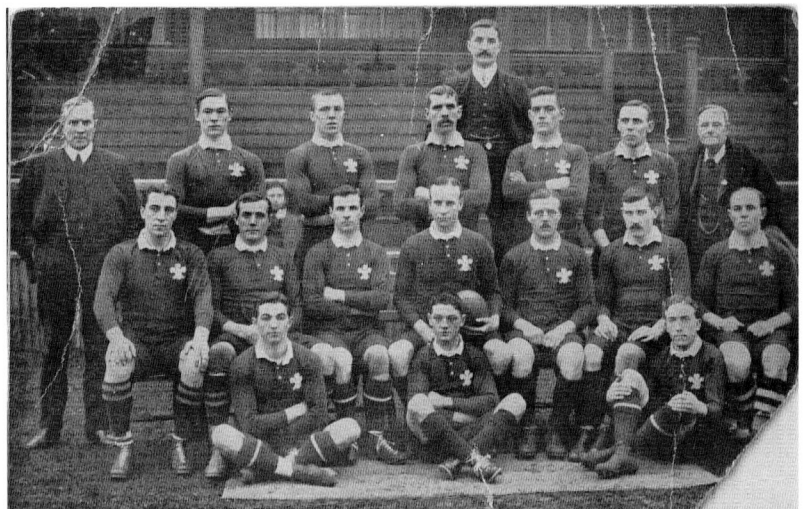

Wales v New Zealand in 1905. The Captain, Gwyn Nicholls (ex-Cardiff Star), is seated with the ball; Ben Winfield (ex-St. Andrews) is seated on his left; Percy Bush (ex-Cardiff Romilly) is third right in the front row.

Llandaff in 1891–2 with the South Wales Challenge Cup. Jack Elliott (Captain), seated with the ball, later played for Cardiff and three times for Wales. Llandaff, who defeated Llanelli A in the final, are the oldest extant club in Cardiff, having been founded in early 1876.

Penarth in 1893–4. Club Captain Herbie Morgan is seated in the centre and Richard Garrett, who won eight caps for Wales, is seated fifth on the right. Club secretary, John Hayes is standing on the far right. Penarth recorded doubles over both Gloucester and Bristol this season.

Roath in 1894–5, winners of Cardiff and District's nine-a-side competition. They also won the District Union Shield this year and the Mallett Cup the following season. Samuel Hill is standing third from right. In 1896–7, C. Smart (with the ball) and P.J. Brady (seated on his left), joined the Northern Union where Brady played for Huddersfield and for Other Nationalities v England in 1904.

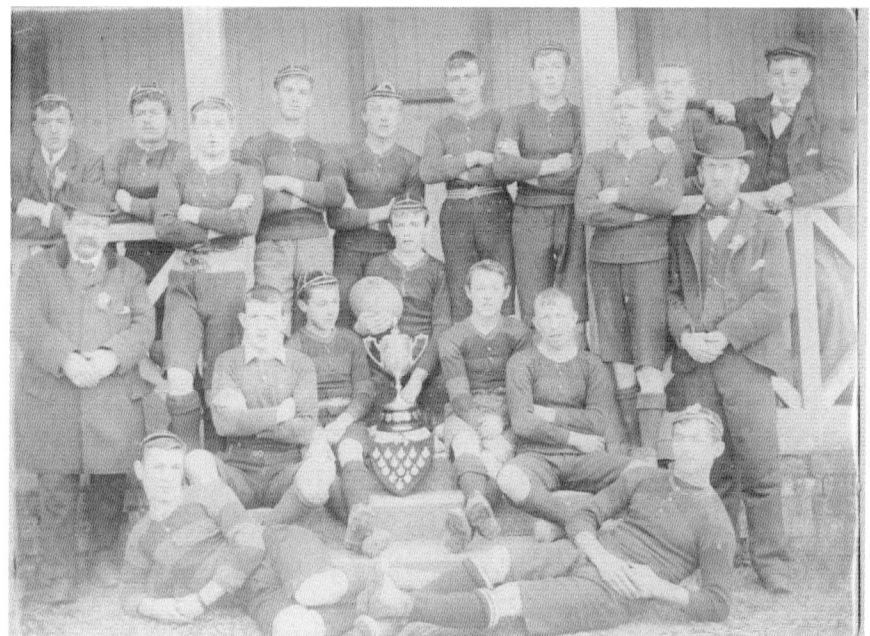

Penarth United in 1898–9 with the Cardiff F.C. Junior Cup. They defeated Grange
Stars in the final at Cardiff Arms Park. The Captain, Edward Best is seated with
the ball. A Penarth United boys team existed as early as 1888.

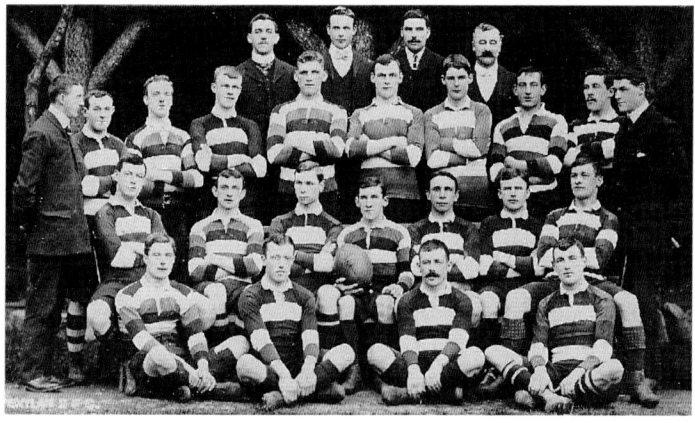

Penylan at Cardiff Arms Park c. 1900. Though members of Cardiff and District,
with a strong fixture list, they did not participate in competitions. Founded
around 1892, Penylan folded in the 1920s because of the lack of a ground.

An 1894–5 handbook advertisement for T. Page Wood's original sports goods market, with the fixture list of one of the stronger District clubs, Cardiff Northern, who won the Mallett Cup this season.

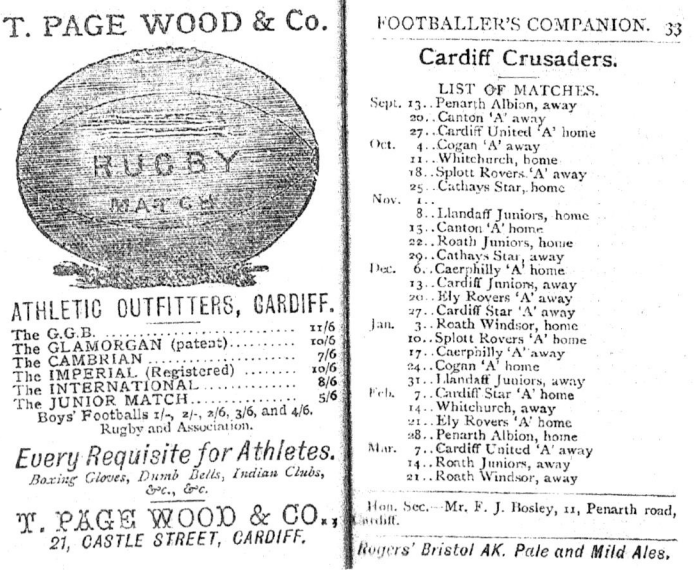

T. Page Wood promoted his footballs in an 1890–1 handbook, alongside the fixture list of a typical neighbourhood club, Cardiff Crusaders, who played all their games in the Cardiff area.

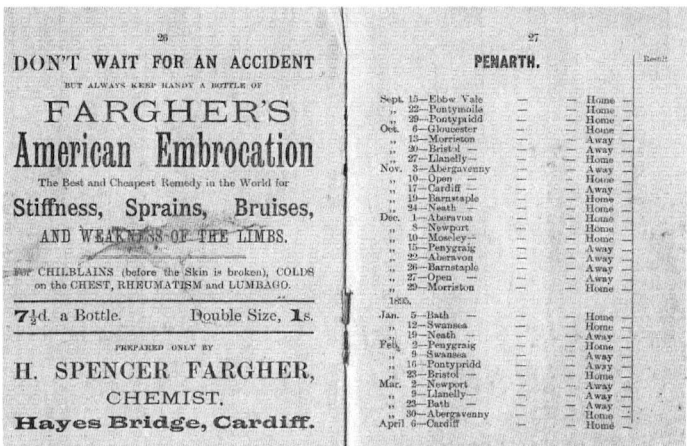

Sports goods retailers weren't the only businesses to benefit from the growth of rugby, as revealed by this 1894–5 handbook advertisement for a cure-all embrocation. It is accompanied by the fixture list for Penarth, who this season recorded doubles over Bath and Gloucester, and also defeated Cardiff, Bristol, Moseley, Llanelli and Neath. Their end of season tour saw victories over Dewsbury, Gloucester and Leicester.

Essential playing equipment advertised in an 1896–7 football handbook.

The Mallett Cup was donated to the Cardiff and District F.U. by Thomas Mallett in 1893–4 and, apart from the war years, it has been successfully organised by the Union every season since.

The Cardiff District Challenge Cup was presented to the short-lived Cardiff District F.U. in 1886–7 by T. Page Wood. It was contested only four times until it was won outright by Penarth in 1888–9.

This Cardiff District Challenge Cup medal, was awarded to an unknown Penarth player after his team defeated Llandaff in the 1887–8 final.

long established mid-week club, Cardiff Rovers, originated as Cardiff
Drapers, whilst Cardiff Assistants and Cardiff Commercials accommodated shop workers and office workers generally. Others were restricted
to one employer like the department store teams Hayes (David Morgan)
and Wharton Wanderers (James Howells), the grocers Liptons Rovers
and the Post Office. These players sometimes took their game seriously.
Three of the twelve teams which competed in the 1888–9 Cardiff Junior
Cup were Wednesday clubs.[108] Mid-week rugby, however, was not
always restricted to specially organised works teams and a number of
clubs, like Cardiff Harlequins, also ran a regular Wednesday XV. Mid-
week rugby was common throughout south Wales whilst in the mining
districts, "Mabon's Day", a holiday for miners on the first Monday in
the month, was also a very popular football day.

The distinctive nature of Cardiff's narrow economic base was, therefore, an influential factor in determining the rather low incidence of
regular workplace teams in the nineteenth century. They had little overall impact, with perhaps only the railway clubs providing any decent
standard of regular rugby. It seems that the majority of workers preferred to play their rugby elsewhere. Significantly, there is no evidence
of any employers providing pitches and accommodation.

There were very few *public house teams* in Cardiff and their numbers
never reached double figures in any year. Of course, these must be distinguished from those clubs which used public houses as their headquarters and of which there were very many, as will be shown in the
following chapter. It is likely that pub teams such as Blue Anchor,
Cottage Rovers, Globe Revellers, Rising Sun, Royal Oak and Rose and
Crown were working class in composition, since the pub was essentially
a working-class institution. These particular teams were based on town
centre pubs, but the Duke of Edinburgh and Green Fields of Erin were
situated in the strongly working-class district of Newtown. However,
public house sides were not necessarily adult teams, as revealed by the
existence of Tredegar Arms Juniors in 1893–4. No doubt the establishment of pub teams often arose on the initiative of the landlord. For
instance, Tom Cooke, the licensee of the *Blue Anchor* was a former
player, who in 1891 claimed to be the oldest member of Cardiff FC.[109]

In contrast to pub teams, *street teams* in Cardiff were very common.
It is highly likely that the majority of these were junior sides, as only a
few of them lasted for more than one season. Teams such as Arabella
Rangers, Broadway Quins, Ethel Street, Glossop Road Rangers,
Gold Street Rangers, Holton Crusaders (Barry), Louisa Street Stars,
Ludlow Street, Merthyr Street Bruisers, Prince Leopold Street Juniors,
Maughan Rovers (Penarth), System Blue Stars, Tin Street Rovers and
many others enjoyed only a brief existence. It would have been natural

for youngsters to form such highly localised teams and then, when they began to grow more financially and socially independent, move to clubs further away from their homes. Alternatively, as suggested by Richard Holt, informal street teams may have developed into organised junior clubs, as was certainly the case with Clyde Juniors and Richmond Road Juniors who survived for several years, and Charles Street Rangers and Tresillian Quins who appear to have evolved into adult clubs.[110] Nevertheless, from the late 1880s, there was a thriving, if constantly shifting, cluster of street teams. There was no particular geographical concentration – they arose in all the working-class residential districts of the town – though there was only a handful recorded in the outlying areas, such as Philog Rovers and College Rovers in Whitchurch and Paradise Rovers in Rumney.

Almost all of the remaining clubs fall into the category of *neighbourhood teams*.[111] Holt stresses the significance of neighbourhood (and street) teams in two particularly important respects, both of which are applicable to Cardiff. Firstly, place-names, he argues, "underline the sustaining role of the neighbourhood in sport: despite vast changes in the city itself, loyalty to a street or parish was deeply held". Local teams could provide an uprooted population with a new sense of belonging and pride. Secondly, the establishment of such a range of clubs was "not the achievement of well-intentioned middle-class reformers; it was the work of the members, of the people themselves".[112]

This was easily the biggest category in the Cardiff area and Stuart Barlow found similar results in his study of Rochdale rugby.[113] Every residential district eventually had its representatives: Roath, Canton, Butetown, Adamsdown, Splott, Cathays, Grangetown, Riverside, Blackweir, Ely, Llandaff, Llandaff North, Penylan, Rumney and Whitchurch. The game had also spread throughout the immediate surrounding district to the neighbouring towns and villages of Barry, Cadoxton, Cogan, Dinas Powys, Penarth, Pentyrch, Tongwynlais and Taffs Well. Indeed, the outward spread of Cardiff in the last three decades of the nineteenth century can be traced in the emergence of its rugby clubs. With the proliferation of teams, it was inevitable that many would share a neighbourhood name in their title, so they were forced to find ways of distinguishing themselves. For example, between 1885 and 1900, there were at least thirty teams which included the residential district of "Roath" in their name.[114]

In adopting names, the Victorians were more far inventive than their modern counterparts: they had to be, as there were so many clubs. Examples of popular name constructions include Adamsdown Crusaders, Canton Wanderers, Cathays Excelsiors, Ely Rangers, Grangetown Stars, Heath Rovers, Moors United, Penarth Harlequins, Roath Windsors and Splott Raglans. Less common names were chosen by Barry Victoria, Canton Lilywhites, Cathays Albions, Penarth Dreadnoughts, Riverside Warriors and Tongwynlais Ramblers. Some clubs dispensed with a local name altogether, for example, Bowry [sic] Boys, Harbour Lights and Maggie Murphy's Pups. There were always some who didn't take themselves too seriously, of course, such as North Central Buffoons, Salmon Tin Rovers and Waistcoat Tearers. The naming of Alpine Rangers was clearly a joke as the club played at East Moors, the lowest and flattest part of the town. Even black humour occasionally had its place. During the Whitechapel Murders, the Jersey Rippers took part in a local nine-a-side tournament.

Borrowing a tradition which originated at Rugby School, many neighbourhood teams were simply named after the emblem worn on their jerseys.[115] These included Blackweir Diamonds, Canton Red Anchor, Cathays Crescent, Grange Thistles, Harp of Erin Juniors and Roath Shamrocks. A surprisingly common practice was for some teams to be named after flowers, such as Cogan White Rose, Grangetown Red Rose, Lily of the Valley, Wild Rose and White Lily. It has to be wondered, though, whether Llandaff Blossoms, Penarth Tulips and Tongwynlais Flowers were short-lived because of recruiting difficulties. The existence of teams like Harp of Erin, Canton Shamrocks, Roath Shamrocks, M'Ginty's Pups and Maggie Murphy's Pups not only provide further evidence of the strong participation of Cardiff's Irish community but also suggests that not all of them necessarily played for parish teams.

There were many clubs, of course, which included "Cardiff" in their title, such as those which adopted Alexandra, Crusaders, Hornets, Mohawks, Northern, Rangers, Star and United as a suffix. Whether these were based in a particular locality or were clubs which drew on a wider catchment area and social background is impossible to establish with certainty, though, given their fixture lists, the likelihood is that the majority were essentially neighbourhood clubs.

There is one further, very small, group of *miscellaneous clubs* with institutional backgrounds which cannot be easily classified in the categories so far discussed. It includes military teams, in particular, the Welsh Regiment Depot and the Volunteers such as 2nd Glamorgan Artillery. The only representatives of higher education were University College Cardiff and Cardiff Medicals. The University rugby club began playing in 1883–4, the year of the college's foundation, and thereafter became a permanent feature of the local rugby scene, often playing important matches at the Arms Park. The Medics, however, only played occasional matches, as did various Liberal and Conservative Working Men's Clubs and the Barry Dock Buffalo Institute. A few clubs were established by special interest groups like Cardiff Cyclists. Old Monktonians were the *only* example of a permanent Old Boys club and this is further evidence of the predominantly working-class nature of the game in Cardiff. Founded in 1894–5, they gave up any formal connection with Monkton House in 1913–14 when they became Glamorgan Wanderers, though they remained a somewhat socially exclusive club until after the Second World War. However, the connection with Monkton House means that the roots of the modern, semi-professional Glamorgan Wanderers club can be traced right back to the very origins of the game in Wales. There were other clubs with a largely predominantly middle-class membership and neighbourhood teams Penylan and Kymin (Penarth) were examples. However, it is virtually impossible to identify others with any great certainty. Such clubs tended to eschew competition but they appear to have made no obvious attempt to create exclusive fixture lists.

To summarise, then, the analysis of Cardiff's Victorian rugby teams reveals a rather different picture from that which has emerged in some studies of soccer in England.[116] Churches, workplaces and pubs were important institutions in the origin of many English soccer clubs. Mason suggests that a considerable proportion of soccer clubs owed their origins to organisations which were previously in existence for another purpose. However, the evidence is that their influence was rather weaker in Cardiff rugby, where the proportion of church, workplace and pub teams never rose above 32% (in 1895–6), and was typically at around 25% or less. This may be explained, at least in part, by religious hostility to rugby and by Cardiff's distinct economic structure.

This difference is further illustrated by a comparison with research findings on the "place of association" of 193 soccer clubs in Teesside in 1888–9. As shown in Table 3, Mike Huggins reveals that 57% of the Teesside clubs could be categorised as church, workplace or pub teams.[117] This was well over double the percentage of rugby clubs in the same categories in Cardiff, where the equivalent figure that season was only 23%. It would appear that in Cardiff, location was of far greater significance in the establishment of teams.

Stuart Barlow argues that in Rochdale, loyalty to the street, neighbourhood or parish was strongly held and that it was the working class,

Table 3: Comparison of Clubs in Teesside and Cardiff in 1888–9

Place of Association	Teesside Soccer		Cardiff Rugby	
	Number	**%**	**Number**	**%**
Workplace	53	27.5	19	11.2
Church/Chapel	46	23.8	16	9.4
Public Houses	12	6.2	4	2.3
Schools	20	10.4	10	5.9
Other	62	32.1	121	71.2
Total	193	100.0	170	100.0

rather than religious or philanthropic members of the middle class, who were responsible for organising many of these local rugby teams.[118] The experience in Cardiff appears to have been similar. From 1880 onwards, neighbourhood and street teams comprised between approximately two-thirds and three-quarters of the total every season. This supports Richard Holt's view that the impact of churches and employers was limited only to a minority and hence there was no effective middle-class imposition in the name of social control.[119] Most clubs were based on the street or neighbourhood and were therefore probably established and organised by and for working people. Neil Tranter also points out that the profusion of local clubs confirms that the spread of football came about as much from efforts from below as from middle-class example and initiative.[120] As Gareth Williams puts it, local teams in Wales "block-built identity upwards".[121] In Cardiff, there is no doubt that strong local allegiances were attracted to neighbourhood teams and these were largely working class in origin and composition. Their emergence also began to influence the wider game, as will be shown in the next chapter.

Notes

1. M.J. Daunton, *Coal Metropolis: Cardiff 1870–1914* (Leicester, 1977), p. 11.
2. *Report of an Enquiry by the Board of Trade into Working Class Rents, Housing and Retail Prices*, 1908, p. 132 quoted in Daunton, *Coal Metropolis*, p. [1].
3. Daunton, *Coal Metropolis*, pp. 2–8; William Rees, *A History of Cardiff* (Cardiff, 1969 edn.), pp. 231–241.
4. Rees, *A History of Cardiff*, p. 271.
5. Daunton, *Coal Metropolis*, p. [1]
6. Daunton, *Coal Metropolis*, p. 11.
7. Daunton, *Coal Metropolis*, p. 7; Rees, *A History of Cardiff*, pp. 296–8.
8. *South Wales Daily News* 22 July 1890.
9. For example, see Rees, *A History of Cardiff*; Daunton, *Coal Metropolis*; Dennis Morgan, *The Cardiff Story: A History of the City from its Earliest Times to the Present* (Cowbridge, 1991).
10. Owing to the unavailability at the time of the research of the *Western Mail* for January to June 1891, the *Evening Express* was used as a replacement. This had broadly the same level of coverage of local rugby as its sister paper. In addition, the figures for the first three seasons up to 1872–3 include the references to Tredegarville and the "Cardiff Club" located in the *Football Annual* 1871 p. 69, 1872 p. 66, 1873 p. 80 and *Cardiff and Merthyr Guardian* 24 Dec. 1870, as discussed in Chapter 2. The number of teams recorded for 1899–1900 may have been affected by the greatly reduced press coverage of sport during the South African War.
11. Appendix 3 (Penarth cup); *WM* 15 Nov. 1892 (Barry).
12. Alan Metcalfe, "Football in the Mining Communities of East Northumberland 1882–1914", *International Journal of the History of Sport*, 5, 3 (1988), p. 274; M. Huggins, "The Spread of Association Football in North-East England, 1876–90: The Pattern of Diffusion", *IJHS*, 6, 3 (1989), p. 303.

13. Michael G. Bassett, *Games of Interchanging Praise: A Centenary History of Rugby Football in Barry* (Barry, 1988), pp. 10–30.
14. Compiled from the *South Wales Daily News* and *Western Mail*. See note 10.
15. Compiled from the *South Wales Daily News* and *Western Mail*. See note 10.
16. Extracted from John Williams, *Digest of Welsh Historical Statistics*, Volume 1 (Cardiff, 1985), pp. 62–4 (figures rounded off).
17. David Smith and Gareth Williams, *Fields of Praise: The Official History of the Welsh Rugby Union* 1881–1981 (Cardiff, 1980), pp. 103–4.
18. Richard Holt, *Sport and the British: A Modern History* (Oxford, 1989), pp. 166–7.
19. See Brian Lile and David Farmer, "The Early Development of Association Football in South Wales, 1890–1906", *Transactions of the Honourable Society of Cymmrodorion*, (1984), pp.193–215.
20. See, for example, Lile and Farmer, "Early Development", p. 195 who incorrectly claim Cardiff RFC initially played soccer; *WM* 8–23 Sept. 1876 (club merger).
21. J.R. Jones, *The Encyclopaedia of Rugby Football* (London, 1960), p. 24 claims Cardiff was founded as an association football club and then turned to rugby in 1876. Since this was one of the earliest rugby reference books, used by many later rugby writers, it may be the source of the widely reported but incorrect account of Cardiff's origins.
22. *Cardiff Times* 1 Oct. 1892 (Swansea); *SWDN* 31 Oct. 1892 (Newport); *Cardiff Times* 3 Sept. 1892 (Cardiff); C.S. Arthur, *The Cardiff Rugby Football Club: History and Statistics, 1876–1906* (Cardiff, 1908); D.E. Davies, *Cardiff Rugby Club: History and Statistics, 1876–1975: "The Greatest"* (Cardiff, 1975).
23. *SWDN* 16 Jan. 1882, *WM* 17 Jan. 1882. In later seasons, they also played soccer matches against both Penarth and Cardiff Harlequins rugby clubs.
24. *WM* 9 Nov. 1883.
25. *WM* 15 Nov. 1883.
26. Martin Johnes and Ian Garland, "'The New Craze': football and society in north-east Wales, c. 1870–90", *Welsh History Review*, 22, 2 (2004), pp. 302–3.
27. *SWDN* 16 Mar. 1885.
28. *SWDN* 25 Mar. 1887. See Table 1 figures for 1886–7.
29. *SWDN* 28 Nov. 1887; *WM* 5 Dec. 1887.
30. *WM* 16 Dec. 1889. They were St. Margaret's, St. Saviour's (Splott), Western Mail and Cardiff Scottish.
31. *SWDN* 25 Nov. 1889; *WM* 25 Nov. 1889.
32. *Cardiff and South Wales Footballer's Companion: 1890–91* (Cardiff, 1890), pp. 3–67.
33. Tony Mason, *Association Football and English Society 1863–1915* (Brighton, 1981), p. 31.
34. *Evening Express* 29 Apr. 1901.
35. *SWDN* 27 Oct. 1890 (isolated effort), 29 Jan. (Socker Player), 31 Jan. 1891 (Enthusiast).
36. Peter Corrigan, *100 Years of Welsh Soccer: The Official History of the Football Association of Wales* (Cardiff, [1976]), p. 10 (league); *SWDN* 8 Apr. 1891 (St. Margaret's).
37. *WM* 7 Aug. 1891 (CAFC), 5 Mar. 1894 and *SWDN* 5 Mar. 1894 (gate money), 4 Nov. 1895 (cups), 17 Jan. 1896 (expulsion).
38. *WM* 8 Oct. 1894.
39. *SWDN* 27 Oct. 1890.
40. *SWDN* 4 Dec. 1893; see also Martin Johnes, "That Other Game: A Social History of Soccer in South Wales c.1906–39" (Ph.D. thesis, University of Wales, Cardiff, 1998), pp. 17–18.

41. Johnes, *Soccer and Society*, p. 3, passim; Johnes, "Other Game" passim.
42. Edward Donovan and Others, *Pontypool's Pride: The Official History of Pontypool Rugby Football Club 1868–1988* (Abertillery, 1988), p. 9; *Star of Gwent* 28 Nov. 1879 (Pontymister); *Bridgend Chronicle* 20 Mar. 1868 (Cardiff).
43. W. Alan Thomas, *Cardiff Cricket Club: 1867–1967* (Cardiff, 1967), p. 20; Cardiff Cricket Club Members Lists 1883 and 1884.
44. Andrew K. Hignell, *A "Favourit" Game: Cricket in south Wales before 1914* (Cardiff, 1992), pp. 217–220.
45. See Mason, *Association Football and English Society*, pp. 21, 24–31; Holt, *Sport and the British*, pp. 150–1; Huggins, "Spread of Association Football", pp. 311–12; Stuart Barlow, "The Diffusion of 'Rugby' Football in the Industrialized Context of Rochdale, 1868–1890: A Conflict of Ethical Values", *IJHS*, 10, 1 (1993), pp. 61–5.
46. Dave Russell, *Football and the English: A Social History of Association Football in England, 1863–1995* (Preston, 1997), pp. 14–15; Johnes, "Other Game", p. 88.
47. Mason, *Association Football and English Society*, pp. 24–31.
48. Holt, *Sport and the British*, pp. 150–1 also draws on Molyneux's research on Birmingham, as well as Tranter's on Stirling, Crump's on Leicester and Rees' on Liverpool.
49. *SWDN* 10 Nov. 1894. See Appendix 3.
50. There are plans for the WRU to absorb all "district" clubs and to dissolve the Welsh Districts RU.
51. At least six of these were street teams: Clyde, Longcross, Railway, Rennie, Saltmede, and (probably) Star.
52. Gordon Westcott, *A Century on the Beat: A History of Police Rugby Football in the South Wales Constabulary Area* (Bridgend, 1992), p. 91.
53. *Cardiff and South Wales Footballer's Companion: 1890–91*, p. 46.
54. *SWDN* 19 Jan., 13 Apr. 1891.
55. *SWDN* 1 Nov. 1889.
56. *WM* 24 Dec. 1877 (Newport), 3 Jan. 1878 (Roath).
57. *SWDN* 10 Mar. 1879.
58. Holt, *Sport and the British*, p. 141.
59. *SWDN* 22 Oct. 1896.
60. *WM* 30 June 1894.
61. *SWDN* 28 Nov. 1884 (Hill); *Evening Express* 15 Sept. 1888 (Young); *WM* 19 Mar. 1892 (Cope); *SWDN* 20 Nov. 1882 (Hybart), 17 Oct. 1884 (Biggs); *Evening Express* 6 Apr. 1901 (Bush), 5 Jan. 1891 (Wesleyan).
62. Carl French, "The History of the Welsh Schools Rugby Union 1903–1939" (M.Ed. thesis, University of Wales, Cardiff, 1991), pp. 1–52.
63. *Cardiff Argus* 26 Sept. 1888.
64. The elementary schools whose matches were reported in the *WM* and *SWDN* between 1885–6 and 1896–7 included: Adamsdown, Albany Road, Canton, Cathays, Court Road, Cogan, Crwys Road, Eleanor Street, Grange, Llandough, Radnor Road, St. David's RC, St. John's, St. Mary's, St. Paul's RC, Severn Road, South Church Street, Splottlands, Stacey Road, Taffs Well, Whitchurch Board, Whitchurch National and Wood Street.
65. See Table 1.
66. David Parry-Jones, *Prince Gwyn: Gwyn Nicholls and the First Golden Era of Welsh Rugby* (Bridgend, 1999), p. 20.
67. T.J. Foster, *Floreat Howardia: The Story of Howard Gardens Schools Cardiff 1885–1990* (Cardiff, 1990), pp. 27, 50–1.

68. *SWDN* 5 Jan. 1896.
69. Lile and Farmer, "Early Development of Association in South Wales", pp. 204–5; *SWDN* 5 May 1900 (Cardiff league), 19 Dec. 1899 (Barry and Penarth).
70. Bassett, *Rugby Football in Barry*, p. [130]; Gwyn Prescott, *The Best and Happiest Team: A History of Cardiff High School Old Boys Rugby Football Club 1929–1978* (Cardiff, 1979), p. 1.
71. *SWDN* 22 Oct. 1896, 10 Feb. 1897.
72. *Cardiff Schools Rugby Union Handbook Season 1987–88* (Cardiff, 1987), p. [4].
73. *WM* 24 Jan. 1894.
74. Mason, *Association Football and English Society*, p. 26.
75. Holt, *Sport and the British*, pp. 150–1.
76. Eric Dunning and Kenneth Sheard, *Barbarians, Gentlemen and Players: A Sociological Study of the Development of Rugby Football* (London, 2005 edn.), pp. 120–3; Daryl Adair, "Competing or Complementary Forces: The 'Civilising' Process and the Commitment to Winning in Nineteenth Century English Rugby and Association Football", *Canadian Journal of History of Sport*, XXIV, 2 (1993), p. 54.
77. Gareth Williams, *1905 and All That: Essays on Rugby Football, Sport and Welsh Society* (Llandysul, 1991), pp. 73–4.
78. Gareth Morgan, "Rugby and Revivalism: Sport and Religion in Edwardian Wales", *IJHS*, 22, 3 (2005), p. 435.
79. Barlow, "The Diffusion of 'Rugby' Football", pp. 54, 63 (italics added).
80. J.V. Hickey, "The Origin and Growth of the Irish Community in Cardiff", (M.A. thesis, University of Wales, Cardiff, 1959), p. 113.
81. Paul O'Leary, *Immigration and Integration: The Irish in Wales, 1798–1922* (Cardiff, 2002), p. 105.
82. *SWDN* 30 Nov. 1891.
83. See Appendix 3 for the competition successes of St. Paul's and St. Peter's.
84. *WM* 21 Aug. 1897; *SWDN* 1 Aug. 1896, 5 Apr. 1899.
85. See D.F. Childs, *One Hundred Years of the "Rocks": the History of St. Peter's R.F.C. 1886/1986* (Cardiff, 1986).
86. *SWDN* 3 May 1897.
87. *WM* 5 Feb. 1894.
88. Anon., "Some Famous Footballers: Cardiff Rugby Football Club", *St. Peter's Magazine*, V, 2 (1925), pp. 43–5.
89. See G.P.T. Finn, "Racism, Religion and Social Prejudice: Irish Catholic Clubs, Soccer and Scottish Society – I The Historical Roots of Prejudice", *IJHS*, 8, 1 (1991), pp. 370–397; G.P.T. Finn, "Racism, Religion and Social Prejudice: Irish Catholic Clubs, Soccer and Scottish Society – II Social Identities and Conspiracy Theories", *IJHS*, 8, 3 (1991), pp. 374–397; Daniel Burdsey and Robert Chappell, "'And If You know Your History …' An Examination of the Formation of Football Clubs in Scotland and their Role in the Construction of Social Identity", *Sports Historian*, 20, 1 (2001), pp. 94–106.
90. David Kennedy and Peter Kennedy, "Ambiguity, Complexity and Convergence: The Evolution of Liverpool's Irish Football Clubs", *IJHS*, 25, 7 (2007), pp. 895, 909.
91. Hickey, *The Irish Community*, passim; O'Leary, *Immigration and Integration*, pp. 304–5.
92. Gareth Williams, "From Popular Culture to Public Cliché: Image and Identity in Wales, 1890–1914" in J.A. Mangan, *Pleasure, Profit, Proselytism: British Culture and Sport at Home and Abroad 1700–1914* (London, 1988), pp. 132–3; Morgan, *Rugby and Revivalism*, pp. 435–6; John Lowerson, *Sport and the English middle classes, 1870–1914* (Manchester, 1993), p. 85 refers to a suggestion that rugby may have been unpopular with evangelicals because of their phobia of bodily contact.

93. Mason, *Association Football and English Society*, p. 25.
94. Morgan, *Rugby and Revivalism*, pp. 449, 434–456.
95. Hignell, *A "Favourit" Game*, pp. 217–220 identifies one Congregationalist and six Wesleyan cricket clubs in Cardiff between 1875 and 1890.
96. Childs, *History of St. Peter's R.F.C.*, pp. 8–9
97. Hickey, *The Irish Community*, pp. 130–8.
98. *SWDN* 15 July 1896.
99. Arthur Llewellyn and Don Llewellyn, *Pentyrch R.F.C.: A Club For All Seasons 1883–1983* (Pentyrch, 1983), pp. 8–12.
100. Anon., *Llandaff Rugby Football Club American Tour Souvenir* (Cardiff, 1968), p. 1.
101. Holt, *Sport and the British*, p. 138; Tony Collins, *Rugby's Great Split: Class, Culture and the Origins of Rugby League Football* (London, 2006 edn.), p. 26.
102. Andrew J. Croll, *Civilizing the Urban: Popular Culture, Public Space and Urban Meaning, Merthyr c. 1870–1914* (PhD thesis, University of Wales Cardiff, 1997), p. 248.
103. M.J. Daunton, "Coal to Capital: Cardiff since 1839" in Prys Morgan (ed.), *Glamorgan County History, Volume VI, Glamorgan Society: 1780–1980* (Cardiff, 1988), pp. 216, 220.
104. See Daunton, *Coal Metropolis*, pp. 37–49 and Rees, *History of Cardiff*, pp. 285–298 for details of Cardiff's main industries in this period.
105. Mason, *Association Football and English Society*, p. 30.
106. Daunton, *Coal to Capital*, p. 220.
107. Daunton, *Coal Metropolis*, pp. 53–4.
108. *SWDN* 17 Oct. 1889. The clubs were Cardiff Rovers, Wharton Wanderers and Post Office.
109. *Welsh Athlete* 19 Oct. 2 Nov. 1891.
110. Richard Holt, "Working-Class Football and the City: The Problem of Continuity", *British Journal of Sports History*, 3, 1 (1986), p. 7.
111. "Town" clubs Cardiff, Penarth and Cardiff Harlequins have been included in this category in Table 1. The Harlequins evolved into a town team over time. Barry did not really become a town club as such for reasons explained in Bassett, *Rugby Football in Barry*, passim.
112. Holt, *Sport and the British*, pp. 150–4.
113. Barlow, "The Diffusion of 'Rugby' Football", pp. 54, 64.
114. They were Roath: Albion, Albion Juniors, Court, Crescents, Crusaders, Elm, Excelsiors, Harlequins, Hornets, Institute, Juniors, Marlborough, Park Juniors, Park Wanderers, Park United, Pouncers (sic), Ramblers, Raglans, Rangers, Star Juniors, Stars, Road, Rovers, Shamrocks, Wanderers, Waterloo, Wednesday, Wednesday Juniors, Windsors and United.
115. Jennifer Macrory, *Running with the Ball: The Birth of Rugby Football* (London, 1991), pp. 78–84. See Parry-Jones, *Prince Gwyn*, p. 96 for a photograph of Cardiff Stars c.1890 which shows a very large star sewn on the jerseys.
116. Mason, *Association Football and English Society*, pp. 24–31.
117. Huggins, "The Spread of Association Football", p. 311. I am grateful to Professor Mike Huggins for giving his permission to use the results of his research published in this article in the compilation of Table 3.
118. Barlow, "The Diffusion of 'Rugby' Football", pp. 61–5.
119. Holt, *Sport and the British*, pp. 352–3.
120. Neil Tranter, *Sport, Economy and Society in Britain, 1750–1914* (Cambridge, 1998), p. 29.
121. Williams, *1905 and All That*, p. 74.

5

ORGANISATION AND
PARTICIPATION

'Administered by the few, played by the many'

While local newspaper coverage of rugby expanded greatly during the Victorian period, the reports concentrated heavily on match details. These do confirm that, as Gareth Williams puts it, the game was administered by a few officials but played and watched by many.[1] However, surprisingly little detail is revealed about the day to day administration of the game and how matches were organised, especially at the local level, so we have to piece together what few clues are available.

Most of the teams identified here were never affiliated to any union. However, as rugby became increasingly popular and competitive, there was an evident need for stronger control over its administration, particularly at a local level. Issues such as match disputes, foul play, crowd control, player transfer, referee appointments and demands for competitive structures all took on increasing importance during the 1890s. Only a very small number of the leading local sides joined the Welsh Football Union. Cardiff, of course, were founder members in 1881, while Penarth and Cardiff Harlequins both joined in 1886. They were followed by Cardiff Star (1891), Llandaff (1891), St. David's (1891), Cathays (1892), Cogan (1892), Grangetown (1893), Barry (1895) and Whitchurch (1895 and 1898). Several of these clubs participated in the South Wales Challenge Cup, which Llandaff won in 1892, after the senior clubs had ceased taking part. All eight, however, dropped out of the WFU at some point during the 1890s and most disbanded at around the same time. Of all the many rugby clubs in the locality, only Cardiff and Penarth can claim continuous membership of the WRU from the nineteenth century.[2]

In order to administer a new competition, known as the Cardiff Challenge Cup, a Cardiff District Football Union was set up in 1886.[3] It was a requirement that clubs wishing to compete had to join this new Union, whose sole function was to organise the competition. A junior cup was added in 1889 but the Cardiff District Football Union was disbanded shortly afterwards when, after three successive victories in the Challenge Cup, Penarth won the trophy outright under the competition rules in 1890.[4] The cup is still in the possession of the Penarth club.

However, it was soon realised that there was a desperate need for an organisation which could both supervise the burgeoning game at a local level and support the growing status of the town club. Thus, in November 1892, a new Cardiff and District Football Union (C&DFU) was formed with much wider terms of reference than its predecessor and which initially embraced "all junior teams within a radius of nine miles of Cardiff", later extended to twelve miles.[5] This body, now renamed the Cardiff and District Rugby Union, has organised local rugby ever since. Its objectives when set up were to: foster rugby; support the Cardiff club; settle disputes; and recognise club and individual merit.[6] A representative District XV was established which played occasional games with senior clubs including Cardiff, Neath, Bristol and Gloucester. In 1893–4, the Mallett Cup was introduced and was won by Cardiff Reserves, from an entry of fifteen teams. It is believed that this is the oldest cup still competed for in Wales and it is certainly one of the oldest competitions for open clubs in Britain. The other clubs which participated in the first ever Mallett Cup included Barry, Canton, Llandaff, Pentyrch and Whitchurch, all of which still exist, while the other entrants were Blackweir, Cardiff Hornets, Cardiff Northern, Cardiff Star, Cathays, Garth, Grangetown, Grange Stars and Splott Crusaders.[7] The following year saw a two division league established.[8] By 1896–7, founder members Barry had moved on to the increasingly competitive Glamorgan League, which was virtually the second division of Welsh rugby.[9] At the end of the century, there were thirty-six local clubs taking part in three leagues and three knock out cups.[10] However, Alan Metcalfe has shown that, as late as 1913, half of the soccer teams in East Northumberland were not affiliated to the county FA nor were they involved in any leagues. This was very similar to Victorian Cardiff, where the majority of rugby teams never belonged to any union, nor played in any organised competitions.[11]

Before long, both Cardiff's First and Second XVs contained many former District players. In 1897, the Cardiff chairman declared that most of the club's players came from "the ranks of her own junior clubs".[12] Many former players with Cardiff and District clubs went on to play for Wales around this time, most notably Percy Bush (Cardiff Romilly), Gwyn Nicholls (Cardiff Star), and Bert Winfield (St. Andrew's), all of whom were key members of the 1905 team which defeated the All Blacks. Others who won Welsh caps in the 1890s and early 1900s included Jere Blake (Blackweir and Whitchurch), John Brown (St. Peter's),

Fred Cornish (Grangetown), Dickie David (Cathays United and Mackintosh), Tom Dobson (Blackweir and Llandaff Yard), Jack Elliott (Llandaff), Dai Fitzgerald (St. David's and Grangetown), Viv Huzzey (Canton), Billy O'Neill (St. Peter's), Joe Pugsley (Grange Stars), Dai Westacott (Grange Stars) and Johnny Williams (Whitchurch).[13]

The importance of the C&DFU to rugby in Wales soon became evident in 1896, when the WFU suggested that it join the Union. This arose because the WFU had no jurisdiction over the transfer of the many District players who were joining WFU clubs, particularly those in the Glamorgan League. In September 1898, the Cardiff and District Football Union became full members of the Welsh Football Union, the first organisation of its kind to do so. Shortly afterwards, the District reported both Penygraig and Pontypridd for using members of C&DFU clubs without transfers. The WFU decided that transfers *were* required but, if refused by the District, clubs could then apply directly to them. Clearly, they were not prepared to delegate too much power to the "junior" union and accepting C&DFU into affiliation was a subtle way of bringing many clubs under the WFU's jurisdiction without massively extending membership. Restricting entry to the Welsh Union was one way in which the control of the game at the top level was retained in the hands of the professional and business middle classes, even though the majority of clubs catered for working men.[14]

Despite the immediate success of the C&DFU, local clubs still rose and fell with remarkable regularity. With little or no gate money, most suffered from financial insecurity. As well as the loss of pitches, however, it was the movement of key officials and players which contributed appreciably to what Alan Metcalfe terms the "chronic instability" of clubs and the "constantly shifting configuration" of the game at the time.[15] Leading clubs were just as vulnerable as the less successful teams. St. David's, for instance, who had fixtures with Bridgend, Bristol and Pontypridd went out of existence when many of their players joined Cardiff.[16] Another challenge facing the sustainability of local clubs was the advent of the professional game in the north of England. As soon as the Northern Union (NU) was established in 1895, District clubs immediately began to lose players, a surprisingly large number of whom became professional during the late 1890s. Grangetown, for instance, lost two players only a month after the NU was founded.[17] In 1899, it was reported that District clubs were affected "acutely" by the number of players "going North".[18] Even some "amateur" English clubs attempted to poach players. Torquay Athletic, for instance, were suspended by the RFU for offering terms to St. Peter's players.[19]

The increasingly ambitious valley clubs, especially those in the Glamorgan League, also enticed players. Undoubtedly, financial inducements or offers of employment were often involved. It is a widely held view in Wales that the Cardiff club's strength has traditionally depended on players from the valleys. Yet, in the 1880s and 1890s, there is no great evidence for this. On the other hand, many of the leading valley clubs relied, to some extent, on players from Cardiff, for example, future Welsh internationals Tom Dobson and Percy Bush captained Llwynypia and Penygraig respectively. In 1899, there were calls to investigate the amateur status of some thirty Cardiff men who were travelling to play for "Rhondda" clubs in the Glamorgan League.[20] Neighbourhood clubs in Cardiff, on the other hand, had virtually no gates and little income and, with many local rivals making claims on their players, they could rarely sustain the playing standard of the best valley clubs, who enjoyed clearly demarcated boundaries of community support and substantially greater revenues.

The organisation of leagues and cups helped to create a more rational structure to the season, though the participants in the competitions varied considerably with the rise and fall of clubs. A highly efficient postal service meant that fixtures could be arranged easily and swiftly. Local newspapers helped by publishing details of clubs with free Saturdays. Annual football handbooks provided another means for advertising open dates, as well as for confirming previously made arrangements. They also reveal that most established clubs arranged their fixture list well before the opening of the season. For C&DFU competitions, it was customary for secretaries to arrange mutually acceptable dates. This was the general practice in other competitions, such as the Glamorgan and Monmouthshire Leagues and it sometimes led to confusion, dispute and uncompleted league tables.

A necessary condition for the expansion of the game in Cardiff was sufficient space in which to play. Croll and Meller have shown in Merthyr and Bristol respectively that the lack of available land might restrict the development of sports.[21] In this respect, Cardiff was fortunate. Four main types of playing field were used: land occupied by a single club on a permanent or semi-permanent basis; land within the built-up area waiting for development; edge of town land; and public parks. But every conceivable piece of ground was used. There are even several reports of matches, presumably between juniors, taking place on the open spaces in the middle of Adamsdown Square and Loudoun Square. The more established clubs like Cardiff, Cardiff Harlequins and Penarth were able to lease and enclose their grounds and charge for entrance. The majority, however, would have occupied under licence, with the possibility of eviction at short notice. The loss of playing fields was a constant threat to many clubs and no doubt contributed to the high turnover. No independent clubs at this time owned the freehold of their ground. Only three city-based clubs, Cardiff, Cardiff High School Old Boys and Glamorgan Wanderers, do so today.

From the very beginning of the game, the central location and convenience of the Arms Park guaranteed that it would be the main focus of any sporting activity. It was here that the Glamorgan and Cardiff Wanderers clubs played in the early 1870s. However, in April 1875 the Bute Estate announced that because of "repeated acts of mischief and injury done to trees and fences in the Cardiff Arms Park, no person will be allowed to enter it without special permission."[22] This decision was to have an effect on the early rugby players of Cardiff. At the start of the next season, one concerned member of the Glamorgan Football Club wrote to the press.

Last year, after several ineffectual attempts, the young men of Cardiff succeeded in forming a football club. The want of an institution of this kind had long been felt in Cardiff, as was shown by the speedy enrolment of upwards of 150 members, who testified their just appreciation of the benefit of their regular attendances on Wednesday and Saturday afternoons in the Cardiff Arms Park to take part in the old English game. Such was the proficiency attained that ... in no single instance did they sustain defeat, thus well upholding the honour of the town ... the prospects of the club [for the forthcoming season] seemed brighter than ever. Unfortunately, however, on applying for the use of the Cardiff Arms Park it was refused, notwithstanding the expressed intention of the club to maintain a man to look after the ground. Mr Corbett [the Bute agent] kindly offered ... to find a suitable field elsewhere, but without success. Thus, for the want of a convenient ground, this club – a real boon to the town – must collapse. Although we have no doubt that Mr. Corbett had his reasons for refusing the Cardiff Arms Park, still we firmly believe that if the Marquis of Bute fully understood, not only the disappointment, but the great injury that this refusal will cause to so many young men in Cardiff, he would, with his usual generosity and desire to further the interests of the town, immediately give the required permission."[23]

This appeal seems to have been considered sympathetically as the Glamorgan club were allowed to continue their use of the Park for most of their matches that season. However, perhaps the vandalism persisted because the following year, the newly formed Cardiff club were able to play only their opening home fixture against Swansea at the Arms Park. Thereafter they spent their first three seasons at Sophia Gardens, though the club's official histories do not refer to this.[24] Hence it was Sophia Gardens, rather than the Arms Park, which hosted the 1878–9 final of the South Wales Challenge Cup against Newport. Even after moving, Cardiff continued to use the Gardens occasionally when playing conditions at the Park were bad. However, since 1879, Cardiff have enjoyed permanent and exclusive use of the Arms Park, though these events demonstrate that they constantly had to be wary of not upsetting the landlord's interest. The ground was shared with the cricket club, who had been using the Park since 1848 though, as the rugby club's use and development of the site grew, there were increasing conflicts between the two. In 1887, for instance, a dispute arose over responsibility for the cost of protecting the cricket pitch from the crowds attending the rugby matches.[25] In 1922, the land was eventually acquired from the Bute Estate for £30,000 by the Cardiff Athletic (i.e. sports) Club, of which the rugby and cricket clubs were the principal sections.[26]

The significance of the strategic location of the Arms Park to Cardiff rugby in the nineteenth century was recognised at the time. In 1896, "Ariel" of the *Western Mail* declared:

> the dear old park … just as muddy and clammy, but just as convenient and get-at-able for everybody as it was when Cardiff was merely aping a large town. The value of this piece of ground to the Cardiff Football Club is really untold, and they will never rightly value it till they have to shift![27]

One hundred and thirteen years later, the club's twenty-first century professional descendents, Cardiff Blues, disregarded the concerns of modern-day Ariels, and decided to "shift" and become tenants of a new soccer stadium at Leckwith. It remains to be seen whether this proves to be a better location for top-class rugby than "the dear old park". As a consequence of the Blues' move, the long-term future of rugby at the Arms Park looks bleak, especially as the local council seem keener to encourage the development of the land rather than maintain it as part of the long-standing heritage of the city over which they profess to have stewardship.

Most local match reports, especially in early years, give little indication of the exact location of many of the grounds used. There are occasional glimpses of games played in Roath, Cathays or Canton on sites subsequently taken for housing. For instance, Windsor, a strong early club, used land in Cathays before it was developed as Senghenydd Road. Ambitious clubs like Cardiff Harlequins sought their own enclosed facilities and occupied various grounds at Penarth Road, North Road and Newport Road.[28] The major landowners in Cardiff generally gave their support to the game, as long as it did not conflict with their wider estate management interests. When Penarth's new ground was opened in 1891, it was provided free of charge by Lord Windsor, whose agent referred to the similar generosity of the Marquis of Bute and Lord Tredegar who were "doing all they can to encourage the game of football". The Arms Park, of course, was Bute land, whilst Cardiff Harlequins' Newport Road ground was owned by the Tredegar Estate.[29] It is interesting to note that the three senior clubs in the Cardiff area all played on land owned by the three principal landowners in the locality.

Clubs on the urban fringe managed to find places to play more easily than those in the urban core. East Moors was a popular venue for Splott and Newtown teams, whilst those in the west used Canton and Ely Commons. Teams in outlying villages, like Llandaff and Whitchurch, with little competition from other clubs or from housing developers, were able to use their grounds exclusively and permanently. The opportunity to take a twelve year lease allowed Whitchurch to erect a stand and enclose their ground at the rear of the *Fox and Hounds* and this enabled them to apply successfully for membership of the WFU.[30]

Most clubs, however, used public playing fields and hence were generally unable to rely on much gate money. By far the most important public facility in Cardiff was Sophia Gardens.[31] Centrally located, close to public houses and transport terminals, it was the home of many rugby clubs, including junior and school teams, from all over the town.[32] The Gardens were opened to the public by the Marquis of Bute in 1858 and shortly afterwards, they were extended to include "Sophia Gardens Field", the site today of the SWALEC cricket stadium and venue for the first Ashes Test in 2009. The contribution of Sophia Gardens to rugby was immense. Not only did it play host to Cardiff for three seasons and to the South Wales Challenge Cup final, more importantly, it was the place where an overwhelming number of Cardiff's Victorian citizens learned and developed their game from the earliest days. Without this large and accessible facility, it is questionable whether rugby would have expanded quite as it did. Contemporary reports show that, on many Saturdays, in the late 1880s and early 1890s, hundreds of young men played rugby there throughout the day.

Sophia Gardens, however, was not the only public space available. During much of the period, some local clubs used the Cathays recreation ground, which was then part of the site acquired by the Corporation for a burial ground. Inevitably, however, as the cemetery grew, the area available for recreation was gradually reduced. Eventually, in 1892, the Burial Board decided to prohibit rugby there because of the "unseemly conduct" of spectators which caused "great annoyance" to those attending funerals.[33] Nevertheless, there were other facilities available nearby, such as the new recreation ground at Roath Park, and Maindy Barracks, which was a particular favourite of railway clubs like Taff Vale Wanderers. An indication of the variety of grounds used can be found in the columns of the *SWDN* during November 1890. These recorded matches played that month at Sophia Gardens, Maindy Barracks, Cathays Recreation Ground, Roath Park, Llandaff Fields; and on pitches now lost to us in Market Gardens Field (Canton), Atlas Ground (Canton), Canton Common, Saltmede (Grangetown), East Moors (Splott), Tynycoed Field (Roath), and Leckwith Common.

We do not know whether clubs had specific pitches at public parks. Given the number of teams playing at the Gardens, it seems unlikely, though one match report does refer to Mackintosh playing "on the patch of ... Ely [Rovers] in the Sophia Gardens."[34] The marking of pitches was probably the responsibility of the home club. There are occasional references to this not having been carried out, such as when Penygraig complained that Llandaff had failed to mark out touch-lines and goal-lines.[35] The absence of barriers frequently resulted in spectators encroaching onto the field. Commenting favourably on the arrangements at Penarth's ground, "Old Stager" wrote in 1886 that he had expected to see supporters interfering with the players: "the sort of thing ... to be witnessed any Saturday at that happy hunting ground of Cardiff district clubs, the Sophia Gardens."[36] What arrangements there were for erecting goal posts can only be guessed at. They may have been kept in situ but the likelihood is they were erected each week. Reminiscing some years later about the first ever South Wales Challenge Cup final held in 1879 at Newbridge Fields cricket ground outside Bridgend, W. Clifford Phillips recalled that he and his fellow Newport committee-men arrived early to check the ground out. It was just as well they did, as it was deserted and no preparations had been made for the match. They discovered "some poles and sticks in the ditch" which they decided to erect and they then "measured out the ground ... [before] returning to Bridgend to greet the Newport team."[37] Goal posts were much smaller and lighter than today and so it would have been relatively easy to carry them from the corner of the field or from the local pub and erect them for each match. If every spare part of Sophia Gardens was used, as it almost certainly must have been, then something like this must have happened. Timber cross bars were not always standard in the early years of the game and tape was often used for this purpose. Sometimes, though, they were dispensed with altogether. When St. David's defeated Bridgend in 1892 at the Barracks, there were no cross bars and there-fore no goal attempts.[38]

There were few on-field facilities for the players. Press correspondence in 1885 throws light on the inadequate conditions at Sophia
Gardens and on the pilfering which went on.

> [There is a] lack of a proper place … for the players' clothes, bags
> etc. The dressing-rooms pertaining to public-houses in the neigh-
> bourhood of the Sophia Gardens Field are quite inadequate for the
> number of our local clubs which play … there every Saturday and
> Wednesday … players [have to] deposit their clothes in a wash-
> house … which might accommodate four persons at the most,
> and on the open field … pilfering goes on at an alarming rate.
> A few weeks ago the members of one club alone lost … over £2 …
> Such trifling articles as a spare football, hats, mufflers … disap-
> pear with annoying frequency. One player recently had his bag
> and contents "lifted" … owing to the nuisance of either having to
> come to the field dressed and go back dirty, or to dress on the field
> and have your things stolen, many men will not "turn up". What
> is wanted is a good large erection in the Sophia Gardens field …
> with conveniences for washing … This would be an incalculable
> boon to the football community.[39]

Another correspondent complained that thefts from players were common. He suggested a Cardiff v District match should be arranged to
raise funds for a building, with a trough for washing.[40] It is not known
whether the authorities responded to these complaints. It seems unlikely
that much was done. Some years later, there were calls for the attendance
of police at matches to deal with the "roughs" who robbed players'
clothes and even stole their footballs.[41] Even after the First World War,
there was little accommodation at Sophia Gardens. Bleddyn Williams
(Cardiff and Wales) recalled playing there for Cardiff Schoolboys
around 1934, when the teams stripped under the trees and washed off
with water from the river.[42]

There were occasions when Sophia Gardens was unavailable for
sport. Nevertheless, despite its being "half a foot deep in snow" in
February 1895, Canton and Grangetown Stars still managed to complete their fixture; and even when Buffalo Bill's Wild West Show colo-
nised the ground in September 1891, "Some of the Junior teams … took
advantage of the stretches of unoccupied land and had 'a kick or two' on
them."[43] When players turned up in September 1895, their matches had
to be abandoned because "the Band of Hope demonstration … occupied
the field." No doubt many happily retaliated in time honoured rugby
tradition by returning to their local pub to celebrate a free afternoon.[44]

Public houses were, after all, vitally important to the game as social meeting places and club headquarters. Because of this, it soon became apparent to the sport's critics that rugby would have little "reforming" influence on the working class.[45] As Tony Collins and Wray Vamplew astutely put it, "Rather than football being an adjunct of the pub, the pub almost became an adjunct of football." They note that breweries recognised that a location near a major football ground was an important asset which increased takings.[46] This must have been true in Cardiff. With their close proximity to both Cardiff Arms Park and Sophia Gardens, town centre pubs, hotels and restaurants were well placed to respond in a variety of ways to the needs of the rapidly increasing numbers of players and supporters.

The nature of the close relationship in Victorian times between rugby and the public house, particularly those in the town centre, can be glimpsed in the advertisements in local football handbooks published during the 1890s. For example, in 1891, the *Cardiff Cottage* in St. Mary Street, still a popular rugby meeting place today, offered patrons a telegraphic results service. Another modern favourite with rugby supporters, the *Blue Bell* (now the *Goat Major*) in High Street promoted itself as being only one minute from both the Arms Park and (presumably if you could run fast) Sophia Gardens. It boasted first class accommodation for visiting teams and it was also where the C&DFU held its meetings. "The Home of Athletes" was the claim made by the proprietor of the *New Market Hotel* (renamed *O'Neill's*) in Trinity Street. It too was one minute from the Arms Park and a rather more realistic five minutes from the Gardens. It was the headquarters of the strong St. David's club in 1891–2 and provided the players with free hot and cold baths. It was here that the Cardiff and District Football Union was founded in 1892, though no blue plaque yet commemorates this significant contribution to the sporting history of Cardiff. The *Three Horse Shoes*, which was located in High Street, accommodated four rugby clubs and provided telegraphic match results for customers. In 1894, the regulars at "the favourite resort of football enthusiasts", the *Philharmonic Restaurant* in St. Mary Street, could receive football results every Saturday, while in the same year, the publishers Mortimer & Co. offered free advertising to all licensed houses which used their telegraphic results service. However, it was its strategic location in Westgate Street overlooking the Arms Park, which gave the fifty bedroom *Grand Hotel* its particular advantages. Its proprietors advertised facilities for football dinners, concerts and meetings; plunge and swimming baths; and special accommodation for touring teams. The *Grand Hotel*'s unique attraction, however, was what may well be the earliest ever example of the hospitality suite: season tickets could be purchased to view matches from the hotel balconies.[47] This was an innovative and enterprising society, after all. It could be a risk for hoteliers to welcome touring teams, however. The Harlequins caused so much damage at the *Angel Hotel* in 1886 that Cardiff broke off fixtures for several seasons. The *SWDN* reported that the "London Harlequins ... have written offering to make good the damage occasioned by them at several Cardiff hotels during their stay in the town. The Cardiff match committee may discontinue fixtures with the Quins following their rowdy conduct." No doubt it was alcohol which fuelled the boorish behaviour of Blackheath's players at the Theatre Royal in December 1896, where they "made idiots of themselves to the general annoyance of the house". The press was generally critical of such incidents. "Dagon" of the *Western Mail*, however, describes Cardiff's uneventful stay in Burton in 1888 in rather ambiguous terms.

> The practical jokes which are a proverbial indication of the presence of a football team in any hotel were of a rather mild and timid character. An uneventful night – a rare incident – was passed and in the morning a visit was made to one of the many breweries in the town, where the team had the opportunity to inspect the works.[48]

The 1890–91 football handbook provides further insights into the interdependence of pubs and Welsh rugby. It contains the fixture lists of twenty-six clubs in the Cardiff area and for nineteen of these it notes the location of their "dressing rooms". Details are shown in Table 4. Seventeen were based in pubs or hotels, one in a coffee tavern and one in a church institute.[49] These are similar to Tony Collins' findings for Yorkshire in 1885–6, where only five out of eighty rugby clubs did not use a pub as headquarters.[50] Though it relates to a season outside the period covered by this book, the official handbook of the Cardiff and District Rugby Union for 1908–9 reveals that clubs then still relied heavily on the public house. Of the twenty senior clubs which gave details of their headquarters, seventeen used pubs or hotels.[51]

Several authors have referred to the practice of football clubs playing on land attached to public houses.[52] There is no evidence for this in the built-up areas of Cardiff but it was probably different in the less densely populated districts. For example, in the village of Whitchurch, the local club played on fields adjoining the *Hollybush* and the *Fox and Hounds*, their headquarters for many years.

Whilst it was common in the north of England for well-known footballers to runs pubs, there is little indication of this happening in Cardiff at the time.[53] One exception was Syd Nicholls (Cardiff and Wales) who became manager of the *Grand Hotel* in 1894–5, with his brother Gwyn

Table 4: Cardiff and District Clubs' Dressing Rooms 1890–1[54]

Club	Dressing Room	Playing Field
Canton	*Rover Hotel*, Wellington Street	Sophia Gardens
Cardiff	*Angel Hotel*, Castle Street	Cardiff Arms Park
Cardiff Cyclists	*Maindy Hotel*, North Road, Maindy	Barracks
Cardiff Harlequins	*Washington Hotel*, GWR Station, Canal Wharf West/ Penarth Road	Penarth Road
Cardiff Juniors (16 years)	*Coldstream Hotel*, Brook St., Riverside	Not known
Cardiff Rangers	*Cattle Market Tavern*, Quay Street	Sophia Gardens
Cardiff Rovers	*Bristol and South Wales Hotel*, Penarth Road	Penarth Road
Cardiff Star	*Coldstream Hotel*, Riverside	Sophia Gardens
Cardiff United	*Grand Hotel Vaults*, Womanby St.	Sophia Gardens
Cathays Rangers	*Maindy Hotel*, North Road, Maindy	Barracks
Cathays Star	*St. Andrew's Institute*, George St.	Cathays Rec'n. Ground
Clyde Rovers (15 years)	*Lord Wimborne Hotel*, Portmanmoor Rd., Splott	East Moors
Cogan	*Cogan Hotel*, Hewell St., Cogan	Not known
Ely Rovers	*Half-Way Hotel*, Penhill Road	Sophia Gardens
Llandaff	*Malsters Arms*, Llandaff Road	Mill Field
St. David's	*Three Horse Shoes*, High Street	Sophia Gardens
St. Peter's	*Flora Hotel*, Cathays Terrace	Barracks
Star Juniors	*Anchor Coffee Tavern*, Custom House Street	Not known
Taff Vale Wanderers	*Woodville Hotel*, Woodville Road, Cathays	Barracks

acting as under-manager.[55] Syd Nicholls had finished playing then, but when Viv Huzzey became the licensee of the *Windsor Arms* in Stuart Street in the Docks in 1899, he was still a Cardiff and Wales player. Reporting this, the *Western Mail* noted that whilst it was very common in the Northern Union to become a licensed victualler, "yet it is only on very [rare] occasions that Welsh players get these chances." This arrangement was probably an unsuccessful attempt to keep Huzzey in

Wales, for a year later he turned professional and joined Oldham in the Northern Union.[56]

The members of rugby clubs based in coffee taverns were not necessarily teetotal. There are references in the press to clubs using coffee taverns on some occasions and pubs at other times. In some cases, it was perhaps just a matter of convenience. Some teams used neither public house nor coffee tavern as their headquarters. In Grahame Lloyd's history of Cardiff City, there is an interesting account of the facilities used by the Riverside soccer club. Their clubhouse was a disused stable at the rear of a house, where members could play billiards and cards. As it was a short walk from Sophia Gardens, the team presumably also changed here.[57]

Players and Administrators

Having explored aspects of how rugby in Cardiff was organised, it would be appropriate to consider now who played and administered the game. It is widely accepted that the overwhelming majority of the first rugby players came from the middle and upper classes. As Gareth Williams has written, "The role of the middle class in establishing rugby clubs in Wales is clear".[58]

Cardiff provides an opportunity to test this with a limited study of the social background of the town's early players during the 1870s. Charles Arthur's 1908 history records the names of many of these and it also includes lists of members for Cardiff's first two seasons.[59] Additional names were obtained from press match reports of the period. As a result, the names of 150 men involved up to 1878 were identified. Census returns, directories, biographies and the internet were then consulted to try to identify individuals. In many cases, this proved impossible, not least because of the large number of players with common Welsh surnames. Sometimes only a surname was available, making a positive identification difficult. Nevertheless, information was traced on fifty-four, over a third of the known members and players associated with Cardiff and its predecessor clubs up to 1878. This is a sufficiently large sample to provide a reliable indication of the typical background of Cardiff's first players. Whilst this exercise largely confirms traditional views about the social class of early rugby players in Wales, it is the first detailed empirical investigation of a Welsh club's playing membership from this period.

Those identified included all the leading players and officials. None was working class, whether judged by occupation, father's occupation, residence or education. The majority were employed in occupations connected with the coal trade rather than the professions. Some were businessmen in their own right, including a newspaper proprietor, a timber merchant, a shipowner and a chain manufacturer. Many were employed in family commercial enterprises such as shipping, timber importing, coal exporting and fuel manufacture. There were mining engineers, colliery agents, land agents, draughtsmen, teachers, an assistant dentist and students. Finally, there was a large group of clerks employed by shipbrokers, solicitors, banks and the post office as well as by coal, railway and insurance companies. Towards the end of the decade, there are indications of an increase in the number of lower status clerks, suggesting perhaps the beginning of the downward shift in the social class of membership. Of course, it is possible that, amongst the unknown two-thirds, there were some working-class players, since they are generally less likely to have left some record of their lives. However, the overwhelming evidence is that in the 1870s Cardiff was predominantly, if not entirely, a middle-class club.

There is also some contemporary evidence which supports this view of an initially narrow social base. In 1878, the club captain, Raoul Foa, wrote to the press about his fellow players, "being *most of them engaged in business*, [they] are unable to absent themselves from the office more than one afternoon a week."[60] Another correspondent suggested that all members could be guaranteed games if internal matches were organised, involving Lloyd's v Coal Trade and Business in Docks v The Rest amongst others, suggesting that players were predominantly office workers.[61] In March 1879, Cardiff met the holders Newport in the final of the South Wales Challenge Cup. Attempting to excuse Cardiff's defeat, the *SWDN* declared that "while the members of [Cardiff] ... are *many of them connected with the offices of commercial and railway companies*, many of the members of the Newport club are artisans and the difference in point of strength was considerable." [62]

This appears to confirm that the club was still largely socially exclusive at the end of the decade, though the *SWDN* was quite wrong about the involvement of working-class players in the Newport team at this time, as has been shown earlier. However, the match report also referred to the many thousands of spectators present and the keen interest which they displayed. Such levels of support would soon entice clubs to overcome any initial reluctance they may have had about selecting working men. It was inevitable that, amongst the growing numbers drawn to these exciting contests, there would have been workers who fancied giving the game a try. Certainly, within two years of the 1879 cup final, working men were appearing in the Cardiff First XV.

Further evidence of the essentially middle-class nature of the game in the 1870s is revealed by the existence of the 10th Glamorgan Rifle

Volunteers (GRV) club. There were also two other volunteer units in Cardiff at the time, the 16th GRV and the 3rd Glamorgan Artillery Volunteers (GAV). According to a local historian writing in 1918, when these were formed, the 16th GRV were known as the "People's Rifle Corps" and had "more moderate and less restrictive terms of entry than the 10th". He added that the 3rd GAV comprised "artisans, shipwrights and other stalwart working men".[63] It is revealing, therefore, that of these three units, it was only the more socially elite 10th GRV which formed a rugby club during the 1870s.

This research into players' backgrounds also provides clues about the process of the early growth of rugby in the town. Schoolmasters may have been instrumental in introducing the game. Then there were the local products of rugby playing public schools. In Cardiff these included Cheltenham, Marlborough, Clifton, Sherborne, Rugby, Christ College Brecon and Monmouth. In addition, old boys of private schools such as Monkton House, Cardiff Collegiate and Bridgend, as well as local grammar schools like Cowbridge were crucially important. Whilst students are often credited with spreading the game, apart from a few who may have played at university or teaching hospital, their influence in Cardiff does not appear to have been particularly strong. The game, however, *was* enhanced by the presence of talented newcomers, like William Graves, who was already an established player with Manchester and who played for the North of England.[64] The influence of one or two gifted individuals like this should not be underestimated.

However, by the early 1880s, Cardiff could no longer depend on its own resources to maintain its growing status in the sport. The club's initial function of merely providing enjoyment for members was giving way to the much stronger need of upholding the town's reputation.[65] In so doing, the club increasingly began to rely on players produced by the newly emerging local "junior" clubs, such as Bute Dock Rangers, Canton, Cardiff Quins, Cardiff Rangers and Windsor. Both working-class and middle-class players joined Cardiff from these clubs who must, therefore, have drawn their players from across the social classes. If working men had reached a good enough playing standard to represent Cardiff by 1881, they probably began playing in local clubs at least by the end of the 1870s. The arrival of the working class, not only in Cardiff but throughout Welsh rugby, came at a time when clear signs of political change in Wales were also emerging. With nine gains in the general election of 1880, Liberal MPs now held twenty-nine of the thirty-three Welsh seats.[66] The movement towards a more democratic Wales in both politics and rugby was underway.

Given the major impact which they subsequently had on the wider game, it is interesting to note the number of former local club players who represented Cardiff in Hancock's record-breaking year. At the end of 1885–6, the *SWDN* published a list of the men who played under Hancock.[67] By searching the press in earlier seasons, it is possible to show that of the seventeen who appeared most frequently in Hancock's team, *at least* eleven had played for local clubs before joining Cardiff. Seven of those eleven went on to win Welsh caps. Former Canton players included Billy Douglas, Albert Hybart, Dick Kedzlie, David Lewis, William Stadden (all Welsh internationals) and Arthur Emery, John Sant and Wyndham Jarman; while Hugh Hughes and George Young (both Welsh internationals) had played for Cardiff Harlequins and Jimmy Mahoney for Cardiff Rangers. Details of the seventeen players are shown in Table 5.

Reminiscing wistfully and perhaps rather fancifully in 1892 about the Cardiff club of 1884–5, "Old Stager" discussed the process of working-class players joining from local junior clubs.

> The game, by that time, had fairly caught on, and became the pursuit of the masses, who in earlier days had been content merely to look on from outside the ropes. Clubs were springing up all over the town, composed mainly of lusty youths many of them working lads or sons of working men, sound of wind and limb, and brimful of pluck and ambition ... [the Cardiff second XV was] recruited almost entirely from one of those minor clubs ... Canton ... [and they] ... upset in a pitched encounter the first fifteen. The result was the precipitate retirement of many of the older members.[68]

Using census returns, biographies and press articles, it is possible to establish the social background of Hancock's side.[69] Examination of Cardiff teams in match reports reveal that the process of working-class participation began *earlier* and was more *gradual* and less dramatic than implied in "Old Stager's" recollections. Of the six men who were working class, Dick Kedzlie (blacksmith) played as early as 1881–2 and Jimmy Mahoney (labourer), Wyndham Jarman (decorator) and William Stadden (labourer) first appeared in 1882–3. Angus Stuart first played in 1883–4 and Hugh Hughes (carpenter) early in 1884–5. There is no doubt, therefore, that during the 1880s, the composition of the Cardiff XV gradually became more socially mixed than the largely exclusive teams of the 1870s. Moreover, the inclusion of Mahoney, a member of Cardiff's Irish Catholic community, is perhaps the best evidence of all that playing ability was becoming more important than social standing. Wing three-quarter Angus Stuart's social background has been difficult to confirm. He was a professional sprinter and joined

Table 5: Cardiff First XV Players 1885–6 [70]

Name	Games Played	Occupation	Former Club(s)	Place of Birth	Honours
Hugh Hughes	27	Carpenter	Star, Cardiff Quins	Meirionydd	Wales
Wyndham Jarman	27	Decorator	Canton	Cardiff	
Alexander Bland	27	Solicitor		Pembs	Wales
William "Buller" Stadden	26	Labourer	Canton, Bute Dock Rangers	Cardiff	Wales
Quinton Dick Kedzlie	26	Blacksmith	Windsor, Canton	Scotland	Wales
Frank Hancock	26	Brewery Director	Wiveliscombe	Somerset	Wales
Arthur Emery	25	Merchant's Clerk	Canton	Cardiff	
James Mahoney	24	Labourer	Cardiff Rangers, Canton, Bute Dock Rangers	Cardiff	
William Douglas	23	Colliery Official	Windsor, Canton	Barry	Wales
Charles Arthur	22	Schoolmaster, Estate Agent	Newton College Devon, Winchester, Dorchester, Cheltenham	Norfolk	Wales
Angus Stuart	22	Labourer?		Scotland	GB & NZ
David Lewis	22	Clerk	Canton, Cardiff Quins	Cardiff	Wales
Henry Simpson	22	Chartering Clerk		Durham	Wales
John Sant	13	Architect	Canton	Cardiff	
Frank Hill	12	Solicitor	Monkton House, Clifton College	Cardiff	Wales
George Young	11	Shipowner's son	Monkton House, Cardiff Quins	Tyneside	Wales
Albert Hybart	10	Timber Exporter	Cardiff Collegiate, Canton, Cardiff Quins	Cardiff	Wales

Dewsbury with Stadden in 1886. Both were employed as mill hands there, suggesting he was working class. In one of the most remarkable playing careers of any era, Scottish-born Stuart, had a Welsh trial on the wing and later played at *forward* for Great Britain (1888) *and* New Zealand (1893).[71] The contribution of these working men to the success of Hancock's team was important, perhaps crucial, and it is noteworthy that of the eight players who appeared most frequently in the First XV in that record breaking season, five were working class. However, the involvement of working-class players was neither sudden nor total.

A strong case can be made for the argument that Cardiff were only able to enjoy and maintain their dominant position in British rugby from the 1880s onwards because they sat at the apex of a large pyramid of local clubs from which they were constantly able to renew their teams. During Hancock's year, Swansea resolved to institute a cup competition to stimulate clubs in their area because it was "generally thought that the unbroken success achieved by the Cardiff first and second fifteens is due in measure to the large number of clubs they can draw from".[72] The frequently asserted and, it is contested, somewhat distorted view that Welsh rugby is essentially valleys rugby ignores the important contribution which these now almost entirely forgotten Cardiff clubs made to the game. From the very earliest days, local Cardiff clubs were producing players who would help to change not only the social character of Welsh rugby but also the way in which the Welsh, and later the rest of the world, would play rugby.

However, importantly, the participation of working men in the Cardiff club did not extend to its management. Arthur's history records the committee members for each season up to 1906 and it is clear that the control of the club was retained firmly by the middle class throughout. For 1899–1900, the final season in this study, eighteen officers are listed. They were all former players but, of the sixteen who can be identified, only one was working class and he was on the committee because he was the vice-captain. Two of the Second XV committee were lower middle class. All the remainder were solicitors, other professionals or businessmen of substance. It was also this class which dominated the WFU and other senior clubs at the time.[73]

Two clubs, from time to time, attempted to challenge Cardiff's dominance as the area's "premier" club. These were Cardiff Harlequins and Penarth.[74] It is a demonstration of the remarkable strength of Cardiff rugby that, for several seasons, these clubs were regarded as being amongst the handful of elite Welsh clubs and were quite capable of defeating some of the strongest teams in the kingdom. But neither was ever able to break the powerful grip which the Cardiff club had on the Cardiff public: it was the "town" team and therefore the focus of enormous civic pride and, as such, it represented the town in a way in which no other team could hope to challenge. As the regional capital of a large hinterland, too, it drew its support from a much wider area than just the borough. When the "premier" team was playing away, neither the Quins nor Penarth could ever attract crowds like Cardiff, even if the opposition were Llanelli, Newport or Swansea.

Cardiff Harlequins was a socially mixed club, which emerged from the obscurity of district rugby in the late 1870s via a series of name changes and mergers. By 1890, together with their close rivals Penarth, the Quins were recognised as one of the seven senior Welsh clubs along-side Cardiff, Neath, Newport, Llanelli and Swansea.[75] This was due in no small measure to the efforts and financial support of their energetic secretary, Alfred J. Davies, a Cardiff stockbroker. A very influential but now forgotten administrator, Davies served on the WFU for many years and also represented Wales on the IRB. In 1896, he was an unsuccessful candidate for the post of WFU secretary. He was largely responsible for establishing the Glamorgan County Football Union, of which he was its first secretary. A prominent referee, Davies officiated in the 1896 English County Championship final and took charge of the Somerset v New Zealand match shortly before he died. He was also active in Welsh athletics.[76] Despite his high profile in the game, he was never involved with the Cardiff club and, on the contrary, A.J. Davies was sometimes regarded as being hostile to the Arms Park interest.

Under his leadership, the Quins were able to record victories over every leading Welsh club except Cardiff, who would rarely give them fixtures, as well as over many English sides including Bath, Bristol, Leicester and Northampton. They produced two Welsh internationals in Percy Bennett and Fred Nicholls as well as several Welsh trialists and county players. Despite these successes, however, they found it difficult to retain many of their more promising players. Several who turned out for the Quins were later capped from Cardiff like Syd Nicholls, W.E.O. Williams, Hugh Hughes, Hugh Ingledew and Norman Biggs. Even Gwyn Nicholls had a couple of games for the club though he was never a regular player as is often claimed. It was both the constant drain of players and heavy financial burdens which eventually led to the club's demise. In 1892, the Quins took over and developed a new ground in Roath, still known today as "The Harlequins", but they severely over-stretched themselves financially in doing so.[77] The crowds were never large enough to sustain this venture and following a major row with Cardiff over yet another transfer of a player, the rugby club virtually folded in 1895, playing only as a Wednesday team for a while. The Quins were later revived on a regular basis but they never regained their former prominence and only played as a local Cardiff and District club at Splott Park without much success. The club finally disbanded in the 1930s.

Formed in 1880 partly on the initiative of Cyril Batchelor, the son of a well-known Cardiff businessman, Penarth were perhaps the most socially inclusive of all Welsh clubs of the period. Players in their earliest teams came from the across the very wide range of social classes found in the town. Engine fitters, boatmen, carpenters, railwaymen, boilermakers, coal-trimmers and labourers, as well as clerks, insurance agents, shop assistants and shopkeepers could be found playing alongside the public school educated sons of wealthy ship and coal magnates. The Penarth club provides strong evidence that, by the early 1880s, Welsh rugby was becoming socially open. Like Cardiff, however, the management of the club was controlled largely by the middle class, though there were perhaps fewer professionals and more small businessmen involved, while John Hayes the secretary from 1881 to 1887 was a docks foreman.[78] Writing to the *SWDN* in 1890 to refute arguments for a merger with Cardiff, a later secretary claimed that many of the town's leading residents were members: "we have a couple of hundred members ... including many of the aristocracy of Penarth".[79]

Under the guidance of stonemason Dickie Garrett and boilermaker George Rowles, both of whom captained the club and were capped by Wales, Penarth enjoyed a dramatic rise to prominence. By the 1890s, the club had recorded victories over all the leading Welsh clubs, apart from Swansea, as well as over London Welsh, Bath, Bristol, Devonport Albion, Gloucester, Leicester, Moseley, St. Helens and Wakefield Trinity. However, as with Cardiff Quins, the club found it difficult to prevent players from moving to their more powerful neighbour in Cardiff. By the end of the century, Penarth were struggling to maintain their previously high standard but, unlike the Quins, they managed to survive, mainly due to their being a town team with strong support from the local community.[80]

Apart from these senior clubs, it is virtually impossible to determine the social background of the administrators and players belonging to the majority of Cardiff's local teams, as no membership records survive. Team lists in the press are of limited use, since without addresses it is difficult to identify individuals with any certainty, especially given the size of Cardiff and the prevalence of common Welsh surnames. However, a limited investigation was undertaken using the addresses of local club secretaries which were published in football handbooks for 1890 and 1891 and those occasionally found in the press between

1889 and 1891.[81] Of the fifty-three identified this way, thirty-eight were traced in the 1891 census and their details are shown in Appendix 5.

The age of most of the secretaries was remarkably low. The majority were teenagers and only one was over twenty-five. This suggests that the officers of local clubs may have been drawn largely from the play-ing membership and therefore grass roots teams, at least, did not rely to any great extent on older enthusiasts to run their affairs. The lack of a committee composed of former players might perhaps partly explain the fragility of many of the clubs. An example of a prominent and yet very youthful administrator was Wilson Tunley, who at seventeen years was the secretary of two clubs, Cardiff Juniors and the very successful St. David's. Whilst still a teenager, he was actively involved in setting up the Cardiff and District Football Union, which he served for some years before joining the committee of Cardiff rugby club.

Seventeen of the thirty-eight secretaries who were traced were born in Cardiff and six elsewhere in south Wales. Of the rest, six came from the west country, eight from other parts of England and one from Scotland. They were predominantly clerks or tradesmen. Two-thirds had white collar occupations. Sixteen were clerical workers and there were also three shop assistants, a commercial traveller, a proof-reader's assistant and an eighteen year old teacher. One was a schoolboy. There was also a hardware merchant who was probably employed in his father's business and who might be classified as middle class, as he lived in Richmond Road, then one of the better addresses, and his club was Cardiff Cyclists. The remaining thirteen were all working men. Their occupations were plumber (three), plumber's apprentice, compositor, printer's appren-tice, coach trimmer, coach painter, baker, currier, hairdresser, plasterer and telegraph messenger. Apart from the hardware merchant, none of the thirty-eight was obviously a member of the professional or busi-ness middle classes or lived in the more fashionable areas of the town. Neither were any from the unskilled labouring classes. It is interest-ing to compare this with the study by Martin Johnes and Ian Garland, who researched seventeen Welsh soccer club secretaries from 1880 and found that they had a predominantly lower middle-class profile, domi-nated by clerks with an age range of nineteen to thirty-eight.[82]

If this group is representative of the wider Cardiff rugby commu-nity around 1890, then it can be argued that the organisation of the game at the local level was largely dominated by young members of the skilled and semi-skilled working class and lower status middle class. This supports the views of earlier researchers, who believe that the growth of football in England in the late nineteenth century came substantially from within the working class rather than from the efforts of the middle class. The evidence above is admittedly limited, but when combined with that on the sheer level of participation across the town, it does suggest that most workers in Cardiff also arranged their own rugby, rather than having it organised for them. It is unlikely that there were many middle-class reformers in the ranks of the secretaries of Cardiff's clubs.[83] Whilst the officials of the WFU and the leading clubs were largely members of the professional and business classes, this was generally not the case at the grass roots of the game.

By 1911, Cardiff had one of the highest proportions of adult males born outside the United Kingdom.[84] However, apart from the Irish and, to a much lesser extent, possibly the Scottish (e.g. Caledonians, Grange Thistles, Penarth Thistles), no other ethnic groups formed their own clubs. As for teams based on English regions or counties, the only clear example was Cardiff Northern, which was originally founded by play-ers from the north-east though, as they later became one of Cardiff's strongest district clubs, their membership was probably not restricted. Surprisingly, given the very large number of Cardiffians who had roots in the west country, there were no teams with names which obviously connected them to Gloucester, Somerset, Devon or Cornwall. This may be an indication of the extent to which newcomers became quickly assimilated into the local rugby community. Of course, that is not to say that players from a particular area of England did not continue to socialise together by playing for the same club. Occasionally, foreign players can be identified in team lists. For instance, Raoul Foa, Cardiff's captain in 1878–9, was half Italian and half French. He was also Jewish. How much black participation there was in nineteenth-century Cardiff rugby is impossible to establish reliably. It is certain that at least one black player, Charles Lewis of Grange Stars, had a few games in the centre for Cardiff First and Second XVs during 1898–9, so it is likely, therefore, though no evidence has yet been found to prove it, that other black players were members of local clubs.[85]

To summarise then, until the early 1880s, the game in Cardiff was dominated by the middle class. Towards the end of the 1870s, how-ever, changes began to take place. New clubs, which working men were able to join, began to emerge and these soon became socially mixed by the first half of the 1880s. Even the Cardiff club admitted workmen by 1881–2 and, by the middle of the decade, they comprised a substantial part of the First XV. By 1890, local clubs were largely dominated by the working and lower middle classes. However, the administration of the senior clubs, including Cardiff, and of the WFU continued to remain in the control of the professional and business middle class. This, and the previous chapter, therefore, provides a detailed confirmation of Gareth Williams' description of Welsh rugby.

Though an educated middle-class elite dominated the higher echelons of the game, lower down the scale clubs were run by working men for working men. Welsh rugby cannot be portrayed merely as a middle-class salvage operation, rescuing a sullen working class from the aimless and morally damaging attractions of the pub or gin-palace. Administered by the few it [was] played and watched by the many.[86]

Notes

1. Gareth Williams, "Community, Class and Rugby in Wales 1880–1914", *Society for the Study of Labour History Bulletin*, 50, Spring, (1985), p. 11.
2. For WFU membership see *South Wales Daily News* and *Western Mail*, 1886–1895 and WFU minutes 1892–1902 passim; *SWDN* 28 Mar. 1892 (Llandaff win Welsh Challenge Cup).
3. *SWDN* 8 Sept. 1886.
4. *SWDN* 17 Oct. 1889. (Junior Cup); *Cardiff District Football Union Handbook 1886–87* (Cardiff, 1886), pp. 3–14; John Musselwhite, *The Butcher Boys of Donkey Island: An Historical Profile of Penarth R.F.C.* (Penarth, 1980), pp. 9, 20; see Appendix 3 for cup winners.
5. *WM* 15 Nov. 1892.
6. *WM* 4 Feb. 1897.
7. *SWDN* 4 Jan. 1894.
8. *SWDN* 10 Nov. 1894. The clubs in the first Senior League were Barry, Canton, Grangetown, Cardiff Northern and Whitchurch; and in the Junior League (i.e. Second Division) they were Blackweir, Cathays United, Grange Star, Pentyrch, Roath and St. Mary's.
9. *SWDN* 14 Aug. 1896.
10. *SWDN* 24, 28 Feb. 1900. See Appendix 3 for the local competitions held in 1899–1900. See also Gwyn Prescott, "Competitive Rugby in Cardiff Before the First World War", *Touchlines (Rugby Memorabilia Society)*, 46, April, (2010), pp. 5-9.
11. Alan Metcalfe, "Football in the Mining Communities of East Northumberland 1882–1914", *International Journal of the History of Sport*, 5, 3 (1988), p. 270.
12. *SWDN* 3 May 1897.
13. *WM* 4 Feb. 1897 (District players); John M. Jenkins, Duncan Pierce and Timothy Auty, *Who's Who of Welsh International Rugby Players* (Wrexham, 1991) passim; *Evening Express* 6 Apr. 1901 (Bush); *SWDN* 18 Jan. 1897 (Winfield), 14 Nov. 1898 (O'Neill); *SWDN* and *WM* match reports 1890–1910 passim.
14. WFU minutes 30 Dec. 1896, 21 Sept. 1898, 7 Nov. 1898.
15. Metcalfe, "Football in East Northumberland", pp. 274, 278–9.
16. *WM* 8 Oct. 1894.
17. *SWDN* 8 Oct. 1895.
18. *SWDN* 18 Sept. 1899.
19. WFU minutes 8 Dec. 1898.
20. *SWDN* 28 Apr. 1899.
21. Andrew J. Croll, *Civilizing the Urban: Popular Culture, Public Space and Urban Meaning, Merthyr c. 1870–1914* (PhD thesis, University of Wales Cardiff, 1997),

pp. 208, 224–6; 142–3; H.E. Meller, *Leisure and the Changing City, 1870–1914* (London, 1976), p. 236.

22. *WM* 17 Apr. 1875.
23. *WM* 15 Oct. 1875.
24. C.S. Arthur, *The Cardiff Rugby Football Club: History and Statistics, 1876–1906* (Cardiff, 1908); D.E. Davies, *Cardiff Rugby Club: History and Statistics, 1876–1975: "The Greatest"* (Cardiff, 1975).
25. *WM* 11 Apr. 1887.
26. See Andrew Hignell and Gwyn Prescott, *Cardiff Sporting Greats*, pp. 33–5, 115–16 for brief histories of the Arms Park and the Cardiff Athletic Club.
27. *WM* 27 Jan. 1896.
28. *SWDN* 10 Oct. 1892.
29. *WM* 5 Oct. 1891.
30. *WM* 17 Sept. 1894.
31. For a detailed history of Sophia Gardens, see Andrew Hignell, *From Sophia to SWALEC: A History of Cricket in Cardiff*, (Stroud, 2009). Andrew Hignell's account of early rugby in Cardiff draws on the research for this book in places.
32. R.H. Morgan, "The Development of an Urban Transport System: The Case of Cardiff", *Welsh History Review*, 13, 2 (1986), pp. 178–181.
33. *SWDN* 5 Oct. 1892; *County Borough of Cardiff Reports of Council and Committees*, Nov. 1891 to Nov. 1892, p. 589.
34. *SWDN* 25 Nov. 1889.
35. *SWDN* 30 Dec. 1889.
36. *SWDN* 20 Sept. 1886.
37. *SWDN* 4 March 1878 (Newbridge Fields), 21 Nov. 1892 (Phillips).
38. *SWDN* 31 Oct. 1892.
39. *SWDN* 10 Feb. 1885.
40. *SWDN* 14 Feb. 1885.
41. *WM* 12 Oct. 1894.
42. Gareth Edwards and Don Llewellyn, "The Williams Family: More Than a 'Rugby Dynasty'", *Garth Domain*, 26, (2004), p. 11.
43. *WM* 4 Feb. 1895 (snow); *Welsh Athlete* 21 Sept. 1891 (Buffalo Bill).
44. *SWDN* 30 Sept. 1895.
45. Gareth Morgan, "Rugby and Revivalism: Sport and Religion in Edwardian Wales", *IJHS*, 22, 3 (2005), p. 435.
46. Tony Collins and Wray Vamplew, *Mud, Sweat and Beers: A Cultural History of Sport and Alcohol* (Oxford, 2002), pp. 13–15; Alan Metcalfe, "The Control of Space and the Development of Sport: A Case Study of Twenty Two Sports in the Mining Communities of East Northumberland, 1800–1914", *Sports Historian*, 15, (1995), p. 27.
47. *The Welsh Athlete and West of England Cycling News Football Handbook 1891–2* (Cardiff, 1891), pp. [61] (*Cottage*), [56] (*Blue Bell*), [54] (*New Market*), [42] (*Three Horse Shoes*), [52] (*Grand*); *Mortimer's Football Guide for South Wales and Monmouthshire: Season, 1894–95* (Barry, 1894), pp. 22 (*Philharmonic*), 49 (results service).
48. *SWDN* 1 Feb., 26 Apr. 1886 (*Harlequins*); *WM* 1 Jan. 1897 (Blackheath); *WM* 22 Oct. 1888 (Burton).
49. *Cardiff and South Wales Footballer's Companion: 1890–91* (Cardiff, 1890), pp.15–66.
50. Tony Collins, *Rugby's Great Split: Class, Culture and the Origins of Rugby League Football* (London, 2006 edn.), p. 27.
51. *Cardiff and District Rugby Union: Official Handbook, Season 1908–9* (Cardiff, 1908), pp. 4–7.

52. Tony Mason, *Association Football and English Society 1863–1915* (Brighton, 1981), p. 27; Collins and Vamplew, *Mud, Sweat and Beers*, pp. 11–22; Metcalfe, "Control of Space", p. 24.
53. Mason, *Association Football and English Society*, pp. 118–119; Collins and Vamplew, *Mud, Sweat and Beers*, p. 13.
54. Compiled from *Cardiff Footballer's Companion: 1890–91*, pp. 15–66.
55. David Parry-Jones, *Prince Gwyn: Gwyn Nicholls and the First Golden Era of Welsh Rugby* (Bridgend, 1999), p. 32.
56. *WM* 23 Jan. 1899.
57. Grahame Lloyd, *C'Mon City! A Hundred Years of the Bluebirds* (Bridgend, 1999), pp. 21–2.
58. Gareth Williams, "Community, Class and Rugby", p. 10.
59. Arthur, *Cardiff Rugby*, pp. 7–21.
60. *WM* 29 Nov. 1878 (italics added).
61. *WM* 2 Dec. 1878.
62. *SWDN* 10 Mar. 1879 (italics added).
63. W.J. Trounce, *"Cardiff in the Fifties": The Reminiscences and Historical Notes of Alderman W.J. Trounce J.P. 1850–1860* (Cardiff, 1918), pp. 88–9.
64. *WM* 29 Mar. 1893, C. Stewart Caine (ed.), *John Wisden's Rugby Football Almanack for 1924–25* (London, 1924), pp. 229, 234 (Graves).
65. See also Collins, *Rugby's Great Split*, p. 15.
66. Kenneth O. Morgan, *Rebirth of a Nation: Wales 1880–1980* (Oxford, 1982 edn.), pp. 12–13.
67. *SWDN* 21 Apr. 1886.
68. *Cardiff Times* 10 Sept. 1892. See Croll, *Civilizing the Urban*, pp. 245–6 for a different interpretation from that presented here.
69. Anon, *Contemporary Portraits: Men and Women of South Wales and Monmouthshire: Cardiff Section* (Cardiff, 1896), pp. 34–5; Jenkins, Pierce and Auty, *Who's Who of Welsh International Rugby*, passim.
70. Compiled from the *South Wales Daily News*, the *Western Mail*, directories, census returns and biographies.
71. *SWDN* 3 Oct. 1886 (Stuart); R.H. Chester and N.A.C. McMillan, *The Visitors: The History of International Rugby Teams in New Zealand* (Auckland, 1990), p. 41.
72. *SWDN* 1 Feb. 1886.
73. Arthur, *Cardiff Rugby*, passim. For the 1899–1900 officers see p. 147.
74. Hignell and Prescott, *Cardiff Sporting Greats*, pp. 158–9 (Cardiff Quins); Musselwhite, *Penarth R.F.C.*, pp. 7–39.
75. *WM* 12 Apr. 1890.
76. *SWDN* 21 Sept. 1896 (WFU); *WM* 21 Feb. 1896 (County Championship); *SWDN* 26 Apr. 1906 (obituary).
77. *SWDN* 10 Oct. 1892.
78. 1881 and 1891 Census; Penarth RFC archive; Musselwhite, *Penarth R.F.C.*, p. 7–8.
79. *SWDN* 22 Nov. 1890.
80. Musselwhite, *Penarth R.FC*, pp. 7–39.
81. *WM* and *Evening Express* 1889–1891 passim; *Cardiff Footballer's Companion 1890–91*, pp. 3–67; *Welsh Athlete Football Handbook 1891–2*, pp. 43–130.
82. Martin Johnes and Ian Garland, " 'The New Craze': football and society in north-east Wales, c. 1870–90", *Welsh History Review*, 22, 2 (2004), pp. 286–7.
83. Richard Holt, *Sport and the British: A Modern History* (Oxford, 1989), p. 135.
84. 1911 census.
85. *WM* 26 Sept. 1898, *SWDN* 26 Sept. 1898, 5 Apr. 1899 (Lewis).
86. Gareth Williams, "Community, Class and Rugby", p. 11.

6

RUGBY'S WIDER IMPACT

'Football, or, Life in Cardiff'

The popularity of rugby in Victorian Cardiff had an impact which went beyond the mere game itself. The large numbers playing and attending matches in the town, for instance, opened up many new opportunities for a range of businesses. Though it is impossible now to provide precise details, there are still numerous indicators of the general economic effect on Cardiff.

Sport was transformed by the improvements in transport which greatly extended the range of support and participation.[1] Transport companies were quick to recognise the commercial attractions of rugby. As soon as large crowds began to attend major matches, rail companies responded with cheap excursions. For instance, in 1886 and only five years after Wales' first ever international, the GWR ran a special day excursion from Cardiff to Blackheath for the England match, "leaving time to visit a theatre."[2] It became a regular practice to run special trains for Cardiff's home and away fixtures, not only with their main rivals Newport and Swansea but also with less powerful opponents like Penygraig.[3] For a Newport v Cardiff game in 1894, attended by 15,000, GWR ran two special trains each with forty coaches and added sixteen extra ones on the regular 1.30 service.[4] The only way that supporters could realistically travel to matches outside their immediate locality was by rail. Fortunately south Wales had one of the most densely developed railway networks in the world and Cardiff was at its centre.[5] The game could not have expanded as it did without this rail infrastructure but it was a mutually beneficial relationship for both rugby and the railway companies.

This was also true for local transport operators. The outward spread of tram and bus services made it much easier for players and supporters to get to matches, whilst at the same time the operators benefited from the increased takings. All the main Cardiff tram routes in the 1880s and 1890s ran close to the Arms Park and Sophia Gardens.[6] One of the reasons why Cardiff Harlequins chose their new ground in Newport Road in 1891 was that it was near a tram terminal at the *Royal Oak*.[7] There was also increased trade for the town's cabmen, ferrying players and supporters between stations, grounds and pubs. In 1896, one Swansea company advertised that it offered "special terms to football teams" for cabs, carriages, phaetons, brakes and hansoms.[8] Spectators at Penarth-Cardiff games not only travelled by bus and train but they also used the boat service across what is now Cardiff Bay.[9] Not every town possessed adequate transport facilities for the exceptional demands created by big matches, however. Previewing the 1893 Ireland international, "Old Stager" complained that getting transport from Llanelli station to Stradey Park was virtually impossible and that most supporters had to make the long journey on foot. He added that there had been similar problems at Swansea a few years earlier.[10]

As Cardiff developed into the regional capital of south Wales from the 1880s, its central area was transformed as a commercial and service quarter.[11] Pubs, restaurants, hotels and theatres close to the Arms Park and Sophia Gardens were readily able to attract the custom of players and supporters. Of the 274 pubs in the borough in 1903, 131 were located in the central area and well over half of these were found in streets immediately surrounding the Arms Park.[12] The existence of this service industry was vital to the development of the game in Cardiff. In 1891, "Old Stager" reported complaints from supporters that there were not enough pubs and hotels in Llanelli to cater for the crowds attending the Ireland international.[13] The Irish FU unsuccessfully requested that the 1893 international be moved from Llanelli because of its inadequate hotel provision.[14] However, this was the last international played by Wales at Stradey Park for over a hundred years.[15]

As in the twenty-first century, success in major matches was the occasion for a great deal of celebration in the town's pubs and hotels. After Cardiff's victory at Swansea in 1888, the team was met at the station by brass bands and carried to the *Angel* "and there was a deal of cheering *and much consumption of liquor*."[16] "Old Stager" wrote after Wales' first ever win over England at Cardiff in 1893:

> The players ... were borne away to the Angel shoulder high ... later on *every hotel bar along the main streets was blocked to the street doors*, and everywhere football was the main topic of conversation. The victory of Wales simply sent the population of Cardiff, plus the thousands of visitors, off their blessed chumps.[17]

Certainly, then, the proprietors of such establishments had every reason to support and encourage this new trade. Tom Mallett was undoubtedly a lover of rugby, but when he presented a cup for competition to the Cardiff and District Football Union in 1893, it was also a smart business move. When he left the *New Market Hotel* to become the new landlord of the *Blue Bell*, the Union's headquarters went with him.[18]

Sports outfitters and photographers were other local entrepreneurs who benefited greatly from the growth of the game. T. Page Wood originally specialised in supplying middle-class and upper-class customers with shooting and fishing equipment, but he swiftly recognised the new lucrative sports goods market offered by football. In 1886, he shrewdly donated a cup for competition amongst local clubs and, as a direct result, the (first) Cardiff District Football Union was set up and he was appointed its president.[19] That Page Wood saw this as essentially a business venture, however, may be confirmed by the reactions of one disgruntled correspondent to the *SWDN* who was rather suspicious of his motives. "One would imagine the Union existed as an advertising medium."[20] Describing the astonishing popularity of rugby, the weekly *Cardiff Argus* commented in 1888:

> There is no kind of out-door amusement which has become so thoroughly popular during the last few years, in South Wales, as Football ... A glance at the stock of "Footballs" just received by [Page Wood] would lead to the conclusion that they were stored there for a century, but they are only "this season's goods", and are of all kinds and sizes, from the "match" balls to the small ones used in the junior clubs connected with our educational establishments.[21]

Another of Page Wood's sporting initiatives was the publication of a football handbook, which ran to at least seven editions by 1891–2.[22] These contained fixture lists and club details but they were also an imaginative way of promoting his goods which now included balls, bladders, jerseys, caps, gloves, shin guards, ankle guards and football insurance policies.[23] Such was the success of these handbooks that he even extended his publishing activities in 1891–2, by launching *The Welsh Athlete*, a weekly sports journal, overwhelmingly devoted to rugby. Sadly for future sports historians, however, this business enterprise was a financial failure and it folded before the end of the season. Other Cardiff outfitters followed Page Wood's lead. Evans and Co, of the Royal Arcade, sold footballs, jerseys, shorts, badges and presentation caps, while Anderson's in Queen Street not only supplied jerseys, boots and bags but also donated gold medals for the Mallett Cup winners.[24]

It became a regular practice to photograph teams at major matches. This was regarded as a tedious and time-consuming business and was invariably described in match reports as an ordeal. There was clearly a market for the products of the photographers' efforts though. A football handbook for 1896–7 included advertisements for Goldie of Cardiff and Dando of Newport, both of whom specialised in supplying team photographs for purchase by the general public.[25] Others, however, found ways of cashing in on the sport which were not always welcomed. "Old Stager" was aghast at the activities of one local insurance agent.

> It has come at last. The ingenious advertiser, noting the popularity of football, has commenced to turn even it to account. On Saturday men were distributing at the Park ... portraits of [Cardiff players] Charley Arthur and Jarman, on the back of which our friend Mr. Henry Perkins, of Cardiff invited all ... to ensure with him against sickness and accident. What next, I wonder?[26]

Kenneth Morgan argues that the *South Wales Daily News* generally gave little prominence to cultural affairs.[27] Nevertheless, on the whole, this Liberal daily tended to cover the game in rather more depth than the Tory *Western Mail*. This may have been partly due to the influence of one of the *SWDN*'s proprietors, Alex Duncan, a former Cardiff player who served on the committees of both Cardiff and the WFU at the time. Both papers were Cardiff based but they also enjoyed a much wider regional circulation. In the maelstrom of Welsh club rivalry, this could sometimes cause tensions within their readership, a problem which didn't usually arise with their more locally based competitors in Llanelli, Newport, Swansea and elsewhere. This sometimes created a conflict of interest which could never really be satisfactorily resolved. Following the reporting of a major dispute involving Cardiff, William Wilkins, the secretary of Llanelli, complained, probably justifiably, "Both the [Cardiff] daily papers, while professing to cater for South Wales, hold a brief for Cardiff first."[28]

As the game's popularity grew, columnists like "Old Stager", "Welsh Athlete", "Dagon", "Goal Post", and "Touchstone" became regular contributors. Their articles would sometimes include highly provocative views on WFU conduct, team selection, player performance and the behaviour of clubs, players and spectators. This would often stimulate much correspondence. Indeed, the press provided a vital forum for participants and supporters to voice their opinions, initiate ideas and resolve disputes of all kinds. Some journalists even became directly involved in the game; for example, H.W. Wells ("Welsh Athlete") was instrumental in setting up the Cardiff and District Football Union and became its president.[29] The local press, therefore, could be viewed as an unofficial but important branch of the sport, helping to promote the game even at the grass roots level.

After being relatively indifferent to rugby in the very early years, the Cardiff press soon began to recognise the commercial advantages of increasing its coverage of the sport. Looking back at this period, the *SWDN* in 1892 recalled that "Pressmen of the old school seemed to have tumbled to the fact that a game which was attracting the attention of thousands week after week was worth shedding ink over."[30] The first accounts of what were clearly rugby matches appeared in the early 1870s but these were very sporadic and brief.[31] Reflecting the growing numbers playing the game, by the mid 1870s, reports began to appear more frequently and in more detail.[32] As early as 1877, what might be described as the first Monday sports page emerged, when the *Western Mail* published four match reports together.[33] Further evidence of the game's increasing hold is revealed a year later when rugby was mentioned in a *Western Mail* editorial for the first time.[34] Events beyond mere on-field activities were now regularly commented on, such as the banquet given in honour of the victorious Newport cup team of 1878.[35] By the end of the decade, both Cardiff papers were full of detail about the game: regular and comprehensive match accounts, team lists, reports of meetings, cup draws, disputes, complaints, letters and dedicated columns in Monday editions. A close study of the Cardiff dailies, therefore, demonstrates just how rapidly interest had grown during the 1870s. Gradually the number of columns devoted to rugby football in the Monday edition increased, so that by 1896 in the *SWDN* at least, rugby reports and analysis sometimes took up nearly two of the paper's eight pages. As Andrew Croll points out, the greater press coverage being given to sport by this time meant that it was difficult for readers – even those with little interest – to ignore it.[36]

A surprisingly large amount of coverage was devoted to the results and even accounts of grass roots matches. The *SWDN* even provided a special form for local clubs to send in match reports post free.[37] In the last decades of the century, the two main papers' evening and weekly titles (*South Wales Echo, Evening Express, Cardiff Times, Weekly Mail*) also dealt with the game more frequently. The evening papers, in particular, began to take on more regular day-to-day coverage with, for instance, further commentary by sports columnists like "Old Stager". The special late Saturday edition was another device adopted to cash in on the seemingly limitless interest in rugby. An early example was the special Saturday edition of the *South Wales Echo* printed for the 1885 international in Edinburgh.[38] The publication of the forthcoming week's fixtures became a regular practice in the 1880s as did that of local team selections in the 1890s. Money prizes for predicting the results of leading Welsh club matches were also sometimes offered.[39] The use of photography would have to wait until the twentieth century but artists' drawings of the scenes at the game occasionally accompanied major match reports, whilst pen pictures of leading personalities became a regular feature of the sports columns from the mid 1880s.[40] However, by the turn of the century the amount of space devoted to rugby began to diminish somewhat, mainly to accommodate the greater coverage being given to soccer, particularly English Football League matches and subsequently local ones. The most affected by this development were *local* rugby clubs, who were less frequently reported than before, though senior rugby was still covered with the same enthusiasm.[41] The amount of space devoted to the South African War during the 1899–1900 season inevitably meant that the reporting of all sport, including major matches, was reduced significantly.

The great interest in rugby in Wales inevitably led to an increased commercialisation of the game itself. By the 1890s, Cardiff had become a major gate-taking club, with a substantial annual income. It was now effectively a business in its own right and this was recognised in 1892, when the club secretary began to be paid for his services.[42] According to "Old Stager" in 1898, a game which should have been a pastime was fast becoming a business.[43] During this decade, five figure attendances at the Arms Park were frequently reported. Commenting on various press estimates of the crowd at the Llwynypia v Cardiff match in 1897, which varied from 6,000 to 16,000, "Welsh Athlete" reminded readers, "Popular estimates of the sizes of football crowds are, as a rule, far too large ... [But it] is a significant fact of the extreme interest taken in football by the masses." Whilst such figures may have been exaggerations, they do indicate that there was a substantial and growing interest in watching the club game.[44] If the reported figures are accepted at face value, then throughout the 1890s, Cardiff often played in front of crowds in excess of 10,000, while key games, especially with Newport, could attract as many as 20,000 supporters. The *Western Mail* even claimed that such was the rivalry between these two clubs that interest in their games sometimes exceeded that of international matches. "Whatever may be the interest attached to international ... games, so far as Cardiff and Newport are concerned, it pales before the fierce fire of enthusiasm that burns on the occasion of matches between the towns." The two clubs were, after all, according to the *Western Mail*, Britain's "leading exponents" of the game.[45] Fixtures against Blackheath and against Christmas and Easter touring sides were also highly popular and could draw crowds of over 15,000. In 1899, 20,000 attended Cardiff's matches with Swansea and the Barbarians.[46]

The social composition of these match crowds is difficult to determine precisely, though given their size and the character of local participation in rugby, there must have been many working-class spectators. References to the mixed social character of the crowds were often made in the press. "Spectators at local games are derived from all classes of society".[47] Workmen's tickets were introduced by Cardiff in 1890 when 968 were sold, equal to the number of members' and season tickets.[48] In 1892, out of 2,700 members' and season tickets sold, nearly 1,700 were workmen's.[49] In 1897, club membership was the largest in Wales at 1,200 and by 1899 this had grown to 2,000.[50] One Cardiff supporter clearly believed the club belonged to the whole community, and not just the elite, when he wrote in 1892 about the "general public, who are in reality the shareholders [of Cardiff]".[51] This is an interesting viewpoint and it contrasts with today's acceptance that modern professional rugby teams can be owned and controlled by a small number of very wealthy patrons.

Throughout the period, there were frequent references in the press to supporters who attempted to gain access to matches without paying and, no doubt serving the prejudices of a predominantly middle-class readership, it was usually implied that these were members of the feckless lower orders. Working-class "hobbledehoy rowdies" were blamed for crowd disturbances, for example, at the Cardiff v Newport match in 1897, when the referee was attacked and the Arms Park suspended as a result.[52] There is also little doubt about whom the *SWDN* had in mind when it reported on the behaviour at the Cardiff and District cup finals in 1897.

[There was] no excuse for the disgraceful language used by a number of roughs who had ensconced themselves at the back of the stand and who, notwithstanding the presence of several ladies, criticised the play of the teams in brutal 'Billingsgate'.[53]

The reference to women attending matches was not unusual. They are mentioned in the very earliest match reports, for example, "several ladies and gentlemen favoured the players with their presence" at a Glamorgan FC game at Sophia Gardens in 1874.[54] When Wales played their first ever away match in Dublin in 1882, *The Irish Times* revealed that two Welsh women had travelled to watch the game.[55] Early references to female supporters may have been made to challenge the belief, widely held at the time, that rugby was an "uncivilised" activity. Numbers are always difficult, if not impossible, to estimate but, for example, "hundreds of ladies" were reported to have been at the 1891 Cardiff v Gloucester fixture which was attended by 7,000.[56] It was customary for women to sit in the stands free of charge. By 1898, there were complaints at the Cardiff AGM that they were monopolising the grandstand. Nevertheless, the policy of allowing women to attend free of charge, so long as they were accompanied by a member, was continued, despite a (presumably jocular) criticism that their hats were too large.[57] Such occasional press reports, therefore, demonstrate that watching rugby in Cardiff was certainly not a totally male preoccupation.

As a result of growing membership and attendances, the Cardiff club's income also rose steadily, although reports of its increasing prosperity were not necessarily always well received. In 1889, there was some falling-out with the Marquis of Bute over match entrance fees. He had become concerned about rumours that Cardiff were using this income on lavish dinners and other benefits for members but he was assured by the committee that the money was needed to maintain and develop the ground in the wider interests of the town's prestige. "The club [is] not an individual enterprise. It was for the honour of the town that they charged for admission."[58] Whatever the truth of this pious argument, it seems to have been accepted by the Marquis. No doubt it was largely for his benefit that it was announced at the 1897 AGM that the club was run purely in the interest of sport and that no other club in Britain could boast of such a good record in charitable donations.[59] There does seem to have been some substance in this last claim, as will be seen.

Cardiff did have considerable financial liabilities in maintaining a ground suitable for first-class club and international matches. The pitch was a particular and a continual problem. The ancient course of the Taff had been diverted from what became the Arms Park not many years earlier, so the playing surface and surrounding areas were frequently muddy and occasionally flooded.[60] After the Llanelli match in 1884, "Old Stager" complained of having to wade through "a dreary expanse of mud and slush" to get to the pitch which was covered in "numerous miniature lakes".[61] In another game the following season, the whole of one side of the pitch was under water and the players' struggles in the wet caused great amusement for the spectators.[62] When Cardiff played the Maoris in 1888, the ground was "in a deplorable state, wet, muddy, with pools of water on the pitch."[63] As late as the Thursday before the Scotland match in 1890, the playing area was still entirely under water.[64] In the depth of winter, it was often necessary to use straw to protect the playing surface from freezing, whilst the arrangements to ensure that the 1893 England international could go ahead have become part of rugby's folk lore and these are discussed later.[65] Eventually in 1895, the poor conditions necessitated taking up the whole of the playing surface, laying new drains and re-turfing the pitch at a cost of over £1,000.[66]

This did not permanently solve the problem and as recently as 1960 the Arms Park suffered from very severe flooding when the entire ground was covered by a metre of water.[67]

With the growing numbers of spectators came increasing demands to improve facilities. There was constant pressure for new accommodation, such as grandstands and standing areas, press boxes, fencing to replace ropes around the pitch, footboards and paths etc. After 20,000 attended the 1894 Newport game, "Old Stager" warned that the club could not afford to be complacent and recommended the building of yet another stand. "That the expenditure on accommodation for visitors ... has been lavish everyone will admit, but the committee must keep in mind the fact that football is increasing in popularity and that the population of the town is growing."[68] C.S. Arthur was secretary of Cardiff at the time and his 1908 club history details the continual annual expenditure on improvements. For instance, the first grandstand was built in 1885 for £362 and two wings were added eight years later at a cost of £437, providing seating for 1,200. In 1890, new standing areas were constructed along the entire length of the ground for £254 and these were enlarged for £106 in 1894. Another £103 was spent on repairing and erecting new stands in 1896.[69] More care had to be taken with the standard of construction following the collapse of a stand at the river end during a match with Swinton in 1893, which resulted in compensation payments being made to several injured spectators.[70] As a result of all this expenditure, the club chairman was able to boast – clearly with the WFU in mind – that only three other grounds in the kingdom, "Crystal Palace, Aston Villa and Everton", could have accommodated the crowd of perhaps 40,000 which attended the Ireland international in March 1899.[71] The WFU appear to have taken note, as in 1900 Cardiff entered into an agreement to increase standing and seating accommodation, with the Union bearing three-quarters of the cost. This began the process which eventually led to the Welsh Rugby Union taking over the ownership of the ground in 1968 when the Cardiff club moved onto to its present site on the adjacent former cricket area. Because of the central location of the Arms Park, these ground developments added a prominent and distinctive new feature to the townscape of Victorian Cardiff.[72]

Improvements to the ground and accommodation, therefore, were a constant drain on the club's resources, but at the same time they provided occasional business for local architects, builders, contractors and suppliers, as well as employment for local tradesmen and casual workers. Although it was the WFU, rather than the Cardiff club, which met the bill, the scale of the arrangements for ensuring the pitch was playable for the 1893 England match is worth mentioning. Some fifty-eight men were employed for five days before the match attending the coal fires in the 500 buckets and the thirty hot boiler plates which were placed around the ground. At noon on match day another fifteen men were taken on to clear the pitch. Around eighteen tons of coal were burned and the total cost of the operation amounted to over £200. This remarkable event is indicative of the importance of coal in the Welsh economy and in the making of Cardiff in particular.[73]

For some clubs, the financial burden of ground costs could be too great to sustain. After Cardiff Harlequins took a lease from the Tredegar Estate on a former brick field in Roath, they spent a massive £2,000 in preparing the football field and cycling track and erecting stands, changing accommodation and fencing.[74] This over-ambitious expenditure certainly contributed to the club's eventual demise, though their enterprise was not totally wasted, as the "The Harlequins" has been used predominantly by rugby teams ever since. It hosted a Welsh trial in 1892, the South Wales Challenge Cup final in 1893, the first ever Mallett Cup final in 1894 and a Glamorgan County rugby match against Lancashire in 1895. For over seventy years, it served as the Cardiff High School sports field, while from 1947 to 1961 it was Cardiff High School Old Boys' rugby ground and is now the home of St. Peter's RFC.[75]

In an age when the State took little responsibility even for the most disadvantaged in society, it is not surprising that Welsh rugby became actively involved in supporting charity, notwithstanding the heavy burdens mentioned above. Cardiff's steadily improving financial position enabled the club to make regular contributions to local charities. Arthur's history shows that from 1890–1 onwards, large donations, often of several hundreds of pounds, were made each year.[76] For instance, in 1892–3, the club established a scholarship at Cardiff University. Sometimes special matches might be arranged, such as that with a Cardiff District XV in 1890 for the Llanerch Colliery disaster fund. Alternatively, the whole proceeds of the gate might be donated, as happened with the 1892 Swansea match, following the Tondu Park Slip Colliery explosion. By 1897, the club had donated over £3,000 to charity which was claimed to be a record for a sports club anywhere in Britain.[77] Even the *Sheffield Daily Telegraph* wrote, "There is a good deal to admire in a club which can be so openhanded as this ... a somewhat refreshing oasis in a dreary wilderness."[78] As well as distributing club funds, Cardiff allowed teams, such as boilermakers and cabmen, to use the Arms Park for specific charities and leading players would often turn out in these games to help boost the takings. The WFU too also contributed to Cardiff charities, for example the Infirmary and the Nazareth House orphanage.[79] Several local Catholic organisations were beneficiaries and this may reflect the anxiety of rugby administrators to gratify their landlord, the Marquis of Bute, who was a prominent convert to Roman Catholicism. That the game was able to display such generosity not only reveals that it was in a healthy condition by the 1890s, but also that it saw itself as an integral part of the social fabric. Such charitable contributions were also important in cementing the wider perception of sports clubs in general, and Cardiff rugby club in particular, as community and civic institutions.

It is sometimes alleged that the commercialisation of the game must have inevitably led to the payment of players. There is no doubt that broken time payments were being paid in Wales, though even the most successful valley clubs did not have huge resources for this. Arranging employment at the local pit may have been as common as making direct cash payments, though it was still a breach of the professional regulations. Eric Dunning and Kenneth Sheard, however, imply that Cardiff must have paid their players during the 1890s, given the substantial sums which the club received from gate money. They draw on the details of Cardiff's gate receipts (though these were hardly representative of Welsh clubs in general as claimed) which were published in *Report on Rugby* (1959) by Morgan and Nicholson.[80] These authors obtained the figures unacknowledged from C.S. Arthur's 1908 club history. Dunning and Sheard quote from *Report on Rugby* that "clubs were soon making enough money to pay players' ... expenses, if not more." Because Cardiff had enough money to pay players, the argument seems to run, they must have done so.

What this does not take into account, however, are the very substantial expenditures which Cardiff regularly incurred in charitable donations, support for local rugby, match expenses and guarantees, and, importantly, ground maintenance and development. Whilst there is no doubt that Cardiff players were looked after very well, not least because an ambitious fixture list involved very heavy travelling and hotel expenditures, there is no *evidence* that the club regularly made direct cash payments and Morgan and Nicholson do not provide any. In 1895, "Welsh Athlete" commented, somewhat critically, that since wealthy Welsh clubs could afford to pay for boots, jerseys, rail fares and hotels and "every tittle tattle of expenses", players were more or less professional compared to earlier times. But he did not accuse clubs of directly paying players, though he did prophesise that while it "may not come for some time" one day it would happen.[81] There are a number of reasons which suggest that it is unlikely that Cardiff regularly paid players as a matter of course. There was the risk that the Marquis of Bute might reconsider their use of the Arms Park, if it became known that they were not operating as an essentially amateur operation. In addition, Dunning and Sheard argue that rugby in Wales was controlled by men who did not "adhere to the amateur ethos". There may be some truth in this but the example of Cardiff is a not a good one. Most of the senior officials who controlled the club at this time probably would not have agreed to the regular payment of players. Some leading Welsh club officials *were* undoubtedly in favour of broken time payments around the time of the Northern Union break-away, but Cardiff (and Newport) were known to be strongly opposed to, or "dead against", the practice.[82] In 1901, the *Evening Express* suggested that "veiled professionalism" was so rampant in south Wales that some believed even Cardiff was not "free from the taint."[83] However, it continued, if that were the case, leading committeemen would resign. Finally, the number of working-class Cardiff players who did sign for professional Northern Union clubs at this time suggests that there was no great financial benefit for them to remain in Cardiff.

A Popular Urban Culture

Clearly, in many ways then, rugby had a much greater impact on the urban life of Victorian Cardiff than has previously been acknowledged by historians of the city. Discussing Cardiff's cultural amenities around the 1850s to the 1870s, Professor William Rees, in his history of Cardiff, refers to the Cardiff Athenaeum, the Classical Society, the Blue Ribbon Choir, the Cardiff Naturalists Society and many other similar worthy organisations. However, apart from a brief reference to the formation of Cardiff Cricket Club, he entirely ignores the new popular culture of sport which, as we have seen, was beginning to develop such a powerful hold on many of the town's citizens. Admittedly, in a footnote, Rees adds, "More organised sport was at this time becoming popular" but the only example he is able to provide of this popularity is a brief account of two Cardiff climbers who died on Mont Blanc.[84] Yet, just as in Yorkshire and Lancashire in the late nineteenth century, rugby became one of the major forms of mass entertainment in the town.[85] In a society where the quality of civic life may have been limited compared to that in older and more prestigious cities, success in sport would have been enthusiastically embraced.

Mitchell and Kenyon's recently discovered films, which portray British urban life around the turn of the century, vividly reveal how important street society was at the time.[86] Therefore, the presence of large numbers of footballers and supporters congregating on public parks or trudging back to their headquarters every Saturday must have been a familiar part of the urban scene to everyone, even the uninterested. Also, the huge crowds of merry, money-spending supporters of all classes, regularly converging on the town centre for major club matches and internationals, quickly became a distinguishing characteristic of life in Cardiff, as it remains to this day.

For the Llanelli game in 1894, "Cosmopolitan Cardiff ... was thoroughly Welsh on Saturday afternoon", while a month later, "Half the male population of Cardiff, and not a few of the gentler sex ... seemed to have found their way to the Park and its neighbourhood" to watch the match against their keenest rivals Newport.[87] In 1895, when Ireland were the visitors to the Arms Park:

On the roofs of the neighbouring business premises, warehouses etc. were hundreds of sightseers; in the trees a large number perched themselves, while some were even daring enough to plant themselves on the roof of the press box.[88]

The *South Wales Daily News'* description of the atmosphere in Cardiff, on the occasion of the 1899 Triple Crown decider against Ireland, is still entirely recognisable in the twenty-first century. "Westgate Street presented an extraordinary appearance. The road would have done credit to a Continental thoroughfare on a fete day."[89] The composition of these crowds reflected Welsh society. At the Scotland match in 1896, the *Western Mail* noted the presence of colliers, tinplaters, Cardiff workmen ("not always Welsh"), Cardiff "mashers", coal-trimmers, "pale young" curates and ladies, who were "beyond description". There were even dissenting ministers, for "all the chapels in the world would not keep folks from the match."[90]

David Smith and Gareth Williams perceptively reveal how Welsh rugby had become the people's theatre.[91] Perhaps it is not surprising, then, that the theatre itself was quick to reflect this new popular culture. To promote their annual pantomimes, the casts of both the Theatre Royal and the Grand Theatre regularly played each other at rugby on the Arms Park. The 1890 pantomime at the Grand included a song about the "bold blue and black" as well as a "Great Football Ballet ... the sensation of Cardiff".[92] The Whitsun production at the Theatre Royal in 1886 was even *set* in the Arms Park during a match, and was called *Football, or, Life in Cardiff.*[93] The *SWDN* announced that "For once the national winter pastime of Wales has changed both its habitat and its season, for during the present week "Football" occupies the boards of the Theatre Royal instead of the Cardiff Arms Park." The play's hit comic song was a version of *Crawshay Bailey's Engine* adapted to the members of Hancock's record-breaking team and it was received with such "enthusiastic acclamation" that several encores had to be given.[94] Here is another vivid example of just how far rugby had entered into the lifeblood of Victorian Cardiff.

As indicated in the report on the Theatre Royal production, by the 1880s, the Welsh press was regularly referring to rugby football as the national sport. Before the England international in Swansea in 1885, "Old Stager" claimed that the game had increased so greatly in popularity over the previous three or four years that it was "now recognised as a national pastime."[95] After the match, which Wales lost, he wrote of "the strong hold football has secured on the affections of a large portion of the inhabitants of South Wales", adding that it monopolised conversation so much that people forgot all about the safety of General Gordon and the Fenian outrages.[96] In Cardiff's pubs and hotels, too, rugby football was often the main topic of conversation, sometimes involving those who weren't even regular followers of the game. As early as 1890, the *SWDN* detected what has become a perennial characteristic of the Welsh. "Football strongly affects our social barometer – one week very stormy, another set fair."[97] The same paper announced on the morning of the 1891 England match in Cardiff that "it has now become the one great popular pastime of the people".[98]

After he had turned out for Richmond against Liverpool in 1893, the Welsh international Norman Biggs made some revealing remarks about the attitudes to rugby in Cardiff compared to those in some other parts of Britain. "What is the great difference between the London match and a Cardiff game? ... At Richmond there was no need to exert myself, and nobody cared much who won – that's the difference."[99] Nobody cared! But not everyone was necessarily impressed with this obsession with mere sport. The *SWDN* columnist "Cosmos" was one such critic, though his remarks are still worth repeating as they reveal a great deal about the place rugby enjoyed in the new popular urban culture. When visiting the *Pier Head Restaurant* at Cardiff docks after the 1891 England international match, he stopped to listen to the conversations of "the usual crowd of loafers" and had this to say about the encounter:

It was not the slackness of times; it was not Parnell; it was not the Disestablishment of the Church; it was not the utilization of the Welsh language, though from their accent, they were purely Welsh; it was not the strike in Scotland; it was not the selection of the head-constable of Glamorganshire; it was not intermediate education; it was not total abstinence; it was not the lowness of freights or the price of coal; it was not the severity of the weather – but what I heard was something about the backs being absolutely superior, and the forwards heeling out. I knew then the most absorbing topic of interest. The fact that there are twelve vessels laid up in Cardiff Docks ... idle; the fact that wages are declining – arts, industry may fade, *but who cares as long as there is a football match, and sixpence with which to see it?*[100]

Notes

1. Neil Tranter, *Sport, Economy and Society in Britain, 1750–1914* (Cambridge. 1998), p. 34.
2. *SWDN* 21 Dec. 1885.
3. *SWDN* 30 Oct. 1890.
4. *SWDN* 15 Jan. 1894.
5. John Williams, *Was Wales Industrialised? Essays in Modern Welsh History* (Llandysul, 1995), p. 42.
6. R.H. Morgan, "The Development of an Urban Transport System: The Case of Cardiff", *Welsh History Review*, 13, 2 (1986), pp. 178–181.
7. *SWDN* 1 Oct. 1891, 4 Apr. 1892.
8. *The Handy Football Guide (Mortimer's) For South Wales and Monmouthshire: 1896–97* (Cardiff, 1896), p.19.
9. *SWDN* 1 Oct. 1891. Spectators travelled "by rail, bus, or boat" to the Penarth v Cardiff match.
10. *SWDN* 10 Mar. 1893.
11. M.J. Daunton, *Coal Metropolis: Cardiff 1870–1914* (Leicester, 1977), p. 54.
12. Licensed Premises (Alehouses and Beerhouses) in Cardiff: Report of the Chief Constable, 1903.
13. *SWDN* 9 Mar. 1891.
14. WFU minutes 11 Feb. 1893.
15. Wales returned to Stradey in February 1998 when Italy were defeated 23–20.
16. *SWDN* 16 Jan. 1888 (italics added).
17. *SWDN* 9 Jan. 1893 (italics added).
18. *SWDN* 9 Nov. 1893. The Mallett Cup is still the premier competition for Cardiff and District clubs.
19. *SWDN* 28 Aug. 1886; *Cardiff District Football Union Handbook 1886–87* (Cardiff. 1886), p. [3].
20. *SWDN* 28 Apr. 1890.
21. *Cardiff Argus* 26 Sept. 1888.
22. *The Welsh Athlete and West of England Cycling News Football Handbook 1891–2* (Cardiff, 1891), p. [5]. The preface refers to its being the seventh edition of the "Football Handbook". Later versions were produced by other publishers.
23. *Cardiff and South Wales Footballer's Companion: 1890–91* (Cardiff, 1890), pp. 28, 30, 32; *Welsh Athlete Football Handbook 1891–2*, p. [2].
24. *Welsh Athlete Football Handbook 1891–2*, p. [47] (Evans); *Mortimer's Football Guide for South Wales and Monmouthshire: Season, 1894–95*, p. 42 (Anderson's); *SWDN* 24 Oct. 1896 (medals).
25. *Handy Football Guide: 1896–97*, pp. [20] (Goldie), [16] (Dando).
26. *SWDN* 14 Oct. 1889.
27. Kenneth O. Morgan, *Rebirth of a Nation: Wales 1880–1980* (Oxford, 1982 edn.), p. 51.
28. *WM* 17 Nov. 1892.
29. *WM* 9 Nov. 1892.
30. *SWDN* 7 Nov. 1892.
31. See for example, *WM* 9 Nov. 1871, *SWDN* 29 Nov. 1872.
32. See for example, *SWDN* 24 Nov. 1874, 18 Jan. 1875.
33. *WM* 26 February 1877. The games were Llandovery College v Carmarthen Wanderers, Roath v Ely, Pontypool v Aberdare and Newport v Hereford. Team lists were included.

34. *WM* 4 Mar. 1878.
35. *WM* 25 Apr. 1878.
36. Andrew J. Croll, *Civilizing the Urban: Popular Culture, Public Space and Urban Meaning, Merthyr c. 1870–1914* (PhD thesis, University of Wales, Cardiff, 1997), p. 257.
37. *SWDN* 13 Sept. 1887.
38. *SWDN* 12 Jan. 1885.
39. *WM* 13 Nov. 1895.
40. See for example *WM* 20 Mar. 1899 (match scenes); *WM* 8 Feb. 1886 (pen picture of Alex Duncan).
41. For example, *SWDN* 16 Jan. 1899.
42. *SWDN* 25 July 1892.
43. *SWDN* 21 Feb. 1898.
44. *WM* 20 Oct. 1897.
45. *WM* 25 Nov. 1895.
46. Match reports *SWDN* and *WM* 1891–1900 passim.
47. *WM* 27 Jan. 1897.
48. C.S. Arthur, *The Cardiff Rugby Football Club: History and Statistics, 1876–1906* (Cardiff, 1908), p. 102.
49. *WM* 18 July 1892.
50. *SWDN* 20 Oct. 1897; *WM* 29 July 1899.
51. *WM* 5 Jan. 1892.
52. *SWDN* 15 Feb. 1897.
53. *SWDN* 15 Mar. 1897.
54. *WM* 26 Oct. 1874.
55. *Irish Times* 30 Jan. 1882.
56. *WM* 16 Nov. 1891.
57. *SWDN* 30 July 1898.
58. *SWDN* 29 Aug. 1889.
59. *SWDN* 31 July 1897.
60. Gareth Williams, *1905 and All That: Essays on Rugby Football, Sport and Welsh Society* (Llandysul, 1991), pp. 56–7. The river was diverted between 1848 and 1856.
61. *SWDN* 22 Dec. 1884.
62. *SWDN* 12 Oct. 1885.
63. Gareth Williams, "Taffs Acre: The Pre-1900 Years", in David Parry-Jones, *Taffs Acre: History and Celebration of Cardiff Arms Park* (London, 1984), pp. 43–4.
64. *SWDN* 3 Feb. 1890.
65. Williams, *Taffs Acre*, p. 43.
66. Arthur, *Cardiff Rugby*, p. 122.
67. D.E. Davies, *Cardiff Rugby Club: History and Statistics, 1876–1975: "The Greatest"* (Cardiff, 1975) p. 141. Most of Cardiff RFC's early records were lost in these floods.
68. *SWDN* 22 Oct. 1894.
69. Arthur, *Cardiff Rugby*, pp. 64–138; *SWDN* 27 Oct. 1890.
70. *SWDN* 29 July 1893.
71. *WM* and *SWDN* 29 July 1899.
72. Arthur, *Cardiff Rugby*, p. 157. See Hignell and Prescott, *Cardiff Sporting Greats*, pp. 31–3, 184–6, 211–12 for the history of developments at Cardiff Arms Park.
73. Williams, *Taffs Acre*, p. 43; *SWDN* 9 Jan. 1893; *WM* 5, 7 Jan. 1893.
74. *SWDN* 10 Oct. 1892.
75. Hignell and Prescott, *Cardiff Sporting Greats*, pp. 158–9.
76. Arthur, *Cardiff Rugby*, pp. 102–128.

77. Arthur, *Cardiff Rugby*, pp. 96, 113; *SWDN* 20 Oct. 1897. See, however, Tony Collins, *Rugby's Great Split: Class, Culture and the Origins of Rugby League Football* (London, 2006 edn.), p. 83 for details of northern clubs' donations to charity.

78. Quoted in *SWDN* 26 Oct. 1897.

79. *SWDN* 14 Apr. 1896.

80. Eric Dunning and Kenneth Sheard, *Barbarians, Gentlemen and Players: A Sociological Study of the Development of Rugby Football* (London, 2005 edn.), p. 191; William J. Morgan and Geoffrey Nicholson, *Report on Rugby* (London, 1959), p. 78.

81. *WM* 12 Aug. 1895.

82. *SWDN* 25 Sept. 1893 ("Dead against" broken time).

83. *Evening Express* 20 April 1901.

84. William Rees, *A History of Cardiff* (Cardiff, 1969 edn.), pp. 326–7, footnote 116.

85. Tony Collins, *A Social History of English Rugby Union* (London, 2009), p. 27.

86. *The Lost World of Mitchell and Kenyon*, (DVD), (BBC, 2005).

87. *SWDN* 12 Feb. 1894 (Llanelli), 5 Mar. 1894 (Newport).

88. *SWDN* 18 Mar. 1895.

89. *SWDN* 20 Mar. 1899.

90. *WM* 27 Jan. 1896. A "masher" was someone who dressed or behaved in a way to attract susceptible young women.

91. David Smith and Gareth Williams, *Fields of Praise: The Official History of the Welsh Rugby Union 1881–1981* (Cardiff, 1980), p. 75; see also David Smith, "People's Theatre – A Century of Welsh Rugby", *History Today*, 31, March (1981), pp. 31–6.

92. *SWDN* 27 Dec. 1890. The "bold blue and black" was a common term for the Cardiff club at the time. They adopted their distinctive Cambridge blue and black colours in 1877. See Arthur, *Cardiff Rugby*, p. 10.

93. *SWDN* 17 June 1886.

94. *SWDN* 15 June 1886.

95. *SWDN* 2 Jan. 1885.

96. *SWDN* 5 Jan. 1885.

97. *SWDN* 22 Nov. 1890.

98. *SWDN* 3 Jan.1891.

99. *WM* 28 Oct. 1893.

100. *SWDN* 6 Jan. 1891 (italics added).

7

CONCLUSIONS

'The noble game is not totally unknown here'

The last three decades of the nineteenth century, therefore, witnessed nothing less than a transformation in the sporting life of Cardiff. By the end of the century, the interest and participation in rugby had reached a level which would have been unimaginable to the pioneers of only thirty years earlier. During the 1860s, football was played across south Wales but it was sporadic and unstructured. Hybrid rules were the norm. The evidence suggests that the participants were middle and upper class. The comparatively late arrival of rugby is partly explained by the relatively small Welsh middle class and by the absence in the main urban centres of any large public schools and universities, which helped to establish the game elsewhere. It was eventually introduced mainly by old boys and masters from the major rugby playing public schools, especially those located in the west country. Locally, private and grammar schools were probably as important as the Welsh public schools.

The arrival of the game coincided with the demographic and industrial transformation of Wales and, during the 1870s, Welsh rugby too changed out of all recognition. What had been a minority and elite leisure pastime at the beginning of the decade was becoming, ten years later, a consuming passion enjoyed across the community. By this time, there were well over a hundred teams in existence.

The first organised rugby clubs began to emerge around 1870. One of the earliest, if not the earliest, was located in Cardiff, thereby placing the town, in contrast to the prevailing view, at the very heart of the origin of the game in Wales. Within a few years, rugby became the established form of football played in south Wales. By the mid 1870s, all the major Welsh clubs had been formed; local organisation of the game was improving; and interest was beginning to spread beyond the game's original narrow social base. For the next two decades, association football remained very much a minority activity. It was, however, mainly in the coastal towns of Cardiff, Newport, Swansea and Llanelli, and not the coalfield valleys as is sometimes assumed, that Welsh enthusiasm for the game first materialised.

The demand for representative and competitive rugby emerged very early and in response to this the South Wales Football Club was founded in 1875 and the South Wales Challenge Cup inaugurated in 1877. Despite the infancy of the game in Wales, this appears to have been the first major open cup competition in Britain. It had an immediate and lasting effect and was widely acknowledged by contemporaries as one of the main reasons for the game's subsequent popularity in Wales. Its early introduction reveals that competitiveness and inter-town rivalry was emerging even *before* the arrival of the working man. This was fuelled by the growing economic and political rivalry between the leading Welsh towns and it resulted in an increasing incidence of match disputes and disruption, sometimes involving violence by both players and supporters. As the events at the Newport-Cardiff cup match in 1880 show, this was happening before participation by working-class players was significant.

The first clubs were founded by the social elite for their own recreation. However, this soon changed. For instance, the merger of Cardiff Wanderers and Glamorgan in 1876 had the specific objective of creating a team which would be more representative of Cardiff in its matches with its rivals. Though hard evidence is difficult to locate, by the end of the 1870s, Welsh working men were beginning to take up rugby.

Increasing competitiveness, especially in the cup, was matched by growing attendances. The two fed on each other. By the end of the decade, match crowds of thousands were being reported at major games. This was probably how many working men were drawn into the game, first as spectators, then as players. The middle class in Wales was relatively small, so as new clubs sprang up, they could not afford to turn potential players away simply because of their social background. Similarly, if senior clubs wished to compete successfully, particularly with strong English teams, they *had* to select from a wider pool. This was a decisive turning point in the history of the Welsh game. Had working-class players been shut out, as happened elsewhere, then rugby in Wales would have stagnated and would never have risen much above English county standard, as was experienced in other sports. But crucially, civic and national pride was more important than social exclusivity. Before long, of course, workmen offered more than just making up the numbers. It was soon recognised that they possessed new and valuable qualities which could enhance the Welsh game. It was such players who would eventually provide sufficient fire and muscle to the pack to enable Wales to unleash Cardiff's four three-quarter system with such effect in the first "Golden Era" of 1899 to 1910 when, following the victory over New Zealand, they were regarded as the unofficial world champions.

The 1880-1 season was a vitally important one as it saw the formation of the Welsh Football Union which could now harness the game's enormous potential and, at the same time, control the wilder excesses of the growing number of its adherents. The same year also saw the first appearance of the Welsh international team. This at last gave a national focus around which the game – in south Wales at least – could coalesce and, within a year, rugby was already being described as the national sport. The Cardiff club was closely involved in both these developments.

The growth in interest in both playing and watching rugby was as strong in Cardiff as anywhere in Wales. Whilst popular sport in the Victorian period has been largely ignored by the city's historians, it is clear that it had a major influence on the life of Cardiff. The emergence of rugby as a popular pastime, enjoyed by all classes in Cardiff, cannot be divorced from the huge economic, demographic and social changes experienced by the town in the second half of the nineteenth century. These were to influence markedly the particular character of rugby in Cardiff.

In some respects, Cardiff's sporting culture was different from that of many other towns in Britain. Rugby dominated; it enjoyed cross-class support; and, at the neighbourhood level, social improvers were not particularly prominent. Within Wales, Cardiff was distinctive in several ways. There was the sheer number of its clubs and players. Though working-class participation was strong, there was, nevertheless, a notable middle-class involvement. The archetypal Welsh club team, comprised entirely of hard-bitten colliers, so beloved of some writers, simply did not exist in Cardiff but there were plenty of teams which included equally tough dockers and coal-trimmers. The pronounced attachment to the game of the town's Catholic schools and parishes was another distinguishing aspect of the local game. These features, and others touched on below, helped to create the distinctive character of Cardiff "district" rugby.

Cardiff became the largest town in Wales from the 1870s, mainly by attracting large numbers of young migrants. Given the town's growing industrial and commercial prominence, these newcomers included many members of the mercantile and professional classes. It should not be a surprise, therefore, that Cardiff was a focus for early Welsh rugby. It is surprising, however, that occasionally some commentators have suggested that Cardiff lagged behind other centres in Wales in taking up the game. Even in 1878, the Cardiff captain, Raoul Foa, was forced to respond to a letter in the local press which suggested that there was no club in the town. Evidently irritated by this, he felt it necessary to reply somewhat understatedly that "the noble game is not totally unknown here."[1]

A close study of local newspapers has revealed a previously unrecognised scale of participation in rugby during the years 1870 to 1900. Whilst the research was largely confined mainly to Cardiff, it does suggest that the extent of rugby's penetration into nineteenth-century Wales was even greater than has previously been assumed. Therefore, simply relying on the number of clubs in membership of the WFU as an indication of the game's popularity clearly grossly underestimates the actual extent of the popularity of the game.

Whilst many of the "clubs" identified were short lived or transient, their existence nevertheless provides a measure of the depth of interest in the game. During the first eight years of the 1890s, there were, on average, over 200 teams each season in the Cardiff locality. The sheer numbers involved in playing the game in the town, therefore, calls into question the often expressed contention that Welsh rugby was essentially a valleys phenomenon. Only by the late 1890s are there signs of a decline in participation in Cardiff. This occurred partly because soccer at last began to penetrate the sporting culture of the town, largely as a result of the introduction of the game in elementary schools and the arrival of migrants from soccer playing regions.

Rugby had become firmly entrenched as the main sporting interest of the town's middle and working classes by the 1880s. It provided an accessible means by which many newcomers could identify with their host community, show allegiance to it and enter into its social life. In so doing, it acted as a "social cement", helping to develop a sense of neighbourhood, civic and national identity amongst a diverse population.

The detailed analysis of the background of clubs contrasts with the results of research into English soccer at this time. Though there *were* many church, workplace and pub teams in Cardiff, their overall importance was much less marked. They comprised only around a quarter of all teams, which was considerably lower than suggested in some studies of English soccer. In addition, with the notable exception of a few Catholic parish clubs, they rarely featured amongst the strongest local adult teams.

The relatively smaller number of church teams may be partly explained by the general opposition to sport and its associated activities by Welsh nonconformists and by the antipathy towards "uncivilised" rugby by religious organisations in general. Catholic authorities seem to have been rather less concerned about this, recognising no doubt that rugby could act as a useful bridgehead for the assimilation of Irish Catholics into the wider community. The relatively low number of workplace teams is partly a reflection of the nature of Cardiff's industrial economy, where there was little manufacturing and where many workers were employed in casual waterfront occupations. Neither case of church nor workplace, therefore, suggests that there was a strong element of middle-class "social control" in the establishment and organisation of rugby in Cardiff. The number of pub teams was insignificant though since most clubs used public houses as their headquarters, their contribution to the game was, nevertheless, still immense.

On the other hand, neighbourhood and street teams were clearly the overwhelming choice of most players. Research into rugby in Rochdale produced similar findings, which may perhaps indicate there were different emphases in club formation in the two branches of football but clearly this requires much further investigation. In one of the most rapidly growing towns in Britain, the popularity of neighbourhood teams was probably a response to the need to accommodate newcomers quickly into the game, avoiding the necessity of membership of a pre-existing organisation, such as a church.

The evidence from local newspapers suggests that large numbers of youngsters were involved in school, street and junior rugby. Most of these teams appear to have been largely organised by the boys themselves. Even with adult clubs, it was apparent that club officials were often very young and certainly predominantly of a playing age.

The investigation into the background of Cardiff's players in the 1870s confirms the widely held view that the game was introduced and initially played by a social elite, largely drawn from the mercantile and professional classes and at least some of whom had been educated at public school. However, this dominance first began to erode by the end of the decade with the arrival of lower status middle-class and working-class players. By the early 1880s, new neighbourhood clubs, in which working men appeared, were springing up. Cardiff were including working men by 1881–2 and by the middle of the decade they comprised a substantial proportion of the First XV. It is significant that the very first working-class Welsh international, William Stadden, came through this system.

Thus, from the mid 1880s, Cardiff sat at the apex of a growing pyramid of local clubs from which it was constantly able to renew its teams. In one sense, then, even though the club was still technically a private organisation, Cardiff can be seen as a "representative" team, embracing the "region" of Cardiff and district. It was certainly regarded as an institution which represented the whole of Cardiff by its many supporters. In this respect, Cardiff was no different from any of the other leading Welsh clubs, all of which acted as the focus of deep civic pride for the various communities which they represented.

Growth at the local club level was stimulated by the continued success of the Cardiff team, playing with a revolutionary new style which it had pioneered. Cardiff now had one of the best club sides in Britain. Since the team was essentially a representative one, local players could aspire to progress via an extensive and comprehensive network of junior and neighbourhood clubs. Though class barriers undoubtedly still existed, the over-riding demand from spectators, the general public and the press was for success on the field, so working-class players could and did find themselves representing their town and even their country.

By 1890, grass roots clubs were largely administered by young members of the skilled and semi-skilled working class and lower status middle class. Amongst the huge number of teams in Cardiff, only a few were exclusively middle class and many middle-class players belonged to socially mixed clubs. This provides strong evidence that the game was largely played and administered by ordinary working people and not the well intentioned middle class. Rugby in Victorian Cardiff was at the centre of working-class culture and this demonstrates that, in Wales at least, it was, above all, a game of the urban working class. However, it was a different story when it came to the administration of the WFU and the senior clubs, as there it was the professional and business classes who continued to control the game and they ensured that it did not fall into the hands of a more democratic representation. With the major gate-taking clubs dominating the Union, by restricting membership and by operating a cartel in the election of officers, they managed to retain overall control of the game in Wales.

The majority of teams which appeared in this period never belonged to any union or participated in any formal competitions. Even of those local clubs which did join the Welsh Football Union or the Cardiff and District Football Union in the 1890s, most enjoyed only a brief existence. There was a very high rate of annual turnover. The condition of the local club game in the period was one of chronic instability, with even successful teams disappearing as quickly as they rose. While financial and ground problems were contributory causes, the main reason seems to have been the frequency with which players and officials moved on. By the late 1890s, district clubs often lost players as a result of financial inducements made by other Welsh clubs or by those in the Northern Union.

The success of the Challenge Cup inspired the establishment of numerous other competitions across south Wales. By the 1890s, the thirst for competition had also extended to the formation of leagues, though not for the senior Welsh clubs. This was as true in Cardiff as elsewhere in Wales. An early district cup was discontinued after four years in 1890 but it was soon replaced by the new Cardiff and District's Mallett Cup – still in existence – from 1893–4. Later, cups for less strong teams and youths teams were successfully inaugurated and a two division league was established in 1894 with a third youth division added in 1899. Similar developments occurred widely throughout the towns and valleys of south Wales, though these competitions were never co-ordinated nationally.

Rugby in Cardiff was facilitated by a range of convenient playing areas. In particular, Sophia Gardens, centrally located and close to pubs and transport routes, provided accommodation for countless teams and players and was even Cardiff's home for its first three years. The strategic location of the Arms Park had an even wider significance for the game in Wales and it still helps to sustain its popularity to the present day. Easily accessible from both within and without the town, it rapidly became – as it remains today in the form of the Millennium Stadium and the Cardiff RFC ground – a conspicuous statement about the importance of rugby football to Cardiff and to Wales.

The level of interest in club and international rugby generated financial benefits for a range of businesses and organisations in the town, including transport operators; public house, hotel, restaurant and theatre proprietors; sports goods suppliers; photographers; newspaper proprietors, publishers and printers; builders and contractors; and charities. Cardiff's new and rapidly expanding role as the regional centre for south Wales meant that the level and range of its transport, commercial and recreational infrastructure was better able to respond to the new demands from rugby than anywhere else in Wales. The close proximity of the Arms Park and Sophia Gardens to the commercial centre only reinforced this. Attendances at club matches at the Park regularly reached five figures by the 1890s and on occasion rose to 20,000. International matches could draw substantially more spectators. These crowds reflected the composition and character of Welsh industrial society – cosmopolitan, socially inclusive, disputatious and sometimes disruptive and disrespectful of authority.

The income of the major clubs rose substantially during the 1890s and this was particularly true of Cardiff. However, the club also incurred high costs in maintaining the playing surface which was especially prone to flooding. In addition, significant sums were spent on continual ground improvements to meet the growing demands of spectators. The club was also very generous in making regular donations to local charities and junior rugby. Players were looked after extremely well in terms of equipment, travel and hotel expenses but there is no firm evidence that direct cash payments were regularly made. This is not to say that it never happened, but given the views of the committee and the possible opposition of the club's ground landlord, it is unlikely that such payments ever became standard in the period. If they were, the evidence so far remains elusive.

For a whole generation of Victorians, rugby union was *the* Cardiff sport. Its early introduction gave it a seemingly unassailable lead over its rivals. The absence of any serious competition from any other team or mass spectator sport for over twenty-five years allowed rugby to become entrenched in the local popular culture. The success of the town team was not only the focus of great civic pride, irrespective of class or even gender, but it also stimulated the growth in participation at a neighbourhood level. As the dominant sport in Cardiff, rugby provided a diverse and uprooted population, whether players or spectators, with a sense of belonging. Just as *Fields of Praise* argues that the sport contributed to a newfound sense of nationhood, it can be claimed that, at a local level, rugby also contributed to a new sense of citizenship.[2] Rugby in Cardiff was a highly visible feature of the urban landscape. Whether it was the central prominence of the Arms Park, the presence of players on public parks and streets, or the large crowds regularly descending on Cardiff for major matches, it would have been difficult for its Victorian citizens to be completely unaware of the game's place in the life of the town.

Victorian Cardiff was a brash and thrusting newcomer on Britain's urban scene. It had a lot of catching up to do. It had no great history or distinguished institutions. "Cardiff was no Edinburgh or Athens of the west".[3] However, success in sport provided one way for Cardiff to make its presence felt apart, that is, from merely being recognised as the country's "Coal Metropolis". Ordinary citizens, businessmen, journalists and politicians – many of them born elsewhere – identified themselves with what was now "their" rugby team, which regularly recorded victories over the representatives of Britain's older and more prestigious cities. Just as the town of Cardiff had ascended from obscurity to become the world's most important centre for the export of coal, so too had its innovative rugby representatives risen to the very forefront of the game.

This study has revealed, for the first time, the extent of involvement in rugby in one locality in Victorian Wales. Cardiff was the largest town by the period but how different its experience was from that of other south Wales urban places needs to be examined in further research. Each town had its own context, of course, which helped to determine its particular rugby character. Cardiff's geographic, demographic, economic, social, educational and religious structure all influenced the particular way in which rugby developed in the town. In a vibrant, competitive and innovative society, Cardiff's aspiring mercantile and professional class introduced the game and continued to control it at the highest level. The location and extent of the town's recreational and commercial infrastructure provided the physical environment in which the game could flourish. A massively expanded and diverse working class adopted the game enthusiastically. They dominated it at its lower levels, took the level of participation to unprecedented heights and thereby contributed strongly to the creation of the socially inclusive version of rugby football which has thrived in Wales ever since. Cardiff was a crucible of the game in Wales. It remained at the very heart of Welsh rugby throughout the Victorian period. Rugby was also at the heart of the life of Victorian Cardiff.

Notes

1. *Western Mail* 14 Oct. 1878.
2. David Smith and Gareth Williams, *Fields of Praise: The Official History of the Welsh Rugby Union 1881–1981* (Cardiff, 1980) passim.
3. Kenneth O. Morgan, *Rebirth of a Nation: Wales 1880–1980* (Oxford, 1982 edn.), p. 22.

APPENDICES

Appendix 1

Welsh Rugby Teams 1880–1

Compiled from the *South Wales Daily News* and the *Western Mail*

Aberavon 1&2
Aberdare
Albion, Cardiff
Alexandra Rangers, Newport
Arnold College, Swansea 1&2
Blaenavon Scarlet Runners
Blaina Ironsides
Bloomfield, Swansea
Brecon
Bridgend 1&2
Builth Wells
Burry Port Juniors
Bute Dock Rangers, Cardiff 1&2
Cadoxton, Neath
Cambrian, Aberdare
Canton Rovers, Cardiff 1&2
Canton Wanderers, Cardiff
Cardiff 1&2
Cardiff Proprietary Collegiate
    School
Carmarthen
Carmarthen Juniors

Carmarthen Training College
Cathays Rangers, Cardiff
Chepstow
Chepstow Grammar School
Christ College Brecon
Cwmavon 1&2
Dare
East Wales (Representative)
Excelsior, Newport
Green Institute, Neath
Haverfordwest
Hirwaun
Lampeter Town
Llandeilo
Llandeilo Academy
Llandeilo Grammar School
Llandovery College 1&2
Llandovery College Old Boys
Llanelli 1&2
Llanelli Juniors
Machen
Maindee, Newport 1&2

Melbourne, Swansea
Merthyr
Monmouth School
Monmouthshire (Representative)
Mountain Ash
Mountain Ash Temperance
Narberth
Neath 1&2
Neath Abbey
Neath Institute
Neath Proprietary School
Neath Rovers
Newport 1&2
Newport Crusaders 1&2
Newport Grammar School
Newport Rovers 1&2
Newport Wanderers
Oakfield, Cwmbran
Old Monmouthians
Pembroke Dock
Penarth
Penarth Juniors
Pontardawe
Pontymister 1&2
Pontymister Rovers

Pontypool 1&2
Pontypridd
Porthcawl
Richmond, Cardiff
Risca Star
Roath, Cardiff 1&2
Roath Collegiate School, Cardiff
Roath Juniors, Cardiff
South Wales FU (Representative)
St. Andrew's College, Swansea
St. David's College, Lampeter
St. Elvan's Aberdare
Star, Aberdare
Star, Roath, Cardiff
Swansea 1&2
Swansea Juniors
Swansea Rovers
Tredegar
United Rhondda Valley
University College Wales,
    Aberystwyth
West Wales (Representative)
Windsor, Roath, Cardiff 1&2
Windsor, Swansea

Appendix 2

Cardiff and District Rugby Teams 1895–6

Compiled from the *South Wales Daily News* and the *Western Mail*

2nd GAV (Cardiff Artillery)
6th Cardiff Boys Brigade 1&2
7th Cardiff Boys Brigade
All Saints Church Lads Brigade
All Saints, Llandaff Yard
Anglo–Bavarian Rovers
Barry 1&2
Barry Barbarians
Barry Boilermakers
Barry Church Lads Brigade
Barry Coal Trimmers (Tippers)
Barry Crescents
Barry Dock Crusaders
Barry Dock Juniors
Barry Excelsiors
Barry Loco
Barry Moulders
Barry Stars
Belgrave 1&2
Belmonts
Bland's Deal Carriers
Bute Docks Workers
Bute Engineers
Cadoxton Crescents
Cadoxton/Stars
Cadoxton United
Caledonians 1&2
Cambrians
Canton 1&2
Canton Hornets
Canton United
Canton Wanderers1&2
Cardiff 1&2
Cardiff Albions
Cardiff Alexandras
Cardiff and District (Representative)
Cardiff Banks

Cardiff Barbarians
Cardiff Boilermakers
Cardiff Boys Brigade
Cardiff Chartering Clerks
Cardiff Clothiers
Cardiff Crescent
Cardiff Crusaders
Cardiff Electrics 1&2
Cardiff Harlequins 1&2&Weds
Cardiff Hibernians (Representative)
Cardiff Hornets
Cardiff (Roath) Marlborough
Cardiff Moulders
Cardiff Northern 1&2
Cardiff Old Westonians
Cardiff Postmen
Cardiff Rangers
Cardiff Saints
Cardiff Star
Cardiff Steam Joinery Men
Cardiff Telegraph Messengers
Cardiff United
Cardiff Villa
Cardiff (& S Wales) Wanderers
Cardiff Wednesday Star
Cardiff Windsor
Cardiff YMCA Wednesday 1&2
Carlton Juniors
Cathays 1&2
Cathays Crescents
Cathays Institute 1&2
Cathays Juniors
Cathays Primrose Juniors
Cathays Rovers (Wednesday)
Cathays Stars
Cathays Wednesday
Cefn Mably

Clifton Rovers
Craddock Juniors
Crescent Juniors
Crescent Stars (not Cres. Juniors)
Crescent United
Depot, Welsh Regiment
Dinas Powys
Docks Cabmen
Docks Juniors
Docks Printers
Docks United
Dowlais Magpies/Stars
Duke Street Rovers
Eldon United/Rovers
Ely Paper Mills
Ely Paper Mills Beaters
Ely Paper Mills Binders
Ely Rangers 1&2
Empire Theatre
Glamorgan Police (E Division)
Gloucester Stars
Gloucester Wagon Works
Grange Albions
Grange Raglans
Grange United 1&2
Grangetown 1&2
Grangetown Harlequins
Grangetown Rovers
Grangetown Workingmen's
    Liberal Club
Grangetown Workmen's
    Conservative Club
Grasshoppers
GWR Crusaders
GWR Excelsiors
Great Western Rangers
Hamilton/Stars
Havelock Stars
Hayes Rovers
Heath Rovers
Holton Juniors, Barry
Howard Crescent
Iestyn Juniors

Inverness Juniors
Lincoln Harlequins
Lisvane
Llandaff 1&2&Past Players
Llandaff Blossoms/Wednesday
Llandaff Boys Brigade
Llandaff Church Lads Brigade
Llandaff Linton
Llandaff Rovers
Llandaff Stars 1&2
Llandaff Working Men's Club
Llandaff Yard
Llandaff Yard Boys Brigade
Loudoun Hornets 1&2
Loudoun Stars
Loudouns 1&2
Louisa Street Stars
Mackintosh
Mackintosh United
May Street Stars
Melingriffith
Merthyr (Street) Stars
Monkton House 1&2
Moorland Stars
North Central Filibusters/Rovers
Oakfield Stars
Old Monktonians
Park Rovers 1&2
Pearl Crusaders
Pearl Street Joinery
Penarth 1&2
Penarth Excelsior
Penarth Hornets (Wednesday)
Penarth Stars 1&2
Penarth Victorias
Penarth White Rose (Wednesday)
Pentyrch
Pentyrch Juniors
Pentyrch Rowdy Boys
Penylan 1&2&3
Penylan Juniors
Picton Stars
Radyr Stars

Red Rose
Rhymney Railway Cleaners
Richmond Crescents
Richmond Road Juniors
Riverside
Roath
Roath Albion (Wednesday)
Roath Albion Juniors (Saturday)
Roath Excelsiors
Roath Park Juniors
Roath Road/ Juniors/Stars
Roath Stars
Roath United
Roath Wanderers
Roath Wednesday
Roath Windsor
Romilly 1&2
Romilly Rangers
Romilly Victorias
Saltmede Crusaders
Sawmills Rovers
Spillers United
Splott Cruaders 1&2
Splott Raglans 1&2
Splott White Star
Spring Wanderers
St. Andrew's 1&2
St. Anne's Rangers (not
     St. Anne's)
St. Anne's/ Stars
St. Catherine's
St. David's
St. David's Crusaders
St.David's Juniors
St. David's Rovers 1&2 (not
     St. David's)
St. Dyfrig's
St. Fagans
St. Fagans Juniors
St. John's
St. Mary's 1&2
St. Mary's Hall School 1&2

St. Michael's 1&2
St. Monica's
St. Paul's
St. Peter's 1&2
St. Peter's Stars
Steam Joinery Juniors
Sydenham Stars
Taffs Well
Taffs Well Juniors
Taffs Well Rovers
Talbot Stars/United
The Windsors (not Cardiff
     Windsors)
Theatre Royal
Tongwynlais
Tongwynlais Juniors
Tongwynlais Stars (not
     Tongwynlais)
Town Cabmen
Town Printers
Town Raglans
Tredegar Stars/Tredegars
Trinity Crusaders
Ty Mawr, Llandaff North
University College Cardiff 1&2
Victoria Stars
Wellington
Wells United, Canton
Western Wagon Works
Wharton 1&2
Wharton Juniors
Whitchurch 1&2
Whitchurch Harlequins
Whitchurch Juniors
Whitchurch Stars
White Lion Rovers
White Star
Windsor Juniors/Stars
Windsor Stars Penarth
Windsor United
Woodlands
Woodvilles

Appendix 3

Competitions in Cardiff[1]

(1) Cardiff District Football Union

Cardiff District Challenge Cup

Year	Winners	Runners-up
1886–7	Cardiff Harlequins	Penarth
1887–8	Penarth	Cardiff Harlequins
1888–9	Penarth	Llandaff
1889–0	Penarth	Ely Rovers

Cardiff District Junior Cup

Year	Winners	Runners-up
1889–0	Cathays Rangers	Grangetown

(2) Cardiff and District Football Union

Mallett Cup

Year	Winners	Runners-up
1893–4	Cardiff Reserves	Canton
1894–5	Cardiff Northern	Canton
1895–6	Roath	Canton
1896–7	Canton	St. Paul's
1897–8	St. Paul's	Canton
1898–9	Mackintosh	St. Paul's
1899–1900	St. Peter's	Roath

Union Shield

Year	Winners	Runners-up
1894-5	Roath	Not Known
1895-6	Mackintosh	Not Known
1896-7	St. Peter's	Adamsdown
1897-8	St. Mary's	St. Andrew's
1898-9	Grange Stars	Cathays United
1899-1900	Roath Reserves	Canton Harlequins

1. Compiled from the *Western Mail* and *South Wales Daily News* 1886–1900 and *Cardiff and District Rugby Union: Official Handbook, Season, 1908–9*, (Cardiff, 1908), p. [1]

Senior League

Year	Winners
1894–5	Cardiff Northern
1895–6	Roath
1896–7	Not Held
1897–8	St. Peter's
1898–9	St. Paul's
1899–1900	Roath

Junior League

Year	Winners
1894–5	Roath
1895–6	Mackintosh
1896–7	Not Held
1897–8	St. Andrew's
1898–9	Grange Stars
1899–1900	Canton Harlequins

Second Junior League

Year	Winners
1899–1900	Cardiff Barbarians

(3) Cardiff Football Club

Cardiff FC Junior Cup

Year	Winners	Runners-up
1896–7	Canton Crescents	Roath Crescents
1897–8	St. Peter's Reserves	Canton Crescents
1898–9	Penarth United	Grange Stars Reserves
1899–1900	Canton Crusaders	St. Mary's Juniors

Appendix 4

Welsh Football Union Competition[1]

South Wales Challenge Cup

Year	Winners	Runners-up
1878–9	Newport	Swansea
1879–0	Newport	Cardiff
1880–1	Swansea	Lampeter College
1881–2	Cardiff	Llanelli
1882–3[2]	Newport	Llanelli
1883–4	Newport	Swansea
1884–5	Llanelli	Newport
1885–6	Newport	Neath
1886–7	Llanelli	Newport
1887–8	Swansea	Llanelli
1888–9	Not Held	–
1889–0	Not Held	–
1890–1	Penygraig	Llanelli A
1891–2	Newport Reserves	Swansea Harlequins
1892–3	Llandaff	Llanelli A
1893–4	Pontymister	Neath A
1894–5	Llanelli A	Pontymister
1895–6	Neath A	Crumlin
1896–7	Pontymister	Llandeilo
1897–8	Llanelli A	Risca
1898–9	Not Held	–
1899–1900	Not Held	–

1. Compiled from the *Western Mail* and *South Wales Daily News* 1878–1900 and David Smith and Gareth Williams, *Fields of Praise*, pp. 485–6
2. This was the last season in which Cardiff competed in the cup. C.S. Arthur, *The Cardiff Rugby Football Club: History and Statistics 1876–1906*, (Cardiff, 2008), p. 52.

Appendix 5

Cardiff and District Club Secretaries 1889–91

Name	Age	Occupation	Place of Birth	Club	Source
Thomas Phillips	19	Travelling salesman	Pentyrch	Pentyrch	WM 89–0
Frank Seager	19	Book-keeper	Cardiff	Tyneside (16–20)	WM 89–0
Isaac Chorley	24	Plumber	Somerset	Footlights	WM 90–1
Anthony Proud	22	Plumber	North Shields	Wanderers	WM 90–1
William Morgan	15	Printer's apprentice	Cardiff	Albany Stars (15)	WM 90–1
Bertie Harris	14	Scholar	Newport	Canton Rovers (11–13)	EE 90–1
Arthur Lloyd	19	Coach trimmer	Cardiff	Cardiff United	FC 90–1
David Hopkins	22	Clerk	Llantrisant	Cardiff Rangers	FC 90–1
Thomas Jones	19	Hardware merchant	Llantrisant	Cardiff Cyclists	FC 90–1
Ernest Thomas	17	Plasterer and paper hanger	Cardiff	St. Peters	FC 90–1
Sidney Smith	22	Baker	Birkenhead	Cathays Stars	FC 90–1
William Gardner	19	Office clerk	Sunderland	Splott Rovers	FC 90–1
Richard Jones	19	Plumber's apprentice	Gloucester	Canton	FC 90–1
Sidney Phillips	24	Ship chandler's assistant	Bath	Ely Rovers	FC 90–1
Edward Davies	16	Clerk	Cardiff	Roath Windsor	FC 90–1
Wilson Tunley	17	Clerk	Cardiff	Cardiff Juniors (16), St. David's	FC 90–1
William Johnston	16	Telegraph messenger	Scotland	Clyde Rovers (15)	FC 90–1

(Continued)

Appendix 5   (Continued)

Name	Age	Occupation	Place of Birth	Club	Source
Fred Hodson	17	Proof-reader's assistant	London	Star Juniors (13–14)	FC 90–1
Henry Hayes	16	Office boy	Cornwall	Penarth Albion	FC 90–1
Samuel Hall	22	Currier	Llandaff	Llandaff	FC 90–1
Frederick Bosley	20	Railway clerk	London	Cardiff Crusaders	FC 90–1
William Rigby	31	Draper's assistant	Lancs	Cardiff Rovers	FC 90–1
Thomas Grant	20	Plumber	Lincs	Cardiff Star	FC 90–1
Henry Cypher	20	Clerk	Wilts	Taff Vale Wanderers	FC 90–1
John Hall	25	Book-keeper	Cardiff	Cogan	FC 90–1
Ernest Carder	19	Builder's clerk	Cardiff	Cathays	WM 91–2
Eli Hopkins	18	Office clerk	Whitchurch	Whitchurch	WM 91–2
Francis John	18	Clerk	St Andrews	Barry	FH 91–2
John Nelms	25	Compositor	Gloucester	Barry and Cadoxton	FH 91–2
George Dyer	15	Clerk	Cardiff	Cardiff Albion	FH 91–2
Robert England	18	Teacher	Cardiff	Canton	FH 91–2
Thomas Lewis	16	Clerk	Swansea	Ely Juniors	FH 91–2
George Parsons	21	Hairdresser	Dorset	Grangetown	FH 91–2
Edward Lewis	21	Chartering clerk	Cardiff	Heath	FH 91–2
Frederick Barrass	17	Merchant's clerk	Newcastle	Kymin, Penarth	FH 91–2
George Pawley	17	Grocer's assistant	Penarth	Penarth United	FH 91–2
John Thomas	18	Clerk	Pembs	Roath Windsor	FH 91–2
John Richards	16	Coach painter	Cardiff	St. Germans	FH 91–2

Key to Sources:
EE (*Evening Express*), FC (*Cardiff and South Wales Footballer's Companion: 1890–91*), FH (*The Welsh Athlete and West of England Cycling News Football Handbook 1891–2*), WM (*Western Mail*).

BIBLIOGRAPHY

Manuscripts

Cardiff Census Returns, 1881, 1891.
Cardiff Cricket Club Members Lists, 1883, 1884.
County Borough of Cardiff Reports of Council and Committees, Nov. 1891 to
    Nov. 1892.
Licensed Premises (Alehouses and Beerhouses) in Cardiff: Report of the Chief
    Constable, 1903 (Unpublished transcript).
Penarth RFC Archive 1885–1900.
Rodway, I.M.F., *History of Canton R.F.C.* (Unpublished transcript, n.d.).
Rugby Football Union Minutes, January 1871–March 1883.
Welsh Football Union (WRU) Minutes, September 1892–September 1902.

Newspapers

Bridgend Chronicle
Cardiff and Merthyr Guardian
Cardiff Argus
Cardiff Times
Evening Express (Cardiff)
Monmouthshire Merlin
North Wales Chronicle
South Wales Argus
South Wales Daily News
South Wales Echo
Star of Gwent
The Irish Times
The Times
The Welsh Athlete
Weekly Mail (Cardiff)
Western Mail

Handbooks

Cardiff and District Rugby Union: Official Handbook, Season 1908–9 (Cardiff, 1908).
Cardiff and South Wales Footballer's Companion: 1890–91 (Cardiff, 1890).
Cardiff District Football Union Handbook 1886–87 (Cardiff, 1886).
Cardiff Schools Rugby Union Handbook Season 1987–88 (Cardiff, 1987).
Mortimer's Football Guide for South Wales and Monmouthshire: Season, 1894–95 (Barry, 1894).
The Handy Football Guide (Mortimer's) For South Wales and Monmouthshire: 1896–97 (Cardiff, 1896).
The Welsh Athlete and West of England Cycling News Football Handbook 1891–2 (Cardiff, 1891).
Welsh Districts Rugby Union 2000–2001 Handbook (Cardiff, 2000).
Welsh Football Union: Year Book, 1889–90 (Newport, 1889).
Welsh Rugby Union 2002–2003 Handbook (Cardiff, 2002).

Annuals

Alcock, C.W., (ed.), *John Lillywhite's Football Annual* (London, 1868).
Alcock, C.W., (ed.), *The Football Annual* (London, 1869–1895).
Jackson, N.L., (ed.), *The Football Handbook 1888–9* (London, 1889).
Owen, O.L. (ed.), *Playfair Rugby Football Annual* (London, 1950–1967).
Stewart Caine, C., (ed.), *John Wisden's Rugby Football Almanack for 1924–25* (London, 1924).

Directories

Butcher's Cardiff Directory (Cardiff, 1875–1883).
Daniel Owen and Co.'s Cardiff Directory (Cardiff, 1887–1895).
J. Wright and Co.'s Cardiff Directory (Cardiff, 1883–1886).
Slater's Post Office Directory of Cardiff and its Suburbs (Cardiff, 1882–1885).
Webster and Co.'s Postal and Commercial Directory of the City of Bristol and Counties of Glamorgan and Monmouth (London, 1865).
Western Mail Cardiff Directory (Cardiff, 1897–1900).

Books

Andrews, David, "Sport and the Masculine Hegemony of the Modern Nation: Welsh Rugby, Culture and Society, 1890–1914", in Nauright, John and Chandler, Timothy J.L. (eds.), *Making Men: Rugby and Masculine Identity* (London, 1996).

Anon., *Contemporary Portraits: Men and Women of South Wales and Monmouthshire: Cardiff Section* (Cardiff, 1896).

Anon, *Marlborough College Register From 1843 to 1904 Inclusive* (Oxford, 1905).

Anon., *Who's Who in Wales* (London, 1933 edn.).

Anon., *Sixty Years of Rugby 1887–1947: Ammanford R.F.C.* (Ammanford, 1947).

Anon., *Llandaff Rugby Football Club American Tour Souvenir* (Cardiff, 1968).

Anon., *Treherbert Rugby Football Club Centenary Year 1874–1974* (Treherbert, 1974).

Anon., *Merthyr Rugby Football Club Centenary Year 1876–1976* (Merthyr, 1976).

Anon., *Penygraig RFC: 100 Years of Valley Rugby 1877–1977* (Penygraig, 1977).

Anon., *The Blues: Loughor Rugby Football Club 1882–1982* (Loughor, 1981).

Anon., *Famous Rugby Footballers 1895* (Harefield, 1997).

Arthur, C.S., *The Cardiff Rugby Football Club: History and Statistics, 1876–1906* (Cardiff, 1908).

Atkinson, Philip T., *One Hundred Years of Rhymney Rugby: The Centenary History of Rhymney R.F.C. 1877–1982* (Rhymney, 1982).

Bale, John, *Sport and Place: A Geography of Sport in England Scotland and Wales* (London, 1982).

Bassett, Michael G., *Games of Interchanging Praise: A Centenary History of Rugby Football in Barry* (Barry, 1988).

Beken, Paul and Jones, Stephen, *Dragon in Exile: The Centenary History of London Welsh R.F.C.* (London, 1985).

Billot, John, *All Blacks in Wales* (Ferndale, 1972).

Billot, John, *Springboks in Wales* (Rhondda, 1974).

Billot, John, *History of Welsh International Rugby* (Cardiff, 1999 edn.).

Birley, Derek, *Sport and the making of Britain* (Manchester, 1993).

Birley, Derek, *Land of sport and glory: Sport and British society, 1887–1910* (Manchester, 1995).

Birley, Derek, *Playing the game: Sport and British society, 1910–45* (Manchester, 1995).

Boucher, David, *Steel, Skill and Survival: Rugby in Ebbw Vale and the Valleys (1870–1952)* (Ebbw Vale, 2000).

Bowker, Barry, *England Rugby* (London, 1978 edn.).

Breeze, Alan, *One Hundred Years of Abergavenny Rugby Football Club* (Abergavenny, 1975).

Broughton-Mainwaring, Rowland, *Historical Record of the Royal Welch Fusiliers* (London, 1889).

Brown, Mike, *Brewed in Northants* (Longfield, Kent, 1998).

Cary, A.D.L. and Stouppe McLance, S., *Regimental Records of the Royal Welch Fusiliers Volume II 1816–1914* (London, 1923).

Chester, R.H. and McMillan, N.A.C., *The Encyclopaedia of New Zealand Rugby* (Auckland, 1981).

Chester, R.H. and McMillan, N.A.C., *The Visitors: The History of International Rugby Teams in New Zealand* (Auckland, 1990).

Childs, D.F., *One Hundred Years of the "Rocks": the History of St. Peter's R.F.C. 1886/1986* (Cardiff, 1986).

Collins, John, Currie, Alan, Currie, Brenda, Walters, Mike and Williams, Clive, *The History of Welsh Athletics Volume I* (Llanelli, 2002).

Collins, Tony, *Rugby's Great Split: Class, Culture and the Origins of Rugby League Football* (London, 1998 edn.) (London, 2006 edn.).

Collins, Tony, "Violence, gamesmanship and the amateur ideal in Victorian middle-class rugby", in Huggins, Mike and Mangan, J.A. (eds.), *Disreputable Pleasures: Less Virtuous Victorians at Play* (London, 2004).

Collins, Tony, *A Social History of English Rugby Union* (London, 2009).

Collins, Tony and Vamplew, Wray, *Mud, Sweat, and Beers: A Cultural History of Sport and Alcohol* (Oxford, 2002).

Collins, W.J. Townsend (ed.), *Newport Athletic Club: The record of half a Century 1875–1925* (Newport, 1925).

Collins, W.J. Townsend, *Rugby Recollections* (Newport, 1948).

Corrigan, Peter, *100 Years of Welsh Soccer: The Official History of the Football Association of Wales* (Cardiff, [1976]).

Coughlan, Kevin, Hall, Peter and Gale, Colin, *Before the Lemons: A History of Bath Football Club RFU 1865–1965* (Stroud, 2003).

Croll, Andy, *Civilizing the Urban: Popular Culture and Public Space in Merthyr, c. 1870–1914* (Cardiff, 2000).

Cunningham, Vanessa and Goodwin, John, *Cardiff University: A Celebration* (Cardiff, 2001).

Daglish, J.R.A., *Red, Blue & Black: The First 125 Years of Liverpool Football Club (Rugby Union)* (Manchester, 1983).

Dargavel, T., *Neath R.F.C. 1871–1971 Centenary Year* (Neath, 1971).

Daunton, M.J., *Coal Metropolis: Cardiff 1870–1914* (Leicester, 1977).

Daunton, M.J., "Coal to Capital: Cardiff since 1839", in Morgan, Prys (ed.), *Glamorgan County History, Volume VI, Glamorgan Society: 1780–1980* (Cardiff, 1988).

Davidson, John Mcl., *International Rugby Union: A Compendium of Scotland's Matches* (Edinburgh, 1994).

Davies, D.E., *Cardiff Rugby Club: History and Statistics, 1876–1975: "The Greatest"* (Cardiff, 1975).

Davies, Iolo, *"A Certaine Schoole": A History of the Grammar School at Cowbridge Glamorgan* (Cowbridge, 1967).

Davies, John, *A History of Wales* (London, 1994).

Davis, Jack, *One Hundred Years of Newport Rugby 1875–1975* (Risca, 1974).

Delaney, Trevor, *The Roots of Rugby League* (Keighley, 1984).

Dicks, Brian, *Portrait of Cardiff and its Valleys* (London, 1984).

Dolan, J. (ed.), *Aberavon Rugby Football Club 1876–1976* (Port Talbot, 1976).

Donovan, Edward, Crane, Arthur, Smith, Allan and Harris, John, *Pontypool's Pride: The Official History of Pontypool Rugby Football Club 1868–1988* (Abertillery, 1988).

Dunning, Eric and Sheard, Kenneth, *Barbarians, Gentlemen and Players: A Sociological Study of the Development of Rugby Football* (Oxford, 1979 edn.), (London, 2005 edn.).

Edwards, R. Wendell, *100 Years of Rugby Football in Bangor* (Bangor, 1980).

Evans, Allan, *Taming the Tourists: How Cardiff Beat the All Blacks, Springboks and Wallabies* (Halifax, 2003).

Evans, Barbara M., *Blaina Rugby Football Club 1875–1976: Memories of Mutton Tump* (Risca, 1976).

Evans, D. Gareth, *A History of Wales 1815–1906* (Cardiff, 1989).

Evans, Denver, *Bont: The Story of a Village and its Rugby Club, Pontarddulais* (Pontarddulais, 1980).

Evans, Howard, *Welsh International Matches 1881–2000* (Edinburgh, 1999).

Evans, Neil and O'Leary, Paul, "Playing the Game: Sport and Ethnic Minorities in Modern Wales", in Williams, Charlotte, Evans, Neil and O'Leary, Paul (eds.), *A Tolerant Nation? Exploring Ethnic Diversity in Wales* (Cardiff, 2003).

Evans, T.L., *Carmarthen Rugby Football Club Centenary Year 1874–1974* (Llandeilo, 1974).

Evans, W. Gareth, *A History of Llandovery College* (Llandovery, 1981).

Farmer, David, *The Life and Times of Swansea R.F.C.: The All Whites* (Swansea, 1995).

Farmer, Stuart and Hands, David, *The Tigers Tale: The Official History of Leicester Football Club 1880–1993* (Leicester, 1993).

Foster, Joseph, *Alumni Oxfordiensis 1715–1886* (4 Volumes) (London, 1887–1888).

Foster, T.J., *Floreat Howardia: The Story of Howard Gardens Schools Cardiff 1885–1990* (Cardiff, 1990).

Gane, Denis, *Cwmbran R.F.C. One Hundred Years of Rugby* (Cwmbran, 1980).

Gardiner, Duncan and Evans, Alan (eds.), *Images of Sport: Cardiff Rugby Football Club 1876–1939* (Stroud, 1999).

Gate, Robert, *Gone North: Welshmen in Rugby League, Volume 1* (Sowerby Bridge, 1986).

Gate, Robert, *Gone North: Welshmen in Rugby League, Volume 2* (Sowerby Bridge, 1988).

Gealy, D.I., "Sport at Llandovery: Rugby Football", in Jones, R. Brinley (ed.), *Floreat Landubriense: Celebrating a Century and a Half of Education at Llandovery College* (Llandovery, 1998).

Glover, Brian, *Prince of Ales: The History of Brewing in Wales* (Stroud, 1993).

Godwin, Terry, *The International Rugby Championship 1883–1983* (London, 1984).

Godwin, Terry, *The Complete Who's Who of International Rugby* (Poole, 1987).

Green, Geoffrey, *The History of the Football Association* (London, 1953).

Griffiths, John, *The Book of English International Rugby 1871–1982* (London, 1982).

Griffiths, John, *The Phoenix Book of International Rugby Records* (London, 1987).

Griffiths, John, *Rugby's Strangest Matches: Extraordinary but true stories from over a century of rugby* (London, 2000).

Grigg, Russell, *History of Trinity College Carmarthen 1848–1998* (Cardiff, 1998).

Harragan, Bob (ed.), *Images of Wales: Llanelli Rugby Club* (Stroud, 1998).

Harragan, Bob and Andrew Hignell, *C.P. Lewis: The Champion Cricketer of South Wales* (Cardiff, 2009).

Harris, C.R.G., *The Statistical History of Cardiff Rugby Football Club 1876–1984* (Cardiff, 1984).

Harris, Gareth, *Amalgamation: Pontypridd R.F.C at Taff Vale Park – The Early Days* (Pontypridd, 1999).

Harris, Gareth, *Taff Vale Park: Memories Lost in Time* (Pontypridd, 2000).

Harris, Gareth and Evans, Alan, *The Butchers Arms Boys: The Early Years* (Neath, 1997).

Harris, H.A., *Sport in Britain: Its Origins and Development* (London, 1975).

Harvey, Adrian, *Football: The First Hundred Years: The Untold Story* (London, 2005).

Hawkins, Frank C. and Seymour-Bell, E., *Fifty Years with the Clifton Rugby Football Club 1872–1922* (Bristol, 1922).

Hignell, Andrew, *From Sophia to SWALEC: A History of Cricket in Cardiff* (Stroud, 2009).

Hignell, Andrew K., *A "Favourit" Game: Cricket in south Wales before 1914* (Cardiff, 1992).

Hignell, Andrew and Prescott, Gwyn (eds.), *Cardiff Sporting Greats* (Stroud, 2007).

Holt, R.J., "Football and the Urban Way of Life in Nineteenth–Century Britain", in Mangan, J.A., *Pleasure, Profit, Proselytism: British Culture and Sport at Home and Abroad 1700–1914* (London, 1988).

Holt, Richard, *Sport and the British: A Modern History* (Oxford, 1989).

Hopkins, Bleddyn, *Images of Sport: Swansea RFC 1873–1945* (Stroud, 2002).

Hoskins, Mark and Fox, Dave, *Images of Sport: Bristol Football Club (RFU) 1888–1945* (Stroud, 2000).

Huggins, M.J., "Leisure and Sport in Middlesbrough, 1840–1914", in Pollard, A.J. (ed.), *Middlesbrough: Town and Community 1830–1950* (Stroud, 1996).

Huggins, Mike and Mangan, J.A. (eds.), *Disreputable Pleasures: Less Virtuous Victorians at Play* (London, 2004).

Hughes, Gareth (ed.), *One Hundred Years of Scarlet* (Llanelli, 1983).

Hughes, Gareth, *The Scarlets: A History of Llanelli Rugby Football Club* (Llanelli, 1986).

Hunter, A.A. (ed.), *Cheltenham College Register 1841–1889* (London, 1890).

Irving, Dennis, *One Hundred Years of Rugby at Narberth* (Narberth, 1982).

James, Danny and Rowlands, P.O.J., *Brecon Rugby Football Club: One Hundred Years of Rugby Football 1879–1979* (Brecon, 1979).

Jarvis, Bernard, *The Origin of Chepstow Rugby Football Club* (Chepstow, 1978).

Jefferies, Horace, *100 Years in Black and White: Cross Keys Rugby Football Club* (Pontypool, 1985).

Jenkins, D.G., *Blaenavon Rugby Football Club Centenary Brochure 1877–1977* (Blaenavon, 1977).

Jenkins, John M. (ed.), *A Rugby Compendium: An Authoritative Guide to the Literature of Rugby Union* (Boston Spa, 1998).

Jenkins, John M., Pierce, Duncan and Auty, Timothy, *Who's Who of Welsh International Rugby Players* (Wrexham, 1991).

Johnes, Martin, *Soccer and Society: South Wales, 1900–1939* (Cardiff, 2002).

Johnes, Martin, *A History of Sport in Wales* (Cardiff, 2005).

Johnson, Martin, *Rugby and All That* (London, 2001).

Jones, Desmond T. (ed.), *Pontypridd Rugby Football Club 1876–1976* (Pontypridd, 1976).

Jones, Elias, "The Palmy Days of Welsh Rugby" (1935), reprinted in Hughes, Gareth (ed.), *One Hundred Years of Scarlet* (Llanelli, 1983).

Jones, Gareth E. and Smith, Dai (eds.), *The People of Wales* (Llandusul, 1999).

Jones, Ieuan, *The First 100 Years: The History of Mountain Ash Rugby Union Football Club 1875–1975* (Mountain Ash, 1975).

Jones, J.R., *The Encyclopaedia of Rugby Football* (London, 1960).

Jones, R. Brinley (ed.), *Floreat Landubriense: Celebrating a Century and a Half of Education at Llandovery College* (Llandovery, 1998).

King, Walter, *Towards the Light: The Story of Cardiff High School for Boys: 1898–1970* (Llanharan, 1992).

Lawrie, W.A.D. (ed.), *Souvenir Brochure to mark the 75th Anniversary Season of the Bridgend R.F.C. 1879–1954* (Bridgend, 1954).

Lawrie, W.A.D., *Bridgend Rugby Football Club: The First Hundred Years* (Bridgend, 1979).

Lewis, Steve, *Images of Sport: Newport Rugby Football Club 1874–1950* (Stroud, 1999).

Lewis, Steve, *The Priceless Gift: 125 Years of Welsh Rugby Captains* (Edinburgh, 2005).

Lewis, Steve and Griffiths, John, *The Essential History of Rugby Union: Wales* (London, 2003).

Llewellyn, Arthur and Llewellyn, Don, *Pentyrch R.F.C.: A Club For All Seasons 1883–1983* (Pentyrch, 1983).

Lloyd, Grahame, *C'mon City! A Hundred Years of the Bluebirds* (Bridgend, 1999).

Lowerson, John, *Sport and the English middle classes, 1870–1914* (Manchester, 1993).

Lush, Peter and Farrar, Dave (eds.), *Tries in the Valleys: A History of Rugby League in Wales* (London, 1998).

Macrory, Jennifer, *Running with the Ball: The Birth of Rugby Football* (London, 1991).

Mangan, J.A. (ed.), *Pleasure, Profit, Proselytism: British Culture and Sport at Home and Abroad 1700–1914* (London, 1988).

Mangan, J.A., *Athleticism in the Victorian and Edwardian Public School* (London, 2000 edn.).

Mangan, J.A. (ed.), *A Sport-Loving Society: Victorian and Edwardian Middle-Class England at Play* (London, 2006).

Marshall, F. (ed.), *Football: The Rugby Union Game* (London, 1894 edn.).

Marshall, F and Tosswill, Leonard R., (eds.), *Football: The Rugby Union Game* (London, 1925).

Marshall, Howard and Jordan, J.P., *Oxford v. Cambridge: The Story of the University Rugby Match* (London, 1951).

Mason, Tony, *Association Football and English Society 1863–1915* (Brighton, 1981).

Mason, Tony, *Sport in Britain* (London, 1988).

Matthews, Brinley E., *The Swansea Story: A History of the Swansea Rugby Football Club 1874–1968* (Swansea, 1968).

McLaren, John, *The History of Army Rugby* (Aldershot, 1986).

McWhirter, Ross and Noble, Andrew, *Centenary History of Oxford University Rugby Football Club* (Oxford, 1969).

Mee, Arthur, *Who's Who in Wales* (Cardiff, 1921 edn.).

Meller, H.E., *Leisure and the Changing City, 1870–1914* (London, 1976).

Metcalfe, Alan, *Leisure and Recreation in a Victorian Mining Community: The Social Economy of Leisure in North-East England, 1820–1914* (London, 2006).

Mitchell, A.T. (ed.), *Rugby School Register, Volume II, From August 1842, To January, 1874* (London, 1886).

Moorhouse, Godfrey, *At the George and Other Essays on Rugby League* (London, 1989).

Moorhouse, Godfrey, *A People's Game: The Official History of Rugby League 1895–1995* (London, 1996).

Morgan, Dennis, *The Cardiff Story: A History of the City from its Earliest Times to the Present* (Cowbridge, 1991).

Morgan, Eifion, *Llandovery RFC Centenary 1881–1981* (Llandovery, 1981).

Morgan, Kenneth O., *Rebirth of a Nation: Wales 1880–1980* (Oxford, 1982 edn.).

Morgan, William J. and Nicholson, Geoffrey, *Report on Rugby* (London, 1959).

Morris, P.J. and Probert, W.G., *Builth Wells Rugby Football Club Centenary Booklet 1882–1982* (Builth Wells, 1982).

Moses, Anthony J. and Moses, Brenda C., *A History of Dinas Powys Rugby Football Club and its Associations with the Village, 1882–1982* (Risca, 1982).

Musselwhite, John, *The Butcher Boys of Donkey Island: An Historical Profile of Penarth R.F.C.* (Penarth, 1980).

Nauright, John and Chandler, Timothy J.L. (eds.), *Making Men: Rugby and Masculine Identity* (London, 1996).

Nicholls, E. Gwyn, *The Modern Rugby Game and How to Play It* (London, 1908).

O'Leary, Paul, *Immigration and Integration: The Irish In Wales, 1798–1922* (Cardiff, 2002 edn.).

Owen, O.L., *The History of the Rugby Football Union* (London, 1955).

Parry-Jones, David (ed.), *Taffs Acre: History and Celebration of Cardiff Arms Park* (London, 1984).

Parry-Jones, David, *The Rugby Clubs of Wales* (London, 1989).

Parry-Jones, David, *Prince Gwyn: Gwyn Nicholls and the First Golden Era of Welsh Rugby* (Bridgend, 1999).

Pelmear, Kenneth, *Rugby Football: An Anthology* (London, 1958).

Phillips, Glyn and James, Gwyn, *"The Old Parish", 100 Not Out 1882–1982: A History of Maesteg Rugby Football Club* (Maesteg, 1982).

Pike, W.T., (ed.), *Glamorgan Contemporary Biographies: Pike's New Century Series No. 20* (Brighton, 1907).

Pollard, Jack, *Australian Rugby: The Game and the Players* (Chippendale, Australia, 1994).

Powell, Terry (ed.), *An Illustrated History of Newbridge R.F.C.* (Risca, 1988).

Prescott, Gwyn, *"The Best and Happiest Team": A History of Cardiff High School Old Boys Rugby Football Club 1929–1978* (Cardiff, 1979).

Price, D.T.W., *A History of Saint David's University College Lampeter, Volume One: To 1898* (Cardiff, 1977).

Price, Mike, *Images of Sport: Neath RFC 1871–1945* (Stroud, 2002).

Rea, Chris, *Rugby: A History of Rugby Union Football* (London, 1977).

Reason, John and James, Carwyn, *The World of Rugby: A History of Rugby Union Football* (London, 1979).

Rees, J. Hywel, *A History of the Gowerton Rugby Football Club* (Gowerton, 1959).

Rees, J. Hywel, *The Gowerton Rugby Football Club 1884–1984: One Hundred Years On* (Gowerton, 1983).

Rees, William, *A History of Cardiff* (Cardiff, 1969 edn.).

Richards, Alun, *A Touch of Glory: 100 Years of Welsh Rugby* (London, 1980).

Richards, Huw, *A Game for Hooligans: The History of Rugby Union* (Edinburgh, 2006).

Richards, Huw, *The Red and the White: The Story of England v Wales Rugby* (London, 2009).

Roderick, Alan, *Newport Rugby Greats* (Newport, 1995).

Ruddick, Ray (ed.), *Images of Sport: Pontypool Rugby Football Club* (Stroud, 2002).

Russell, Dave, *Football and the English: A Social History of Association Football in England, 1863–1995* (Preston, 1997).

Ryan, Greg, *Forerunners of the All Blacks: The 1888–89 New Zealand Native Football Team in Britain, Australia and New Zealand* (Christchurch, New Zealand, 1993).

Ryan, Greg (ed.), *Tackling Rugby Myths: Rugby and New Zealand Society 1854–2004* (Dunedin, New Zealand, 2005).

Ryan, Greg, *The Conquest for Rugby Supremacy: Accounting for the 1905 All Blacks* (Christchurch, New Zealand, 2005).

Samuel, Michael, *Lampeter Town Rugby Football Club 1875 Centenary Year Brochure* (Llanelli, 1975).

Sewell, E.H.D., *Rugger: The Man's Game* (London, 1944).

Smith, Dai, *Wales: A Question for History* (Bridgend, 1999).

Smith, David and Williams, Gareth, *Fields of Praise: The Official History of the Welsh Rugby Union 1881–1981* (Cardiff, 1980).

Smith, Jed, *The Original Rules of Rugby* (Oxford, 2007).

Smith, Sean, *The Union Game: A Rugby History* (London, 1999).

Starmer-Smith, Nigel (ed.), *Rugby – A Way of Life: An Illustrated History of Rugby* (London, 1986).

Stephens, Meic (ed.), *New Companion to the Literature of Wales* (Cardiff, 1998).

Strickland, Jack, *Risca Rugby: Days of Glory* (Newport, 1983).

Thomas, Clem, *The History of the British Lions* (Edinburgh, 1996).

Thomas, E.T., White, V.T., et al. (eds.), *Glyncorrwg Rugby Football Club 1880– 1980: A Brief Summary of the First Hundred Years* (Glyncorrwg, 1980).

Thomas, Huw, *Discovering Cities: Cardiff* (Sheffield, 2003).

Thomas, Irene and Thomas, Keith, *Abertillery Rugby Football Club 1883–1983: The Centenary Book* (Barry, 1983).

Thomas, J.B.G., *The Men in Scarlet: The Story of Welsh Rugby Football* (London, 1972).

Thomas, J.B.G., "In the Beginning" in Western Mail in Association with the Welsh Rugby Union, *100 Years of Welsh Rugby* (Cardiff, 1980).

Thomas, J.B.G. and Harding, Rowe (eds.), *Rugby in Wales* (Swansea, 1970).

Thomas, W. Alan, *Cardiff Cricket Club: 1867–1967* (Cardiff, 1967).

Thomas, Wayne, *A Century of Welsh Rugby Players* (Birmingham, 1979).

Thorburn, A.M.C., *The Scottish Rugby Union: Official History* (Edinburgh, 1985).

Thorburn, Sandy, *The History of Scottish Rugby* (London, 1980).

Thorn, J. Lot (ed.), *Souvenir Programme to Mark the 75th Anniversary Season of the Penarth R.F.C.* (Penarth, 1954).

Titley, Uel A. and MacWhirter, Ross, *Centenary History of the Rugby Football Union* (London, 1970).

Toulouse, H.C., *Monmouth School Rugby Football Club: One Hundred Years* (Newport, 1973).

Tranter, Neil, *Sport, Economy and Society in Britain 1750–1914* (Cambridge, 1998).

Trounce, W.J., *"Cardiff in the Fifties": The Reminiscences and Historical Notes of Alderman W.J. Trounce J.P. 1850–1860* (Cardiff, 1918).

Vamplew, Wray, *Pay up and play the game: Professional Sport in Britain 1875– 1914* (Cambridge, 1988).

Van Esbeck, Edmund, *The Story of Irish Rugby* (London, 1986).

Van Esbeck, Edmund, *Irish Rugby 1874–1999: A History* (Dublin, 1999).

Venn, J.A., *Alumni Cantabrigienses Part II* (6 Volumes) (Cambridge, 1940–1954).

Vincent, Geoffrey T., "'To Uphold the Honour of the Province': Football in Canterbury c. 1854 – c. 1890", in Ryan, Greg (ed.), *Tackling Rugby Myths: Rugby and New Zealand Society 1854–2004* (Dunedin, New Zealand, 2005).

Wakefield, W.W. and Marshall, H.P., *Rugger* (London, 1927).

Walvin, James, *Leisure and Society 1830–1950* (London, 1978).

Wemyss, A., (ed.), *Barbarian Football Club: History and Complete Record of Results and Teams 1890–1955* (London, 1956).

Westcott, Gordon, *A Century on the Rugby Beat: A History of Police Rugby Football in the South Wales Constabulary Area* (Bridgend, 1992).

Williams, Chris, *Capitalism, Community and Conflict: The South Wales Coalfield 1898–1947* (Cardiff, 1998).

Williams, Gareth, "Taffs Acre: The Pre-1900 Years", in Parry-Jones, David, *Taffs Acre: History and Celebration of Cardiff Arms Park* (London, 1984).

Williams, Gareth, "From Popular Culture to Public Cliché: Image and Identity in Wales, 1890–1914", in Mangan, J.A., *Pleasure, Profit, Proselytism: British Culture and Sport at Home and Abroad 1700–1914* (London, 1988).

Williams, Gareth, "Sport and Society in Glamorgan 1750–1980", in Morgan, Prys (ed.), *Glamorgan County History, Volume VI, Glamorgan Society 1780–1980* (Cardiff, 1988).

Williams, Gareth, *1905 and All That: Essays on Rugby Football, Sport and Welsh Society* (Llandysul, 1991).

Williams, John, *Digest of Welsh Historical Statistics*, Volume 1 (Cardiff, 1985).

Williams, John, *Was Wales Industrialised? Essays in Modern Welsh History* (Llandysul, 1995).

Williams, Stewart, *Stewart Williams' Cardiff Yesterday*, 36 Volumes (Cardiff 1980–2000).

Articles

Adair, Daryl, "Competing or Complementary Forces: The 'Civilising' Process and the Commitment to Winning in Nineteenth Century English Rugby and Association Football", *Canadian Journal of History of Sport*, XXIV, 2 (1993), 47–67.

Anon., "Rugby Football in Wales: An Estimate", *Welsh Outlook*, 1, 1 (1914), 17–20.

Anon., "Some Famous Footballers: Cardiff Rugby Football Club", *St. Peter's Magazine*, V, 2 (1925), 43–5.

Bale, J., "Sport and National Identity: A Geographical View", *International Journal of the History of Sport*, 3, 1 (1986), 18–41.

Barlow, Stuart, "The Diffusion of 'Rugby' Football in the Industrialized Context of Rochdale, 1868–1890: A Conflict of Ethical Values", *International Journal of the History of Sport*, 10, 1 (1993), 49–67.

Burdsey, Daniel and Chappell, Robert, "'And If You Know Your History …': An Examination of the Formation of Football Clubs in Scotland and their Role in the Construction of Social Identity", *Sports Historian*, 20, 1 (2001), 94–106.

Campbell, J.D., "'Training for Sport is Training for War': Sport and the Transformation of the British Army, 1860–1914", *International Journal of the History of Sport*, 17, 4 (2000), 21–58.

Chandler, Timothy J.L., "Games at Oxbridge and the Public Schools, 1830–1880: The Diffusion of an Innovation", *International Journal of the History of Sport*, 8, 2 (1991), 171–204.

Collins, Tony, "Myth and Reality in the 1895 Rugby Split", *Sports Historian*, 16, (1996), 33–41.

Collins, Tony, "History, Theory and the 'Civilizing Process' ", *Sport in History*, 25, 2 (2005), 289–306.

Collins, Tony, "The Ambiguities of Amateurism: English Rugby Union in the Edwardian Era", *Sport in History*, 26, 3 (2006), 386–405.

Collins, Tony and Vamplew, Wray, "The Pub, the Drinks Trade and the Early Years of Modern Football", *Sports Historian*, 20, 1 (2000), 1–17.

Curry, Graham, "The Trinity Connection: An Analysis of the Role of Members of Cambridge University in the Development of Football in the Mid-Nineteenth Century", *Sports Historian*, 22, 2 (2002), 46–73.

Curry, Graham, Dunning, Eric and Sheard, Kenneth, "Sociological Versus Empiricist History: Some Comments on Tony Collins's 'History, Theory and the Civilizing Process' ", *Sport in History*, 26, 1 (2006), 110–123.

Dunning, Eric and Curry, Graham, "The Curate's Egg Scrambled Again: Comments on 'The Curate's Egg Put Back Together'!", *International Journal of the History of Sport*, 19, 4 (2002), 200–204.

Edwards, Gerald and Llewellyn, Don, "The Williams Family: More Than a 'Rugby Dynasty' " , *Garth Domain*, 26, (2004), 1–40.

Evans, A.L., "Some Reflections on Local Sport", *Port Talbot History Society Transactions*, 13, 2 (1981), 22–49.

Evans, Neil, "The Welsh Victorian City: The Middle Class and Civic and National Consciousness in Cardiff, 1850–1914", *Welsh History Review*, 12, 3 (1985), 350–387.

Finn, G.P.T., "Racism, Religion and Social Prejudice: Irish Catholic Clubs, Soccer and Scottish Society – I The Historical Roots of Prejudice", *International Journal of the History of Sport*, 8, 1 (1991), 72–95.

Finn, G.P.T., "Racism, Religion and Social Prejudice: Irish Catholic Clubs, Soccer and Scottish Society – II Social Identities and Conspiracy Theories", *International Journal of the History of Sport*, 8, 3 (1991), 374–397.

Gouldstone, John, "The Working-Class Origins of Modern Football", *International Journal of the History of Sport*, 17, 1 (2000), 135–143.

Harris, Jonathan, "The Early History of Association Football in Breconshire", *Brycheiniog*, XXVIII, (1996), 127–135.

Harvey, Adrian, " 'An Epoch in the Annals of National Sport': Football in Sheffield and the Creation of Modern Soccer and Rugby", *International Journal of the History of Sport*, 18, 4 (2001), 53–87.

Harvey, Adrian, "The Curate's Egg Put Back Together: Comments on Eric Dunning's Response to 'An Epoch in the Annals of National Sport' ", *International Journal of the History of Sport*, 19, 4 (2002), 192–199.

Harvey, Adrian, "Curate's Egg Pursued by Red Herrings: A Reply to Eric Dunning and Graham Curry", *International Journal of the History of Sport*, 21, 1 (2004), 127–131.

Harvey, Adrian, "The Oldest Rugby Football Club in the World?", *Sport in History*, 26, 1 (2006), 150–2.

Holt, Richard, "Working-Class Football and the City: The Problem of Continuity", *British Journal of Sports History*, 3, 1 (1986), 5–17.

Huggins, M., "The Spread of Association Football in North-East England, 1876–90: The Pattern of Diffusion", *International Journal of the History of Sport*, 6, 3 (1989), 299–318.

Huggins, Mike, "Second-Class Citizens? English Middle-Class Culture and Sport 1850–1910: A Reconsideration", *International Journal of the History of Sport,* 17, 1 (2000), 135–143.

Hutchinson, John, "Sport, Education and Philanthropy in Nineteenth-century Edinburgh: The Emergence of Modern Forms of Football", *Sport in History*, 28, (2008), 547–565.

Jackson, Lorna, "Patriotism or Pleasure? The Nineteenth Century Volunteer Force as a Vehicle for Rural Working-Class Male Sport", *Sports Historian,* 19, 1 (1999), 125–139.

Johnes, Martin, "Eighty Minute Patriots? National Identity and Sport in Modern Wales", *International Journal of the History of Sport,* 17, 4 (2000), 93–110.

Johnes, Martin, " 'Poor Man's Cricket': Baseball, Class and Community in south Wales c.1880–1950", *International Journal of the History of Sport,* 17, 4 (2000), 153–166.

Johnes, Martin and Garland, Ian, " 'The New Craze': football and society in north-east Wales, c. 1870–90", *Welsh History Review*, 22, 2 (2004), 278–304.

Kennedy, David and Kennedy, Peter, "Ambiguity, Complexity and Convergence: The Evolution of Liverpool's Irish Football Clubs", *International Journal of the History of Sport*, 24, 7 (2007), 894–920.

Lile, Brian and Farmer, David, "The Early Development of Association Football in South Wales, 1890–1906", *Transactions of the Honourable Society of Cymmrodorion,* (1984), 193–215.

Martens, James W., " 'To Throttle the Hydra': The Middle Class and Rugby's Great Schism", *Canadian Journal of History of Sport*, XXII, 1 (1991), 52–76.

Martens, James W., " 'They Stooped to Conquer': Rugby Union Football, 1895–1914", *Journal of Sports History*, 20, 1 (1993), 25–41.

Metcalfe, Alan, "Football in the Mining Communities of East Northumberland 1882–1914", *International Journal of the History of Sport,* 5, 3 (1988), 269–291.

Metcalfe, Alan, "The Control of Space and the Development of Sport: A Case Study of Twenty Two Sports in the Mining Communities of East Northumberland, 1880–1914", *Sports Historian,* 15, (1995), 23–33.

Morgan, Gareth, "Rugby and Revivalism: Sport and Religion in Edwardian Wales", *International Journal of the History of Sport,* 22, 3 (2005), 434–456.

Morgan, R.H., "The Development of an Urban Transport System: The Case of Cardiff", *Welsh History Review*, 13, 2 (1986), 178–193.

Prescott, Gwyn, "Competitive Rugby in Cardiff Before the First World War", *Touchlines (Rugby Memorabilia Society)*, 46, April (2010), pp. 5–9.

Rivington, R.T., "W. Webb Ellis and Ashbourne Football", *International Journal of the History of Sport*, 8, 1 (1991), 133–9.

Roese, H.E., "Cardiff and its Port Facilities", *Morgannwg*, XXXIX, (1995), 50–71.

Russell, David, "'Sporadic and Curious': The Emergence of Rugby and Soccer Zones in Yorkshire and Lancashire, c. 1860–1914", *International Journal of the History of Sport*, 5, 2 (1988), 185–205.

Seward, Andy, "Cornish Rugby and Cultural Identity: A Socio-Historical Perspective", *Sports Historian*, 18, 2 (1998), 78–94.

Smith, David, "People's Theatre – A Century of Welsh Rugby", *History Today*, 31, March (1981), 31–6.

Tranter, N.L., "The Social and Occupational Structure of Organized Sport in Central Scotland during the Nineteenth Century", *International Journal of the History of Sport*, 4, 3 (1987), 301–314.

Williams, Gareth, "Community, Class and Rugby in Wales 1880–1914", *Society for the Study of Labour History Bulletin*, 50, Spring, (1985), 10–11.

Theses

Croll, Andrew J., "Civilizing the Urban: Popular Culture, Public Space and Urban Meaning, Merthyr c.1870–1914" (Ph.D. thesis, University of Wales, Cardiff, 1997).

Evans, Kenneth, "A Historical Study of the Formative Years of the Welsh Rugby Union 1870–1900" (M.Ed. thesis, University of Liverpool, 1981).

French, Carl, "The History of the Welsh Schools Rugby Union 1903–1939" (M.Ed. thesis, University of Wales, Cardiff, 1991).

Hickey, J.V., "The Origin and Growth of the Irish Community in Cardiff" (M.A. thesis, University of Wales, Cardiff, 1959).

Hignell, Andrew K., "Suburban Development in North Cardiff, 1850–1919: A Case Study of the Pattern and Processes of Growth in the Parishes of Llanishen, Lisvane and Whitchurch" (Ph.D. thesis, University of Wales, Cardiff, 1987).

Johnes, Martin, "That Other Game: A Social History of Soccer in South Wales c. 1906–39" (Ph.D. thesis, University of Wales, Cardiff, 1998).

Stroud, Raymond J., "The Landscape of Popular Recreation in Newport, Monmouthshire, 1888–1914" (M.A. thesis, University of Wales, Cardiff, 1993).

Website

http://cricketarchive.com

Audiovisual

DVD: *The Lost World of Mitchell and Kenyon* (BBC, 2005).

INDEX